PRINT MEDIA AND PHOTO JOURNALISM

PRINT MEDIA AND PHOTO JOURNALISM

Monita Singh

CENTRUM PRESS
NEW DELHI-110002 (INDIA)

CENTRUM PRESS
H.O.: 4360/4, Ansari Road, Daryaganj,
New Delhi-110002 (India)
Tel: 23278000, 23261597, 23255577, 23286875
B.O.: No. 1015, Ist Main Road, BSK IIIrd Stage,
IIIrd Phase, IIIrd Block, Bangalore-560085 (INDIA)
Tel: 080-41723429
Email: centrumpress@gmail.com
Visit us at: www.centrumpress.com

Print Media and Photo Journalism

First Edition, 2010

ISBN 978-93-80836-19-5

PRINTED IN INDIA

Printed at Mehra Offset Press, Delhi

Contents

Preface

Print Media - a medium that disseminates printed matter, medium - a means or instrumentality for storing or communicating information to public, press - the gathering and publishing of news in the form of newspapers or magazines. Photojournalism as a descriptive term often implies the use of certain bluntness of style or approach to image making.

This assumes 'photojournalism' is an accepted category of photographic practice. It is an essentially contested category - there are a number of different accounts of what is or isn't photojournalism, many photographers are happy to wear the label and may are not. This encompasses what others call documentary or editorial photography, but excludes works of visual fiction produced with computer-generated images.

Of all the journalistic forms said to have died, none have had their demise declared more often than photojournalism. The traditional model of print distribution and direct editorial funding has been unravelling from the 1970s onwards, ever since weekly pictorial magazines like Life folded. This demonstrates photojournalism that required an editorial paymaster was in trouble long before the Internet was an issue or the global recession added to its woes.

As a community of practice photojournalism does not have a single voice with a consensus view. There are photographers attuned to the new media economy and working in new ways. There have recently been a number of notable comments that indicate the world of photojournalism is paying minimal attention to contemporary debates about the revolutions in the media economy, or resorting to some commonly circulated but ill-founded views on how to proceed.

Chapter 1

Introduction

Photojournalism is a particular form of journalism (the collecting, editing, and presenting of news material for publication or broadcast) that creates images in order to tell a news story. It is now usually understood to refer only to still images, and in some cases to video used in broadcast journalism or for personal use. Photojournalism is distinguished from other close branches of photography (such as documentary photography, street photography or celebrity photography) by the qualities of:

- *Timeliness:* The images have meaning in the context of a recently published record of events.
- *Objectivity:* The situation implied by the images is a fair and accurate representation of the events they depict in both content and tone.
- *Narrative:* The images combine with other news elements to make facts relatable to the viewer or reader on a cultural level.

Like a writer, a photojournalist is a reporter but he or she must often make decisions instantly and carry photographic equipment, often while exposed to significant obstacles (physical danger, weather, crowds). *Journalism* is the production of news reports and editorials through media such as newspapers, magazines, radio, television and the Internet.

Journalists—be they writers, editors, photographers, broadcast presenters or producers—serve as the main purveyors of information and opinion in contemporary society. From informal beginnings in Europe of the 18th century, stimulated by the arrival of mechanized printing—

in due course by mass production and in the 20th century by electronic communications technology—today's journalistic enterprises include large corporations with global distribution.

The formal status of journalism has varied historically and still varies greatly from country to country. The modern state and hierarchical power structures in general have tended to consider unrestricted flow of information as a potential threat, and inimical to their own proper function. Censorship, governmental restriction or even active repression of individual journalists and non-state organs of communication continue to cause, at best, intermittent trouble in most countries.

Few formal democracies and no authoritarian governments make provision for protection of press freedom implied by the term *Fourth Estate*. The rise of internet technology, in particular the advent of blogging and social networking software, further destabilize journalism as defined traditionally, and its practitioners as a distinct professional category. Combined with the increasing transfer of advertising revenue from print and broadcast media to the internet, the full effect of the arrival of the "citizen journalist" — potentially positive (proliferation having thus far proved more difficult to police) as well as negative— is not yet known. A story is a single article, news item or feature, usually concerning a single event, issue, theme, or profile of a person.

Correspondents report news occurring in the main, locally, from their own country, or from foreign cities where they are stationed. Most reporters *file* information or write their stories electronically from remote locations. In many cases, *breaking stories* are written by staff members, through information collected and submitted by other reporters who are out on the field gathering information for an event that has just occurred and needs to be broadcast instantly.

Radio and television reporters often compose stories and report "live" from the scene. Some journalists also interpret the news or offer opinions and analysis to readers, viewers, or listeners. In this role, they are called commentators or columnists. Reporters take notes and also take photographs or shoot videos, either on their own, or through a photographer or camera person. In the second phase, they organize the material, determine the focus or emphasis (identify the peg), and finally write their stories.

The story is then edited by news or copy-editors, who function from the *news desk*. The headline of the story is decided by the news desk, and practically never by the reporter or the writer of the piece. Often, the news desk also heavily re-writes or changes the style and tone of the first draft prepared by the reporter/writer originally.

Finally, a collection of stories that have been picked for the newspaper or magazine *edition*, are laid out on dummy (trial) pages, and after the *chief editor* has approved the content, style and language in the material, it is sent for publishing. The writer is given a *byline* for the piece that is published; his or her name appears alongside the article.

This process takes place according to the frequency of the publication. News can be published in a variety of formats (broadsheet, tabloid, magazine and periodical publications) as well as periods (daily, weekly, semi-weekly, fortnightly or monthly). In a broadcast system (television), journalists or reporters are also involved with editing the video material that has been shot alongside their research, and in working on the visual narrative of the story.

Broadcast journalists often make an appearance in the news story at the beginning or end of the video clip. In television or broadcast journalism, news analysts (also called news-casters or news anchors) examine, interpret, and broadcast news received from various sources of information. *Anchors* present this as news, either videotaped or live, through transmissions from on-the-scene reporters (news correspondents). News films ("clips") can vary in length; there are some which may be as long as ten minutes, others that need to fit in all the relevant information and material in two or three minutes. News channels these days have also begun to host special documentary films that stretch for much longer durations and are able to explore a news subject or issue in greater detail.

The desk persons categorise news stories with various formats according to the merit of the story. Such formats include AVO, AVO Byte, Pkg, VO SOT, VOX POP, and Ancho Visual.

- The AVO, or Anchor Voice Over, is the short form of news. The story is written in a gist. According to the script visual is edited. The anchor reads the news while the visual is broadcast simultaneously. Generally, the duration of an AVO is 30 to 40 seconds. The script is three to four lines. At first the anchor starts to read the news, and, after reading one or one-and-a-half lines, the visual is aired, overlapping the face of anchor.
- The AVO Byte has two parts: An AVO, and one or more bytes. This is the same as an AVO, except that as soon as the AVO ends, the Byte is aired.
- The Pkg has three parts: Anchor, Voice Over, and Sign Off. At first a Script is written. A voice over anchor reads the anchor or anchor intro part.

"Wire services" are typically news agencies that provide news to publications, broadcasters and media houses by the minute. They work through technical tie-ups and arrangements with practically all mainstream news organizations, who pay them for the content that they provide.

The public does not have direct access to this content, unless it is featured by a local newspaper or television channel. Most of these agencies, like Agence France-Presse, Reuters or the Associated Press for instance, work on international, local, and national fronts.

Often, *routine news* is sourced directly from these agencies, by the news desk. Routine news is information related to announcements, press conferences, statements made by government or corporate officials, and any other mundane facts. The news desk receives updates from agencies every few minutes.

Information related to the outbreak of a calamity, or important developments concerning national issues is usually obtained from agencies itself. These news items often go without any reporter's byline, that is, the credit is given to the newspaper in general, or is attributed to the agency that has sent out the information (or "broken the story"). If not very impactful, they are carried as small *news briefs*.

On television, these items are the snippets displayed on the *ticker*: the rolling text at the bottom of the screen. Reporters who work for agencies do not usually get any credit for their work, as it is sent out as an "agency copy". Wire agencies are extremely important to the functioning of journalism; they are the backbones of most news organisations today, who heavily depend on them for important, routine content.

They provide the material that an organisation may not be able to cover through its own limited resources alone. *Exclusive stories* on the contrary, are the stories or news items that a publication or channel has obtained through its own resources; it is when a reporter associated with a particular organization has found certain information through personal *sources*, and not through public announcements or from PR officials.

The exclusivity of a story is also dependent on the condition that no other news channel or publication carries it simultaneously. Often, a reporter may find an exclusive story, but finds that it has lost its exclusivity when his or her source gives out that information to other newspapers and channels.

While routine stories may provide the basic material that is required, exclusive stories are the ones that form the editorial identity or the voice of the newspaper. Morning newspapers are obliged to carry both routine and exclusive news; afternoon editions usually have to go a step further and work hard on *follow-ups* and their own exclusive stories. Most afternoon dailies do not carry routine news at all. Their content is lighter, and is meant to be a second reflection of the day's events. Magazines and weeklies also focus entirely on features and exclusive stories.

The Internet has allowed the formal and informal publication of news stories through mainstream media outlets as well as blogs and other self-published news stories.

Journalists working on the Internet are J-Bloggers, a term coined by Australian Media Academic Dr Nicola Goc to describe journalists who [blog] and [blog]gers who produce journalism.

"J-Bloggers: Internet bloggers acting in the role of journalists disseminating newsworthy information, who subscribe to the journalistic ideals of an obligation to the truth and the public's right to know". The web has also seen the development of Online Newspapers and Online magazine. Many of these could be the way forward for local media.

Newscasters function at large stations and networks that usually specialize in a particular type of news, such as sports or weather. Weathercasters, also called weather reporters, report current and forecast weather conditions. They gather information from national satellite weather services, wire services, and local and regional weather bureaus.

Some weathercasters are trained meteorologists and develop their own weather forecasts. Sportscasters select, write, and deliver sports news. This may include interviews with sports personalities and coverage of games and other sporting events. Articles are written about topics that are considered notable by the editors of the publication, with notability varying depending on the focus and audience of the publisher.

Large agencies or companies may have reporters that are specialized to discuss specific topics (a *beat*); smaller agencies are more likely to have a small number of reporters covering all areas of interest. Investigative reports may cover lengthy stories that require days or weeks to gather sufficient information.

Articles must be produced to meet a limited deadline determined by the broadcast or print time of the specific publication and working hours may vary according to the deadlines set and depending on projects or last-minute developments may be long or irregular.

Newspapers and periodicals often contain features written by journalists, many of whom specialize in this form of in-depth journalistic writing. Feature articles are usually longer forms of writing; more attention is paid to style than in straight news reports. They are often combined with photographs, drawings or other "art." They may also be highlighted by typographic effects or colours.

Writing features can be more demanding than writing straight news stories, because while a journalist must apply the same amount of effort to accurately gather and report the facts of the story, he or she must also find a creative and interesting way to *write* it. The *lead* (or first two paragraphs of the story) must grab the reader's attention and yet accurately embody the ideas of the article.

In the last half of the 20th Century the line between straight news reporting and feature writing has blurred. Journalists and publications today experiment with different approaches to writing. Tom Wolfe, Gay Talese, Hunter S. Thompson are some of these examples. Urban and alternative weekly newspapers go even further in blurring the distinction, and many magazines include more features than straight news.

Some television news shows experimented with alternative formats, and many TV shows that claimed to be news shows were not considered as such by traditional critics, because their content and methods do not adhere to accepted journalistic standards. National Public Radio, on the other hand, is considered a good example of mixing straight news reporting, features, and combinations of the two, usually meeting standards of high quality. Other US public radio news organizations have achieved similar results. A majority of newspapers still maintain a clear distinction between news and features, as do most television and radio news organizations.

Sports journalism covers many aspects of human athletic competition, and is an integral part of most journalism products, including newspapers, magazines, and radio and television news broadcasts. While some critics don't consider sports journalism to be true journalism, the prominence of sports in Western culture has justified the attention of journalists to not just the competitive events in sports, but also to athletes and the business of sports. Sports journalism in the United States has traditionally been written in a looser, more creative and more opinionated tone than traditional journalistic writing; the emphasis on accuracy and underlying fairness is still a part of sports journalism. An emphasis on the accurate description of the statistical performances of athletes is also an important part of sports journalism.

Science journalism is a relatively new branch of journalism, in which journalists' reporting conveys information on science topics to the public. Science journalists must understand and interpret very detailed, technical and sometimes jargon-laden information and render it into interesting reports that are comprehensible to consumers of news media.Scientific journalists also must choose which developments in science merit news coverage, as well as cover disputes within the scientific community with a balance of fairness to both sides but also with a devotion to the facts.

Investigative journalism, in which journalists investigate and expose unethical, immoral, and illegal behaviour by individuals, businesses and government agencies, can be complicated, time-consuming and expensive — requiring teams of journalists, months of research, interviews (sometimes repeated interviews) with numerous people, long-distance travel, computers to analyse public-record databases, or use of the company's legal staff to secure documents under freedom of information laws.

Because of its inherently confrontational nature, this kind of reporting is often the first to suffer from budget cutbacks or interference from outside the news department. Investigative reporting done poorly can also expose journalists and media organizations to negative reaction from the subjects of investigations and the public, and accusations of gotcha journalism.

When conducted correctly it can bring the attention of the public and government to problems and conditions that the public deem need to be addressed, and can win awards and recognition to the journalists involved and the media outlet that did the reporting. New Journalism was the name given to a style of 1960s and 1970s news writing and journalism which used literary techniques deemed unconventional at the time.

The term was codified with its current meaning by Tom Wolfe in a 1973 collection of journalism articles. It is typified by using certain devices of literary fiction, such as conversational speech, first-person point of view, recording everyday details and telling the story using scenes. Though it seems undisciplined at first, new journalism maintains elements of reporting including strict adherence to factual accuracy and the writer being the primary source. To get "inside the head" of a character, the journalist asks the subject what they were thinking or how they felt.

Because of its unorthodox style, new journalism is typically employed in feature writing or book-length reporting projects. Many new journalists are also writers of fiction and prose. In addition to Wolfe, writers whose work has fallen under the title "new journalism" include Norman Mailer, Hunter S. Thompson, Joan Didion, Truman Capote, George Plimpton and Gay Talese.

Gonzo journalism is a type of journalism popularized by the American writer Hunter S. Thompson, author of *Fear and Loathing in Las Vegas, Fear and Loathing on the Campaign Trail '72* and *The Kentucky Derby is Decadent and Depraved,* among other stories and books. Gonzo journalism is characterized by its punchy style, rough language, and ostensible disregard for conventional journalistic writing forms and customs.

More importantly, the traditional objectivity of the journalist is given up through immersion into the story itself, as in New Journalism, and the reportage is taken from a first-hand, participatory perspective, sometimes using an author surrogate such as Thompson's Raoul Duke. Gonzo journalism attempts to present a multi-disciplinary perspective on a particular story, drawing from popular culture, sports, political, philosophical and literary sources.

Gonzo journalism has been styled eclectic or untraditional. It remains a feature of popular magazines such as *Rolling Stone* magazine.

It has a good deal in common with new journalism and on-line journalism. Another area of journalism that grew in stature in the 20th Century is 'celebrity' or 'people' journalism, which focuses on the personal lives of people, primarily celebrities, including movie and stage actors, musical artists, models and photographers, other notable people in the entertainment industry, as well as people who seek attention, such as politicians, and people thrust into the attention of the public, such as people who do something newsworthy.

Once the province of newspaper gossip columnists and gossip magazines, celebrity journalism has become the focus of national tabloid newspapers like the *National Enquirer*, magazines like *People* and *Us Weekly*, syndicated television shows like *Entertainment Tonight, Inside Edition, The Insider, Access Hollywood,* and *Extra,* cable networks like E!, A&E Network and The Biography Channel, and numerous other television productions and thousands of websites. Most other news media provide some coverage of celebrities and people.

Celebrity journalism differs from feature writing in that it focuses on people who are either already famous or are especially attractive, and in that it often covers celebrities obsessively, to the point of these journalists behaving unethically in order to provide coverage. Paparazzi, photographers who would follow celebrities incessantly to obtain potentially embarrassing photographs, have come to characterize celebrity journalism.

An emerging form of journalism, which combines different forms of journalism, such as print, photographic and video, into one piece or group of pieces. Convergence journalism can be found in the likes of CNN and many other news sites. *The Washington Post* has a notable amount of this.

Ambush journalism refers to aggressive tactics practiced by journalists to suddenly confront and question people who otherwise do not wish to speak to a journalist. The practice has particularly been applied by television journalists, on news shows like The O'Reilly Factor and 60 Minutes and by Geraldo Rivera and other local television reporters conducting investigations.

The practice has been sharply criticized by journalists and others as being highly unethical and sensational, while others defend it as the only way to attempt to provide those subject to it an opportunity to comment for a report. This can usually be discerned by the level of physical aggression the journalist displays and in the time allowed for an uninterrupted answer.

ROLE OF JOURNALISM IN A DEMOCRACY

In the 1920s, as modern journalism was just taking form, writer Walter Lippmann and American philosopher John Dewey debated over the role of journalism in a democracy. Their differing philosophies still characterize a debate about the role of journalism in society and the nation-state.

Lippmann understood that journalism's role at the time was to act as a mediator or translator between the public and policy making elites. The journalist became the middleman. When elites spoke, journalists listened and recorded the information, distilled it, and passed it on to the public for their consumption.

His reasoning behind this was that the public was not in a position to deconstruct the growing and complex flurry of information present in modern society, and so an intermediary was needed to filter news for the masses. Lippman put it this way: The public is not smart enough to understand complicated, political issues. Furthermore, the public was too consumed with their daily lives to care about complex public policy. Therefore the public needed someone to interpret the decisions or concerns of the elite to make the information plain and simple.

That was the role of journalists. Lippmann believed that the public would affect the decision-making of the elite with their vote. In the meantime, the elite (i.e. politicians, policy makers, bureaucrats, scientists, etc.) would keep the business of power running. In Lippman's world, the journalist's role was to inform the public of what the elites were doing.

It was also to act as a watchdog over the elites, as the public had the final say with their votes. Effectively that kept the public at the bottom of the power chain, catching the flow of information that is handed down from experts/elites. Dewey, on the other hand, believed the public was not only capable of understanding the issues created or responded to by the elite, it was in the public forum that decisions should be made after discussion and debate.

When issues were thoroughly vetted, then the best ideas would bubble to the surface. Dewey believed journalists should do more than simply pass on information. He believed they should weigh the consequences of the policies being enacted. Over time, his idea has been implemented in various degrees, and is more commonly known as "community journalism."

This concept of *community journalism* is at the centre of new developments in journalism. In this new paradigm, journalists are able to engage citizens and the experts/elites in the proposition and generation of content. It's important to note that while there is an assumption of equality, Dewey still celebrates expertise.

Dewey believes the shared knowledge of many is far superior to a single individual's knowledge. Experts and scholars are welcome in Dewey's framework, but there is not the hierarchical structure present in Lippman's understanding of journalism and society.

According to Dewey, conversation, debate, and dialogue lie at the heart of a democracy.

While Lippman's journalistic philosophy might be more acceptable to government leaders, Dewey's approach is a better description of how many journalists see their role in society, and, in turn, how much of society expects journalists to function.

Americans, for example, may criticize some of the excesses committed by journalists, but they tend to expect journalists to serve as watchdogs on government, businesses and other actors, enabling people to make informed decisions on the issues of the time.

According to *The Elements of Journalism*, a book by Bill Kovach and Tom Rosenstiel, there are nine elements of journalism. In order for a journalist to fulfill their duty of providing the people with the information they need to be free and self-governing. They must follow these guidelines:

- Journalism's first obligation is to the truth.
- Its first loyalty is to the citizens.
- Its essence is discipline of verification.
- Its practitioners must maintain an independence from those they cover.
- It must serve as an independent monitor of power.
- It must provide a forum for public criticism and compromise.
- It must strive to make the significant interesting, and relevant.
- It must keep the news comprehensive and proportional.
- Its practitioners must be allowed to exercise their personal conscience.

In the April 2007 edition of the book, they have added one additional element, *the rights and responsibilities of citizens* to make it a total of ten elements of journalism. In the UK, all newspapers are bound by the Code of Practice of the Press Complaints Commission.

This includes points like respecting people's privacy and ensuring accuracy. However, the Media Standards Trust has criticised the PCC, claiming it needs to be radically changed to secure public trust of newspapers.

This is in stark contrast to the media climate prior to the 20th Century, where the media market was dominated by smaller newspapers and pamphleteers who usually had an overt and often radical agenda, with no presumption of balance or objectivity.

There are several professional organizations, universities and foundations that recognize excellence in journalism in the USA. The Pulitzer Prize, administered by Columbia University in New York City, is awarded to newspapers, magazines and broadcast media for excellence in various kinds of journalism. The Society of Professional Journalists gives the Sigma Delta Chi Award for journalism excellence. In the television industry, the National Academy of Television

Arts & Sciences gives awards for excellence in television journalism.

Such a code of conduct can, in the real world, be difficult to uphold consistently. Journalists who believe they are being fair or objective may give biased accounts—by reporting selectively, trusting too much to anecdote, or giving a partial explanation of actions.

Even in routine reporting, bias can creep into a story through a reporter's choice of facts to summarize, or through failure to check enough sources, hear and report dissenting voices, or seek fresh perspectives. A news organization's budget inevitably reflects decision-making about what news to cover, for what audience, and in what depth.

Those decisions may reflect conscious or unconscious bias. When budgets are cut, editors may sacrifice reporters in distant news bureaus, reduce the number of staff assigned to low-income areas, or wipe entire communities from the publication's zone of interest. Publishers, owners and other corporate executives, especially advertising sales executives, can try to use their powers over journalists to influence how news is reported and published.

Journalists usually rely on top management to create and maintain a "firewall" between the news and other departments in a news organization to prevent undue influence on the news department. One journalism magazine, Columbia Journalism Review, has made it a practice to reveal examples of executives who try to influence news coverage, of executives who do not abuse their powers over journalists, and of journalists who resist such pressures.

Self-censorship is a growing problem in journalism, particularly in covering countries that sharply restrict press freedom. As commercial pressure in the media marketplace grows, media organizations are loath to lose access to high-profile countries by producing unflattering stories. For example, CNN admitted that it had practiced self-censorship in covering the Saddam Hussein regime in Iraq in order to ensure continued access after the regime had thrown out other media.

CNN correspondent Christiane Amanpour also complained of self-censorship during the invasion of Iraq due to the fear of alienating key audiences in the US. There are claims that the media are also avoiding covering stories about repression and human rights violations by the Israeli and Iranian regimes in order to maintain a presence in those countries.

Generally, publishers and consumers of journalism draw a distinction between reporting — "just the facts" — and opinion writing, often by restricting opinion columns to the editorial page and its facing or "op-ed" (opposite the editorials) page. Unsigned editorials are traditionally the official opinions of the paper's editorial board, while op-ed pages may be a mixture of syndicated columns and other contributions, frequently with some attempt to balance the voices across some political or social spectrum.

The distinction between reporting and opinion can break down. In the UK, the Press Complaints Commission states that "the Press, whilst free to be partisan, must distinguish clearly between comment, conjecture and fact" but some commentators have suggested there can sometimes be a blurring of opinion and fact. Complex stories often require summarizing and interpretation of facts, especially if there is limited time or space for a story.

Stories involving great amounts of interpretation are often labelled "news analysis," but still run in a paper's news columns. The limited time for each story in a broadcast report rarely allows for such distinctions. Journalists around the world often write about the governments in their nations, and those governments have widely varying policies and practices towards journalists, which control what they can research and write, and what press organizations can publish.

Many Western governments guarantee the freedom of the press, and do relatively little to restrict press rights and freedoms, while other nations severely restrict what journalists can research and/or publish. Journalists in many nations have enjoyed some privileges not enjoyed by members of the general public, including better access to public events, crime scenes and press conferences, and to extended interviews with public officials, celebrities and others in the public eye.

These privileges are available because of the perceived power of the press to turn public opinion for or against governments, their officials and policies, as well as the perception that the press often represents their consumers. These privileges extend from the legal rights of journalists but are not guaranteed by those rights.

Sometimes government officials may attempt to punish individual journalists who irk them by denying them some of these privileges extended to other journalists. Nations or jurisdictions that formally license journalists may confer special privileges and responsibilities along with those licenses, but in the United States the tradition of an independent press has avoided any imposition of government-controlled examinations or licensing.

Some of the states have explicit shield laws that protect journalists from some forms of government inquiry, but those statutes' definitions of "journalist" were often based on access to printing presses and broadcast towers. A national shield law has been proposed.

In some nations, journalists are directly employed, controlled or censored by their governments. In other nations, governments who may claim to guarantee press rights actually intimidate journalists with threats of arrest, destruction or seizure of property (especially the means of production and dissemination of news content), torture or murder.

Journalists who elect to cover conflicts, whether wars between nations or insurgencies within nations, often give up any expectation of protection by government, if not giving up their rights to protection by government. Journalists who are captured or detained during a conflict are expected to be treated as civilians and to be released to their national government.

Journalists' interaction with sources sometimes involves confidentiality, an extension of freedom of the press giving journalists a legal protection to keep the identity of a source private even when demanded by police or prosecutors; withholding sources can land journalists in contempt of court, or in jail.

The scope of rights granted to journalists varies from nation to nation; in the United Kingdom, for example, the government has had more legal rights to protect what it considers sensitive information, and to force journalists to reveal the sources of leaked information, than the United States. Other nations, particularly Zimbabwe and the People's Republic of China, have a reputation of persecuting journalists, both domestic and foreign.

In the United States, there has never been a right to protect sources in a federal court. Some states provide varying degrees of such protection. However, federal courts will refuse to force journalists to reveal sources, unless the information the court seeks is highly relevant to the case, and there's no other way to get it. Journalists, like all citizens, who refuse to testify even when ordered to can be found in contempt of court and fined or jailed.

RIGHT OF ACCESS

Journalists often depend on freedom of information legislation to access information held by the government. These rights also vary from nation to nation. In the United States, the Freedom of Information Act guarantees journalists the right to obtain copies of government documents, although the government has the right to black out some information from these documents.

Other federal legislation also controls access to information. Some states have more open policies for making information available, and some states have acted in the last decade to broaden those rights. New Jersey has updated and broadened its freedom of information legislation to better define what kinds of government documents can be withheld from public inquiry.

In India, the Right to Information Act was passed in 2005, giving citizens the right to access state and national records. There exist several organizations that use journalism as a form of media development. Such organizations include Search for Common Ground, BBC World Service Trust, and Journalists for Human Rights.

In 2008, journalism came under heavy fire. The decline of print newspapers has led to a sharp increase in job cuts for journalists. In 2008 alone, approximately 16,000 journalists were terminated – a budgetary response to declining subscription dollars and the inability to adapt to a free-news-driven society. With advertising revenues taking a harsh rapping from the transitional shift of a subscription-based/advertising model to online ad placements, the discrepancy in advertising revenue is making it difficult for traditional newspapers to survive.

The Tribune Company (owner of the LA Times) filed for Chapter 11 bankruptcy; The Rocky Mountain Times (one of the countries oldest newspapers) closed its doors after 150 years of business; The Christian Science Monitor transitioned from its daily newspaper edition to online distribution; 120 newspapers closed their doors in the first three months of 2009; newspaper circulation is down 7% in the first six months of 2009.

Newspapers are forced to maximize their current staff in a response to declining advertising and circulation revenue. As formerly relied upon revenues shore-up, newspapers are exploring radically new ways of reaching readers. The New York Times has partnered with Amazon's Kindle DX to bring current subscribers and Kindle users NYT content. This, along with other social media properties, are ways in which traditional media are fighting to stay relevant in the digital age.

Chapter 2

The Photojournalism and Ethics

Photojournalism is a particular form of journalism (the collecting, editing, and presenting of news material for publication or broadcast) that creates images in order to tell a news story. It is now usually understood to refer only to still images, and in some cases to video used in broadcast journalism. Photojournalism is distinguished from other close branches of photography (such as documentary photography, street photography or celebrity photography) by the qualities of:

- *Timeliness*: The images have meaning in the context of a recently published record of events.
- *Objectivity*: The situation implied by the images is a fair and accurate representation of the events they depict in both content and tone.
- *Narrative*: The images combine with other news elements to make facts relatable to the viewer or reader on a cultural level.

Like a writer, a photojournalist is a reporter but he or she must often make decisions instantly and carry photographic equipment, often while exposed to significant obstacles (physical danger, weather, crowds).

FOUNDATIONS

The practice of illustrating news stories with photographs was made possible by printing and photography innovations that occurred between 1880 and 1897. While newsworthy events were photographed as early as the 1850s, printing presses could only publish from engravings until the 1880s.

Early news photographs required that photos be re-interpreted by an engraver before they could be published.

The first photojournalist was Carol Szathmari who did pictures in the Crimean War (1853 to 1856). His albums were sent to European royals houses. Just a few of his photography survived. The next ones were British press reporters,in the same war. William Simpson of the *Illustrated London News* and Roger Fenton were published as engravings.

Similarly, the American Civil War photographs of Mathew Brady were engraved before publication in *Harper's Weekly*. Because the public craved more realistic representations of news stories, it was common for newsworthy photographs to be exhibited in galleries or to be copied photographically in limited numbers.

On March 4, 1880, *The Daily Graphic* (New York) published the first halftone (rather than engraved) reproduction of a news photograph. Further innovations followed. In 1887, flash powder was invented, enabling journalists such as Jacob Riis to photograph informal subjects indoors, which led to the landmark work *How the Other Half Lives*. By 1897, it became possible to reproduce halftone photographs on printing presses running at full speed.

Despite these innovations, limitations remained, and many of the sensational newspaper and magazine stories in the period from 1897 to 1927 were illustrated with engravings. In 1921, the wirephoto made it possible to transmit pictures almost as quickly as news itself could travel. However, it was not until development of the commercial 35mm Leica camera in 1925, and the first flash bulbs between 1927 and 1930 that all the elements were in place for a "golden age" of photojournalism.

GOLDEN AGE

In the "golden age" of photojournalism (1930s–1950s), some magazines (*Picture Post* (London), *Paris Match* (Paris), Arbeiter-Illustrierte-Zeitung (Berlin), Berliner Illustrierte Zeitung (Berlin), *Life* (USA), *Sports Illustrated* (USA)) and newspapers (*The Daily Mirror* (London), *The New York Daily*

News (New York)) built their huge readerships and reputations largely on their use of photography, and photographers such as Robert Capa, Alfred Eisenstaedt, Margaret Bourke-White and W. Eugene Smith became well-known names.

Henri Cartier-Bresson is held by some to be the father of modern photojournalism, although this appellation has been applied to various other photographers, such as Erich Salomon, whose candid pictures of political figures were novel in the 1930s. Soldier Tony Vaccaro is also recognized as one of the pre-eminent photographers of World War II.

His images taken with the modest Argus C3 captured horrific moments in war, similar to Capa's soldier being shot. Capa himself was on Omaha beach on D-Day and captured pivotal images of the conflict on that occasion. Vaccaro is also known for having developed his own images in soldier's helmets, and using chemicals found in the ruins of a camera store in 1944.

Until the 1980s, most large newspapers were printed with turn-of-the-century "letterpress" technology using easily smudged oil-based ink, off-white, low-quality "newsprint" paper, and coarse engraving screens. While letterpresses produced legible text, the photoengraving dots that formed pictures often bled or smeared and became fuzzy and indistinct.,

In this way, even when newspapers used photographs well — a good crop, a respectable size — murky reproduction often left readers re-reading the caption to see what the photo was all about. The *Wall Street Journal* adopted stippled hedcuts in 1979 to publish portraits and avoid the limitations of letterpress printing.

Not until the 1980s had a majority of newspapers switched to "offset" presses that reproduce photos with fidelity on better, whiter paper. By contrast *Life*, one of America's most popular weekly magazines from 1936 through the early 1970s, was filled with photographs reproduced beautifully on oversize 11×14-inch pages, using fine engraving screens, high-quality inks, and glossy paper.

Life often published a United Press International (UPI) or Associated Press (AP) photo that had been first reproduced in newspapers, but the quality magazine version appeared to be a different photo altogether. In large part because their pictures were clear enough to be appreciated, and because their name always appeared with their work, magazine photographers achieved near-celebrity status.

Life became a standard by which the public judged photography, and many of today's photo books celebrate "photojournalism" as if it had been the exclusive province of near-celebrity magazine photographers. *The Best of Life* (1973), for example, opens with a two-page (1960) group shot of 39 justly famous *Life* photographers.

But 300 pages later, photo credits reveal that scores of the photos among *Life's* "best" were taken by anonymous UPI and AP photographers. Thus even during the golden age, because of printing limitations and the UPI and AP syndication systems, many newspaper photographers laboured in relative obscurity.

FARM SECURITY ADMINISTRATION

From 1935 to 1942, the Farm Security Administration and its predecessor the Resettlement Administration were part of Franklin Roosevelt's New Deal, and were designed to address agricultural problems and rural poverty associated with the Great Depression.

A special photographic section of the agency, headed by Roy Stryker, was intended merely to provide public relations for its programs, but instead produced what some consider one of the greatest collections of documentary photographs ever created in the U.S.

Whether this effort can be called "photojournalism" is debatable, since the FSA photographers had more time and resources to create their work than most photojournalists usually have.

ACCEPTANCE BY THE ART WORLD

Since the late 1970s, photojournalism and documentary

photography have increasingly been accorded a place in art galleries alongside fine art photography. Luc Delahaye, VII Photo Agency and Chien-Chi Chang are among many who regularly exhibit in galleries.

PROFESSIONAL ORGANIZATIONS

The Danish Union of Press Photographers (Pressefotografforbundet) was the first national organization for newspaper photographers in the world. It was founded in 1912 in Denmark by six press photographers in Copenhagen. Today it has over 800 members.

The National Press Photographers Association (NPPA) was founded in 1946 in the U.S., and has about 10,000 members. Others around the world include the British Press Photographers Association (BPPA) founded in 1984, then relaunched in 2003, and now has around 450 members.

Hong Kong Press Photographers Association (1989), Northern Ireland Press Photographers Association (2000), Pressfotografernas Klubb (Sweden, 1930), and PK – Pressefotografenes Klubb (Norway).

News organisations and journalism schools run many different awards for photojournalists. Since 1968, Pulitzer Prizes have been awarded for the following categories of photojournalism: 'Feature Photography', 'Spot News Photography'.

Other awards are World Press Photo, Best of Photojournalism, and Pictures of the Year as well as the UK based The Press Photographer's Year.

ETHICAL AND LEGAL CONSIDERATIONS

Photojournalism works within the same ethical approaches to objectivity that are applied by other journalists. What to shoot, how to frame and how to edit are constant considerations. Often, ethical conflicts can be mitigated or enhanced by the actions of a sub-editor or picture editor, who takes control of the images once they have been delivered to the news organization. The photojournalist often has no control as to how images are ultimately used.

The emergence of digital photography offers whole new realms of opportunity for the manipulation, reproduction, and transmission of images. It has inevitably complicated many of the ethical issues involved. The U.S. National Press Photographers Association, and other professional organizations, maintains codes of ethics to specify approaches to these issues.

Major ethical issues are often inscribed with more or less success into law. Laws regarding photography can vary significantly from nation to nation. The legal situation is further complicated when one considers that photojournalism made in one country will often be published in many other countries.

THE IMPACT OF NEW TECHNOLOGIES

Smaller, lighter cameras greatly enhanced the role of the photojournalist. Since the 1960s, motor drives, electronic flash, auto-focus, better lenses and other camera enhancements have made picture taking easier. New digital cameras free photojournalists from the limitation of film roll length, as thousands of images can be stored on a single microdrive or memory card.

Content remains the most important element of photojournalism, but the ability to extend deadlines with rapid gathering and editing of images has brought significant changes. As recently as 15 years ago, nearly 30 minutes were needed to scan and transmit a single colour photograph from a remote location to a news office for printing.

Now, equipped with a digital camera, a mobile phone and a laptop computer, a photojournalist can send a high-quality image in minutes, even seconds after an event occurs. Video phones and portable satellite links increasingly allow for the mobile transmission of images from almost any point on the earth.

There is some concern by news photographers that the profession of photojournalism as it is known today could change to such a degree that it is unrecognizable as image-capturing technology naturally progresses. There is also concern that fewer print publications are commissioning serious photojournalism on timely issues.Civilization is a stream with banks.

The stream is sometimes filled, with blood from people killing, stealing, shouting and doing things historians usually record, while on the banks, unnoticed, people build homes, make love, raise children, sing songs, write poetry. The story of civilization is the story of what happened on the banks- Will Durant In a fitting tribute to the power and prevalence of photojournalism images, Time magazine recently produced the first issue in its history on a single topic with a single advertiser.

Measured from the dual technological achievements announced in 1839 of Louis Daguerre's daguerreotype and Henry Talbot's calotype, the 150th year of photography has been celebrated throughout the world with gallery exhibitions and feature articles in all manner of media.

Life magazine, a publication responsible for photojournalism's rise in respect, published an anniversary issue titled, " 150 Years of Photography: Pictures that Made a Difference". American Photographer, a magazine that regularly features works by newspaper and magazine photojournalists, devoted its cover and over 30 pages to the subject of photojournalism.

Marianne Fulton, associate curator of photographic collections at the International Museum of Photography at the George Eastman House in Rochester, New York, was the editor of a well-researched and richly illustrated book on photojournalism, Eyes of Time: Photojournalism in America.

Jim Dooley, photography editor and chief for the Long Island newspaper, Newsday, remarked that "newspaper photojournalism is in its heyday. It's going through a tremendous renewal".

Professor of Photojournalism at the University of Missouri, Bill Kuykendall, also feels that there is now a photojournalism renaissance. "I think there has been a rebirth," said Kuykendall, "of interest in candid photojournalism".

Just as discussions of photojournalism have received an abundance of media treatment, professional ethics has also received widespread attention in magazines, books and from experts in the field. Ethical issues are hot topics in today's media-conscious society.

Questions currently debated in formats that vary from newspaper articles to public forums broadcast on public television stations include: Is insider trading a result of greedy individuals or does it foretell a problem with the entire system of business? Are the temptations from profit motives too great for government employees to manage without outside monitoring?

Should the organs from aborted fetuses be used for medical purposes? Does the media concentrate too much on scandals or other sensational events and miss the underlying issues that may be ultimately more important?

ICONS WITH ETHICAL PROBLEMS

When photojournalism and ethics are combined as a topic for discussion, Time magazine's, "150 Years of Photojournalism" issue should be analysed in a more critical manner. After consulting with experts in the field, the editors of the photojournalism issue reproduced in the introduction, "The Ten Greatest Images of Photojournalism." "There are hundreds of unforgettable news pictures," the subhead explains. "Some record great events, others the small but resonant ones. In our view these ten-images of war and peace, love and hate, poverty and triumph-are the ones indelibly pressed upon the mind and heart".

Ironically, 8 of the 10 photographs have ethical problems associated with them or the photographer. Another "unforgettable news picture" is made more unforgettable through computer digital manipulation.

Civil War photographer Alexander Gardner moved a corpse to illustrate, in separate images, a Union and a Confederate soldier. Robert Capa and Joe Rosenthal were accused of stage managing their famous photographs. Dorothea Lange and Alfred Eisenstaedt were criticized by their subjects for not paying them for their famous poses. The pictures of Bob Jackson and Eddie Adams were considered too gruesome by many members of the general public.

Gene Smith regularly posed his subjects and manipulated his prints with a variety of techniques that included double printing. And finally, in a demonstration of the manipulative potential of computer technology, a photograph of the solitary moonscape portrait of Edwin Aldrin by fellow astronaut Neil Armstrong is transformed at the end of the issue to an invasion of the moon by a platoon of moon-walkers.

There is no doubt that for older Americans, the 10 images are among the strongest and most visually memorable icons of the 20th century. A committee from Britain or France might not have seven American-related images. A group of younger students of photography might include photographs more recent than 1971. Another panel might not have five pictures that are war-related, a portrait of a destitute family, an international disaster, a political assassination and a mercury deformed child.

Ethical arguments are usually not satisfying. There is no clear winner or loser when perspective guides a determination. But there must be some way to defend your action to a reader who does not share your personal perspective. Writers and photographers for newspapers follow the same ethical principle of truthfulness outlined in ethics codes.

Journalists would view as unethical a reporter who fabricated quotations. Likewise, a photographer who uses darkroom tricks to make a false image would probably be fired. The principle of truthfulness is easily defended by both writers and photographers.

IT IS HARD TO HIDE A CAMERA

Ethical worlds often collide, however, because of the fundamental techniques the two reporters use to gather information. During a controversial news event, when a father grieves visibly over the loss of a drowned child, a writer can stay behind the scenes with pen and paper hidden. Facts are gathered quietly and anonymously. A photographer is tied to a machine that must be out in the open and obvious to all who are present. A videographer during the 1967 riots in Newark, New Jersey said, 11 a newspaper guy can huddle in a doorway or get it over the phone. But we've got to be in it to get it".

Long lenses or hidden camera techniques can be used, but the results are usually unsatisfactory. Focus, exposure, and composition problems are increased with the use of telephoto lenses or hiding a camera.

Besides being on ethically shaky ground, the use of hidden cameras is illegal in Delaware, Georgia, Hawaii, Maine, Michigan, New Hampshire, South Dakota, and Utah. The photographer, unlike the hidden writer, can be the target of policemen, family members, and onlookers who vent their anger and grief on the one with the camera.

No call to journalistic principles of truthfulness will convince a mob not to attack a photographer in such an emotionally charged situation. Because photographers must be out in the open to take pictures, the photographer's ethical orientation must be more clearly defined than with writers who can report over the telephone. A photographer must have a clear reason why an image of a grieving parent is necessary.

PHOTOJOURNALISM AS A PROFESSION

Although photojournalism is filled with many dark moments, the history of the field is also rich with pride and professionalism. Cliff Edom (1976), one of the most well respected photojournalism educators in the country, credited Frank Mott, dean of the Journalism School at the University of Missouri, with inventing the term, photojournalism. In 1942, Mott helped establish a separate academic sequence for photojournalism instruction. For the first time, photojournalism was considered "as important to the field of communication" as its word equivalent.

In 1946, Joseph Costa, staff photographer for the New York Daily News, was elected president of the first national organization for newspaper photographers, the National Press

Photographers Association (NPPA). Editor & Publisher magazine at the time wrote that the aim of the new organization was "to combine all elements of the working photographic press in America to raise and maintain the high levels of photography necessary to the advancement of pictorial journalism." Shortly thereafter, the first issue of News Photographer, the official publication of the NPPA, was printed.

Academic standing, professional membership, and literature unique to the organization are fundamental criteria for the definition of a professional group. Since the early days of the NPPA, members of the photojournalism profession have seen academic sequences begun at universities across the country.

NPPA membership has grown from a handful at their first meeting in Atlantic City to more than 9,000. News Photographer magazine has grown in coverage and stature to become one of the leading trade publications in the business. Another standard of professionalism is the amount of self-criticism that occurs within the organization for the betterment of its members.

From the first issue of News Photographer, articles have been written, not simply to introduce technical advances, but to critically examine the ethical behaviour of press photographers. From relations with the police to the coverage of tragic events, ethical issues get a fair hearing within the pages of News Photographer.

Reactions to controversial issues are a result of the underlying principles that guide a person. Many times photographers and the general public are on opposite sides of a philosophical wall. As part of the journalism community, photographers see their role as providing readers with a record of each day's events.

The community at large is benefited. That mission often leads to the taking and printing of disturbing, graphically violent images. Such an underlying philosophy at work for journalists could be interpreted as a form of Utilitarianism. Many members of the general public, however, are disturbed by such images. Readers often complain that they either do not wish to see such gruesome photographs in their morning newspaper or are concerned that the pictures will contribute to the grief of the victim's family and friends. The underlying philosophy for those letter writers is most probably the Golden Rule.

It is important to understand that the two conflicting philosophies have long been debated by philosophers without a satisfactory resolution. Emotional issues find little room for compromise. Again, a person's perspective guides a response to a controversial photograph.

PHOTOJOURNALISM ASSIGNMENTS AND TECHNIQUES

When asked to describe a photojournalist, most people would probably tell of a slightly disheveled, camera-weighted, young photographer who scurries to troubled areas anywhere in the world to produce images that capture people in crisis. Quite a romantic view. The reality is different. Most photojournalists, according to a 1982 survey, work for a daily newspaper, are college-educated men, have families, own homes, are in their mid-30s, and make under $25,000 a year.

Photojournalists should consider themselves to be on an equal status as word journalists. Photojournalists are reporters. But instead of pen, notebook, or tape recorders, these reporters use a camera and its accompanying selection of technical devices to record events for each day's printed record. As reporters, photojournalists must have a strong sense of the journalistic values that guide all reporters.

Truthfulness, objectivity, and fairness are values that give the journalism profession credibility and respect. From getting the names spelled correctly in a group portrait to not misrepresenting yourself or a subject, truthfulness is a value that gives the public a reason to rely on the accuracy of the news they read and see in their newspaper. If you are economically, politically, or emotionally involved with a subject, your objectivity will be put into question.

A photographer's credibility will suffer if free gifts from

a subject are accepted or if political views or personal opinions cloud news judgments. To be fair, a journalist tries to show both sides of a controversial issue, prints stories and photographs proportionate to their importance, and if mistakes are made, prints immediate, clear, and easily found corrections.

A photojournalist, from experience and education, must know what is and what is not news. The media are often criticized for concentrating their efforts on negative, often tragic events in their community. Journalism professors Ted Glasser and Jim Ettema (1989) reviewed the most commonly held news values: "prominence, conflict, oddity, impact, proximity, and timeliness."

In their article, Glasser and Ettema argued that a journalist should also use common sense, taught in journalism schools or through work experiences, to decide what is news. Unfortunately, tragic events usually fit into most news value categories. Successful picture taking is a combination of a strong news and visual sense. It is no easy proposition. As reporters, photographers use their sense of news judgment to determine if a subject is worth coverage and to present a fresh or unusual angle to an ordinary event.

As visual recorders, photographers must use their sense of visual composition to eliminate distracting and unnecessary elements in the frame. As technicians, they must have a high level of expertise to use their machine to expose correctly and in focus that peak news moment.

The French photojournalist Henri Cartier-Bresson used the phrase, "the decisive moment" to describe the same idea. The decisive moment is an instant when the subject and the compositional elements form a union. For a newspaper photographer, the moment may come when a subject expresses in a minor facial gesture or an overt action the essence of his or her situation and when the foreground and background visual elements contribute to a reader's understanding of that subject's emotional state.

A confident news and visual sense is essential when covering any of the many assignments a photographer may face. Photojournalistic maturity elevates an ordinary picture taker to a journalist with a clear communicative goal. Whether the assignment is a ground-breaking ceremony at a local high school or a five-alarm fire at a nursing home, a mature photojournalist will find a way to capture in photographs a fresh and decisive summation of the event.

There are six basic types of assignments a photographer faces. News, features, sports, portraits, illustrations, and picture stories each present a photographer with a different set of challenges.

NEWS ASSIGNMENTS

News is the assignment most people probably think of with the term photojournalism. Crossing police lines to get to the heart of a raging fire or head-on collision, photojournalists often risk physical harm with the news assignments they cover.

TYPES OF NEWS ASSIGNMENTS

News is actually divided into two parts: spot and general. Spot News. Spot news is any unplanned event where little advanced planning is possible. Photographers will often learn of spot news events through a radio call from their photography editor or directly from a police and fire scanner in their car. Because photographers are often driving in their car, spot news is sometimes found through coincidental circumstances. Although emotions are high when driving to a spot news scene, special care must be taken to drive safely.

Traffic laws must be obeyed. Most likely, arriving an extra minute sooner because of a high speed chase will not make a difference in capturing the most dramatic moments. Almost always, spot news is an assignment where subjects will be injured or in physical trouble. The photographer must be prepared to help the injured if no rescue workers are on the scene.

To get quickly through police lines, an identification card is usually connected to a small chain and hung around the neck. Police officials are supposed to allow news photographers access to news events. Understanding and tact are often necessary by photographers during heated emotional moments on both sides of the police line. A photographer who obstructs the work of the police or rescue workers runs the risk of arrest.

For news and most other assignments, a photographer must be prepared for any type of film, lighting, and lens requirement. One camera bag should contain two 35mm single lens reflex (SLR) camera bodies. At least one of the cameras should have a motor driven mechanism to automatically advance the film.

The bag should contain at least three lenses (wide-angle, normal, and telephoto), a portable flash unit with a fully charged battery pack, a portable radio for communication to the photo editor, a pen and notebook for caption information, and a variety of 36exposure film in an assortment of film speeds (100, 400, and 3200 ASA).

Colour or black-and-white film depends on the requirements of the individual newspaper. Whenever possible, both cameras should be loaded with fresh film so that there are plenty of exposures for fast action. Depending on the situation, one camera should have a 35mm wide-angle lens and the other a 180mm or 300mm telephoto lens attached. Most photographers will take an initial wide-angle, scene-setting picture. After a few moments, an assessment of the salient elements of the event is made and the photographer switches to a telephoto lens for a close-up perspective.

There is a debate among photographers whether zoom lenses should be used. As opposed to fixed focal lenses, a photographer can move the focal length in or out for a variety of close-up and wide-angle views. Zoom lenses typically save a beginning photographer money because they can take the place of several lenses.

Most professional newspaper photographers, however, do not use zoom lenses. Many find that zoom lenses do not focus as sharply as fixed focal lenses. With their typically small aperture openings they are not practical in low-lighting situations. Zoom lenses also make photographers worry about another technical consideration when shooting. While making aperture, shutter speed, and focus corrections, a photographer with a zoom lens must also decide whether to zoom in or out. A fleeting subject can be lost if valuable seconds are used to make those decisions. For sensitive news situations, funerals, or courtroom scenes, where the photographer wants to remain as inconspicuous as possible, some photographers carry a small, rangefinder camera in their bag.

A rangefinder, without the mirror mechanism of an SLR camera, is quiet and useful for low-light situations. As with the other assignments, the best images will show the emotional struggle on the faces of those involved at the scene. Tired and dedicated rescue workers helping dazed and confused victims is a visual image that often shows more clearly than words ever can the emotions of concern and fear associated with spot news events.

Often, spot news assignments occur at night just before a press deadline. To get a picture quickly to the photo desk, some photographers will overexpose their images with their flash, underdevelop their film at drastically reduced times, print their negatives while they are wet, and turn in a print that has only slightly been fixed and washed.

From unloading the film from the camera to turning in a print with caption information to the night city editor, the time can be cut by half.

Afterward, the photographer should fix and wash the film. The negatives should be carefully filed and labeled within a protective sleeve.

General News. General news assignments give photographers a chance to prepare. Special film, camera lenses, and lighting needs can be anticipated. General news assignments usually take the form of a politician's press conference or a group of donors to a local charity. A photographer's main concerns with such assignments are typically arriving on time to get a good vantage point, making sure that names in a group picture are spelled correctly, and having enough energy and curiosity to produce an unusual, yet telling moment.

A picture of a politician or lecturer will always be more visually interesting if an emotional facial expression or hand gesture is captured on film. A standing group of business persons all smiling at the camera, a milk bottle picture as a photo editor used to say, is a visually dull image. Take care to find angles or activities that will not only show the physical appearance of a group, but will reveal their personalities.

Be on your toes. Even during the most banal news conference, strange events happen. Still and video journalists covered the Dwyer news conference that suddenly turned tragic. A photojournalist must always be prepared for the unusual and the newsworthy.

FEATURE ASSIGNMENTS

With feature assignments a photographer needs the sharp reflexes honed by spot news events. The trouble with features, however, is that a photographer usually cannot anticipate where the assignment will take place. It is no wonder that many undergraduate photography students often complain that they cannot find meaningful feature pictures to photograph.

Feature assignments are usually self-generated ones. Photo editors, with no other assignments, will tell the photographer to shoot "wild art" or "a colourful enterprise picture for Page 1."

An ordinary photographer might drive to a public park and capture the usual scenes: a child rides a swing, a young woman reads a book, two men talk on a bench. These pictures are made to show readers nothing more than that the weather was nice and people enjoyed the day.

A more mature photographer anticipates the need for a feature picture by the photo editor and has already scouted an area of town or a particular subject that is both visually interesting and filled with meaningful content.

TYPES OF FEATURE ASSIGNMENTS

There are two types of feature assignments: human interest and pictorial.

Human Interest

These features show persons being natural and unique. The images cannot be anticipated. They are one of a kind moments that capture a person or group being themselves: odd, humourous, and natural. Cute kids, animals, and nuns are traditional subject cliches.

Features offer an opportunity for a page to be highlighted with a pleasant, happy picture that may offset the tragic events of the day. A photographer looking for human interest features thinks like a hunter. Keenly aware and observant, knowledgeable on matters of basic human nature, quiet and unassuming, and technically competent to capture quick and fleeting moments, the photographer stalks the city looking for pictures that go beyond the cliche.

Photographers have several techniques they use to take pictures of people. Some will use a 35mm. wide-angle lens and get close to their subjects. Others use telephoto lenses to keep a far and undetected distance from their subjects. They will either identify themselves immediately or wait until the subject asks for an explanation.

There are two things that happen when you ask a person if you can take their picture and both of them are bad. Either they say no and you don't get the picture or they say yes and stare and smile at you like they were posing for a snapshot. When you see some unusual action, get an initial picture. Afterward, you can identify yourself, get their names, and take addition photographs after they become accustomed to your presence.

Pictorials

The other type of feature picture is the much maligned pictorial. Traditionally, the pictorial is a silhouette of two standing, arm-in-arm lovers at sunset. Pictorials rely on the graphic elements of composition and lighting more than subject matter. Many times pictorial feature pictures, when combined with bold page layout design, can educate unsophisticated readers to the artistic forms and lighting characteristics within their world.

A photojournalist should never become distracted by shapes and shadows. Personal artistic expression in the form of pictorial feature pictures has a limited place in the photographer's portfolio. It is far better to take pictures that combine the striking visual qualities of the pictorial with human interest moments.

Because feature assignment photographers often are their own reporters, much of the responsibility for the caption is left to the photographer. Names and locations are a minimal requirement. Quotations from subjects bring more interest to an otherwise ordinary picture/caption package and increase the chances for larger, front-page treatment.

SPORTS ASSIGNMENTS

Although most persons would link photojournalism with news assignments, a recent survey of newspaper photographers revealed that the most common assignment is actually sports. Sports assignments combine the action and excitement of news within a clearly defined structure. The key for successful sports photography is to know that structure.

You have to be familiar with the rules of the game to predict dramatic moments. You should also know the backgrounds of some of the key players and anticipate their contribution. If you know that a rookie kicker is about to attempt his first field goal for an NFL team you should concentrate your telephoto lens on his sideline preparations. In an instant, his face may reveal his nervousness that would make a good picture.

TYPES OF SPORTS ASSIGNMENTS

Sports Action and Sports Feature are categories within the sports assignment. Sports Action is a photograph of any moment that occurs on the playing field during the run of the game. Sports Feature is a picture that shows anything else: an angry coach in the locker room, a frustrated player on the sideline, an anxious fan in the stands.

As implied by the name, the same procedure applies to

sports feature hunting as with human interest features. A photographer tries to capture a peak, dramatic event not happening on the playing field.

Most sports involve a ball and at least two opposing players. The best sports photographs not only show the ball, but reveal the determination in body language and facial expressions each player's struggle to out-perform the other. Readers are aware of the overhead perspective offered by television of the linebacker blitzing a quarterback.

A successful sports photographer gets beyond the uniform and the helmet and into the eyes of the players. A reader should be able to see the passionate, determined eyes of that blitzing linebacker or the frustrated expression of the soon-to-be-sacked quarterback.

For most sports, long lenses are a necessity. Fast shutter speeds are also in order. Because many sports are played at night or indoors under artificial lighting, expensive telephoto lenses that let in as much light as possible are necessary.

A fast ASA film or a film that is pushed to a higher ASA with high speed developer is as necessary as a fast telephoto lens. These techniques are valuable because a photographer wants the most depth of field and the fastest shutter speed possible from a film and lens combination. Focus is a problem with fast moving players. If the lens is wide open, there is no room for focus error. Stopped action without blurring is almost mandatory for sports pictures.

Some photographers use an electronic flash on their cameras where it is permitted by sports officials. Players and television videographers may object to the flash as it causes a brief flash of light that may distract from the game. Flash, however, has been used successfully during basketball games when the electronic strobes are mounted in the four comers of the arena and controlled through a radio frequency on the camera by the photographer at courtside.

Of course the cost of such a system is prohibitive. When using flash, make sure that the power output dial is set low (1/16 of second on some units) and the portable battery pack is fully charged. Sports action happens quickly. A low power setting will make sure that the recycle time is quick enough to capture that action.

A photographer should also use a camera that synchronizes its shutter with the flash at 1/250th of a second. Ghosting, an undesirable bluffing effect, can occur when a player moves faster than a shutter speed can stop. For example, at 1/60th of a second, a common shutter to flash synchronization, ghosting would certainly occur with any player moving faster than a walk.

To round out a photographer's equipment list, cameras should include motor drives for fast film advancement, a unipod to help support the telephoto lens, and a players' roster for caption information. Many photographers keep track of key plays by shooting the scoreboard immediately afterward.

TIPS FOR SHOOTING VARIOUS SPORTS

It is difficult to give guidelines for shooting sports because they are so different. Knowing the rules of the game will help you find a spot where the key action is most likely to occur. Here are some general rules, but always look for an unusual angle. Suggestions are included.

Football photographers usually squat about 5 yards either side of the line of scrimmage with a 300mm telephoto lens on a unipod. When a team is within 10 yards of the goal, photographers usually stand behind the outside boundary of the end zone. Another camera with a wide angle lens is ready for close-up, sideline action or features.

To facilitate mobility, many shooters use a small, stomach bag to carry film, another lens, and a flash. Pay strict attention to the movement of the players. Several photographers have been hit and their equipment damaged by a 210-pound running back. Play your hunches. A quarterback may be ready to throw a "bomb." Get away from the pack and catch the reception.

Basketball photographers seldom locate themselves on the sidelines. They are most likely found on one side or the other of the net with a 35mm lens for close-up action and a

300mm lens for action farther down the court. Try an 85mm lens with a straight-ahead perspective. Or you might use a telephoto lens from a high, sideline position.

Baseball is a difficult sport to cover because the action is usually quick with long periods of dull innings. Photographers are usually confined in a special area behind first and third base. The usual equipment configuration is to have one camera on a tripod that is fixed on second base with a second camera around the neck. Pay attention. Foul balls can hurt if they are a surprise.

Use your fixed position to take pictures with your wide angle lens of fans reacting to key plays. Soccer photographers roam from the sidelines to the goal looking for headers. You may want to use an extreme low angle through the netting of the goalie attempting to stop a score. Hockey photographers try to get high enough with long lenses to avoid the protective shield around the playing area.

Use a wide angle lens up against the plastic protector to capture a hard check or scuffle. Tennis is best photographed while kneeling at one side of the net. However during professional matches photographers are limited to an area at a courtside location. As with baseball, try to get crowd feature pictures. Swimming events are often photographed with a flash and a long lens wit favourable results. Use an underwater camera to record the other side of a dive or turn.

Most track and field events require a long lens and knowledge of the individual event. You might use an extremely long telephoto lens and take close-ups of key actions-the relay hand-off, the pole vaulter's grip, or the shot put thrower's grimace. Whenever there is doubt on how to cover an event, look at the positions and equipment of other, more experienced photographers. Then, think of a position based on your knowledge of the game. Above all, keep in focus, minimize blurring, and show the drama of competition in the players' eyes.

PORTRAIT ASSIGNMENTS

Readers want to know what people in the news look like.

The portrait assignment is an opportunity for photographers to capture a person's personality. It is no easy task. Important and ordinary newsmakers tend to hide behind a facade of friendliness. Seldom does a photographer get the luxury to spend long periods of time with a busy businessman. All the photographer's instincts and technical competence come into play to watch for a moment when the subject's personality is revealed.

TYPES OF PORTRAIT ASSIGNMENTS

There are two kinds of portrait pictures: mug and environmental. Mug shots, those little head and shoulder, close-up portraits, have staged a comeback on the pages of newspapers. A recent research study revealed that the front pages of five large circulation newspapers are filled with the tiny face photographs. It seems that photographers must learn to live with the small images.

Mug Shots

The term mug shot comes from the definition, "to make faces." The challenge for photographers is to make the mug shot more than a picture of a subject smiling for the camera. Despite its small size, the picture can and should be a telling record. The portrait can be taken in the newspaper's studio where the lighting and background can be rigorously controlled or in the subject's office or home. A short telephoto lens, in the range between 85mm and 105mm, is the best choice for the close-up portrait. The subject is likely to be nervous.

With a telephoto, the photographer need not get too close in order to fill the frame with the person's face. A telephoto also tends to have shallow depth of field. A close-up mug shot should not contain distracting background elements. Don't be hesitant to take pictures of hand gestures that occur close to the face. Unusual angles including a side view might be tried. Cropping on the face can also be tighter than normally expected to add interest to the portrait.

Expect to take a 36 exposure roll of film for a variety of

facial gestures. If a subject is outgoing, an editor may be convinced to print a series of three head portraits for a more interesting and revealing layout. Be sure to take pictures from each side and in front for a variety of views.

The Environmental Portrait

The environmental portrait not only shows what the subject looks like, but also reveals aspects of the sitter's personality by the foreground and background objects the person displays. Personal mementos on a desk or hung on a wall let the reader know more about the subject than a simple portrait can reveal.

It is a picture of a person AND that person's environment-NOT simply a picture of a person in an environment. Some photographers specialize in the environmental portrait with wonderful results. Arnold Newman and John Loengard make photographs that reveal a subject's personality through facial expressions and background clues.

Because the environment in which a person lives, works, or plays is a necessary part of the photograph, a wider lens is needed than for a mug shot.

The depth of field should be more extreme because the background needs to be in focus. A wide angle lens choice in a range from 20mm to 35mm is most preferred by photographers.

If a large, picture window is available, use that soft, natural light for the portrait. Often, however, the available lighting must be supplemented with electronic flash. A bare-bulb flash simulates soft, window light and is an excellent flash choice. If the ceiling is of moderate height and lightly coloured, a flash head aimed at an angle will bounce the light off the ceiling and create a soft, even glow.

If possible, a photographer may want to bring an umbrella or a light box and a stand for the flash. The photographer should try to avoid the flash mounted on the camera and pointed directly at the subject unless the personality of the subject warrants such a technique. Direct flash creates bright, blinding light and harsh shadows that are inappropriate for most portraits.

Some photographers stage manage their environmental portrait subjects. They tell them where to sit or stand, whether to look at the camera or away, and to hold a prop. The clich6 environmental business person's portrait always has the subject pretending to talk on the telephone. Such a picture always looks phony and is a result of laziness or a photographer's much too prevalent ego who assumes he or she knows how the subject should look.

The best method is to have plenty of time for picture taking, have a reporter interview the subject so that the photographer can work more freely, and if asked by the subject where to stand or what to do, simply tell him or her to decide. It is always better to not create or stage manage a portrait session.

Even if a pen and pencil set on a desk or a large, leafy, potted palm is in the way, avoid the temptation to move those objects. Part of the challenge of being a photojournalist is to work with the limitations that are presented during a shooting session. Distracting visual elements are a part of the subject's personality and should be left in the composition.

ILLUSTRATION ASSIGNMENTS

Consisting of food, fashion, and editorial subjects, the illustration assignment has come under criticism by leaders in the field who worry about the rise in the use of set up, contrived and computer manipulated images. The judges for the 47th Annual Pictures of the Year, one of the most prestigious photographic competitions in the world, announced that because of a concern for photographic credibility, the editorial illustration category would be eliminated.

In addition, "photos that portray the subject realistically will be preferred to those that illustrate a lever headline or concept". Such trends have come and gone throughout the history of photojournalism. It is certainly hoped that a photographer who works on an illustration assignment does not carry those techniques to the other types of assignments. A fashion assignment, for example, lets the photographer work with an art director to create images that show models and clothing in pleasing compositions.

The nature of an illustration is such that it demands much pre-planning. Locations, models, and clothing must be selected. During the shoot, poses must be managed. The ethical danger lies when the photographer, fresh from a fashion shoot, is asked to make an environmental portrait and uses those same techniques to manipulate the subject for an editorial story.

The photographer's credibility may suffer. Readers who notice the name of a photographer who created an illustration may also see the same photographer taking pictures for other assignment categories and assume those pictures were set up as well. The rise of the illustration assignment can be directly related to the rise in the use of colour.

Newspapers have invested heavily in colour printing technology to attract readers and advertisers. Colour printing in newspapers has increased steadily in quality and quantity to the point where readers expect to see colour photographs and graphics everyday. To keep up with the demand, many photography staffs have switched to shooting all colour negative film, bought colour enlargers and film and print processors, and purchased portable lighting equipment powerful enough to be used in poor lighting situations with low ASA colour films.

New films on the market, however, have made the shooting of colour as easy and worry free as with black-and white film products without complicated electronic flash techniques. Some staffs have hired or made a photographer responsible for all the illustration assignments, thus avoiding an ethical conflict of interest.

The photographer is trained in 120mm and large format colour negative and transparency lighting and shooting techniques.

From an idea originated from a reporter or editor, the photographer is asked to illustrate a vague concept through an arrangement of props and models usually in a studio location. Many photographers enjoy the creative challenges offered by the illustration assignment. Problem solving is an absolute necessity as props get lost, food wilts or melts, and models complain.

The use of illustrations should be kept to a minimum by a newspaper. Whenever possible, illustrations should be made in realistic settings. Above all else, a photographic illustration should be clearly labeled as such in the caption and techniques that are special to the illustration should never carry over to another assignment category.

PICTURE STORY ASSIGNMENTS

With all other assignments, the pressure to produce pictures on a tight deadline sometimes causes photographers to hurry themselves through a shooting session. The picture story assignment gives a photographer a chance to slow down and produce a package of pictures over a longer period of time. Although not as numerous as some of the other assignments, picture stories should be essential components in a photographer's portfolio.

At its best, a picture story illuminates a serious city-wide social problem through the telling in words and pictures a particular person's plight. Picture story ideas come from an editor, a reporter, or a photographer. Gene Smith, one of the most respected photojournalists and producers of picture stories until his death in 1978, said that "Thc best way to find ideas for photo essays is to be immersed in enough activities and different people so that you keep your mind stimulated".

A curious and energetic mind will always find stories worth telling. There may be a pressing story in a foreign country with many of the newspaper readers concerned about the situation.

An editor will send a reporter/ photographer team to report their findings. Closer to home, a reporter or a photographer may have an idea for a story based on his or her own interests or previous assignments that warrant a longer treatment.

In some cases, a photographer has the opportunity and the talent to produce both the words and the pictures. Once a topic is decided upon, one of the first and crucial next steps is to conduct research on the topic. What has been written on the subject in the newspaper or in magazines and books?

What can social workers, city officials, or persons in similar situations tell? Before contact is made with a subject, the photographer should read and talk to as many sources as possible in order to get as thorough an understanding as possible. Part of the research process is to decide on the film and equipment that will be necessary for the completion of the assignment. Is the project a black-and-white or colour film story?

Will special lighting or camera equipment be required? Will permission from subjects be necessary? Another crucial part of proper picture story planning and yet often overlooked is the deadline. There should be some kind of forced completion date for the project.

Even if the story is self-imposed and the photographer shoots the pictures on his or her own time, a strictly enforced deadline upheld by a caring editor will prevent a photographer from spending too much time on the story. Many serious and professional photojournalists have sacrificed their careers because they became emotionally involved with the subject of a picture story.

One photographer worked for over a year on a story of a little girl dying of cancer. When she died, the photographer decided to continue with the story and show how a family copes with the death of a child. The photographer could have used a strong editor to help manage the story and prevent the photographer from becoming obsessed. The next step is to make contact with the subject. Some photographers do not bring cameras with them to the first meeting.

Others take their cameras, but leave them in the trunk of their car. Most photographers will bring a camera with a 35mm lens on a strap around a shoulder to get the subject used to the picture taking process. Most persons think of photography as a means to prove they were at a famous landmark, to document the growth of a child, or to record the smiles of family members and friends.

A photographer must take care to explain to the subject the purpose and intended outcome for the pictures. More importantly, the subject needs to understand that tiny, revealing moments only come if a subject is willing to be revealed and a photographer is willing to be a fly on the wall quietly observing and recording. A picture story usually has five kinds of pictures: an overall scene-setter, a medium distance interaction, a portrait, a close-up, and an ending picture.

The overall scene-setter describes in one picture the essence of the story. The photograph should readily place the main subject in the context for the reader. The medium distance interaction picture should show the subject communicating with some other person connected with the story. A portrait is usually a candid moment that reveals the subject's personality.

The close-up photograph can be a tightly cropped detail of an object or a person that tends to symbolize the person's situation.

Finally, the ending picture sums up and concludes the set of pictures. A photographer tells a story with words and pictures. There should be a logical beginning, middle, and end. Once the pictures are taken, some photographers give contact sheets to an editor for the final decision.

Others make 8 X 10 work prints of their favourites, called 11 selects" and let the editor chose from them. Many photographers work with an editor to produce a layout together. The editor concept, the idea that someone not emotionally involved in the story selects the pictures for the final layout, is a strong and valid one. An editor should keep the reader in mind.

The photographer still has the subjects in mind. An editor should know from experience the pictures that best communicate a story. But a confident editor should never object to a photographer's input. Perhaps the best compromise is for a photographer to make prints of the favourites and for an editor to select from those images with a photographer's gentle prodding.

NEW TECHNOLOGICAL ADVANCES

Photojournalists are not only social historians with a camera, they are competent technicians who must keep abreast of the changing technology and the acceptable ethical considerations associated with that technology. In the 1940s, it was ethically acceptable to pose many subjects because the commonly accepted technology of the day, the awkward 4 X 5 press camera with a portable flash, was a poor recorder of the candid moment.

Also, without a 36 exposure film cassette, photographers were forced to make every picture count. Photographers commonly use cropping, exposure, contrast, dodging, and burning techniques in the darkroom to make the meaning of a picture more clear.

Cropping can be accomplished during shooting by the choice of lens, distance from the subject or angle chosen, in the darkroom by changing the height of the enlarged image or moving the blades of an adjustable easel, or by marking the white borders of a print to show the area of the final, printed image.

With manipulations in aperture and shutter speed combinations or the use of filters when shooting, times and temperatures when processing the film, aperture and time settings with an enlarger, and filter or paper grade selections in the darkroom, photographers can alter the original tones of the scene dramatically.

By preventing light from exposing on a certain area of a print with a tool or by hand, the area can be "dodged" to appear to be lighter. Conversely, by adding more light to a specific area, the print appears to be darker or "burned." Dodging and burning can also be accomplished with concentrated developer or chemical bleaches.

Some photographers have resorted to a simple technique to manipulate an image-flopping. A negative is turned upside-down in the enlarger carrier to produce a picture that is reversed, or flopped. Sometimes the angle of a subject's face or hand fits a layout design more pleasingly if the angle is reversed as if viewed in a mirror.

The practice is dangerous because right-handed people can be made to appear left-handed, a wedding ring is seen on a right hand, and words in the picture are reversed. Photographers should notice the best angles while shooting without resorting to flopping a negative.

With computer technology, the picture manipulations cited here are possible without ever entering a darkroom. Newspapers and national news bureaus are experimenting with technologies that in a few years will be commonly thought of as the industry standard.

Whether a subject is photographed with negative film or by electronic still video cameras where photographers are able to record their images on a 2-inch floppy disk, the pictures can be converted to computerized, digital images. The photographer can then make exposure, colour balance, and cropping adjustments on a television or computer screen, type caption information, and send their words and photographs via a telephone line to the photo editor's computer terminal.

Once in the newsroom's computer, the pictures can be readied for the printing process. The photo editor can make exposure, colour, and cropping corrections. Computer-controlled colour separations are then automatically performed with the pictures ready for the printing press. At the present time, the new technology saves time, yet is expensive with the quality not as high as present, traditional methods.

But the day will come when the technology becomes affordable for even university photojournalism programs. There are certain principles that should remain constant despite technological advances. The guiding principle for such manipulations should always be the content of the photograph. Is the content or intent of the image drastically altered by the manipulation?

Will an exposure adjustment, angle or perspective change, tight crop, colour correction, filter selection, flopped negative, or a dodged or burned area mislead a reader? If the answer is yes, the manipulation should not occur. Whether by traditional or new technological methods, the underlying principle of not fooling the public should never be compromised.

Credibility forms the distinction between a respected chronicle of a community's best and worst moments and a supermarket tabloid. A modem photojournalist is a mixture of reporter, artist, and craftsperson. A photographer is expected to determine in 1/500th of a second, whether a subject is newsworthy, aesthetically pleasing, and technically possible to record on film.

Assignments during any one shift can run from coverage of a five-alarm fire to a meeting with the governor. Consequently, photojournalists should be well-educated, curious, and cool under stressful situations. Photographers must also be humane, caring individuals aware of the many ethical concerns that are a part of any news assignment.

Chapter 3

A Philosophical Perspective

The problem with photojournalism ethics is that answers are not easily found when they are most needed. What answers there are, are often derived from emotional outbursts rather than from the calm of reason. Surveys are mailed to photographers with situations detailed. Respondents are asked to rate the actions of photographers in hypothetical situations.

For example, in one study, 38% of professional photographers in a national survey said the actions of a photographer during a specific situation are ethical. However, 34% rate the same action as unethical. Which group is right? Can the right answer ever be determined? How are right answers derived?

The introduction to Approaches to Ethics, states, "Ethics is not primarily concerned with getting people to do what they believe to be right, but rather with helping them to decide what is right". Such a definition implies that there is an overall right thing to do regardless of a person's conflicts with values, principles, and loyalties.

A photographer may have a very different ethical orientation than an editor or a reader depending on the situation. Taking a picture of a stressful subject is a photographer's choice. Printing the picture on the front page is an editor's choice. A reader may find such choices offensive if he or she is concerned with privacy rights and humanitarian ethics.

Can there be an ethic that will satisfy all groups involved? No. But ethics "is not concerned at all with what public opinion or moral matters actually happen to be, just as the scientist is not concerned with what people believe about the shape of the earth but with its actual shape".

Yet photographers, particularly student photographers, frequently ask if an action during a specific situation is correct. There needs to be some method that solves the ethical dilemma. To further complicate the issue, different philosophers and writers report different definitions of ethical behaviour. Some definitions are based on an ideal derived from general moral rules.

Other definitions are interpreted as being specific guidelines of proper ethical behaviour. Different ethical belief systems with their guiding values, principles, and loyalties are discussed later in a journalistic context. It should be made clear at the outset that no specific course of action will be right for every individual and for every situation. However, confronting general ethical principles is the first step when evaluating whether the shooting and publishing of a controversial situation was ethical.

STUDY HYPOTHETICAL SITUATIONS

There have been few studies specifically related to photojournalism ethics. Brink, Hartley, and Wilcox sent surveys to a large number of students, readers, photographers, editors, and educators. Respondents rated the situations described in those surveys as ethical, questionable, or unethical.

The problem with the surveys was that one never knew why a respondent made a particular ethical judgment. An action was rated ethical, for example, but a reader of the survey never learned how the respondent came to that conclusion. Are upbringings, journalistic principles, reader concerns, newsroom pressures, or ethical orientation responsible for a survey subject's decision?

The answer is not known. Several other researchers have conducted studies of journalism ethics. For example, Barney focused on journalists' ethical orientations, moral development, and dogmatism as possible ethical decision makers. Mills discovered that a number of journalists use the conflicting principles of the public's right to know versus an individual's right to privacy as contributing factors.

Izard found that journalists take into account readers' reactions more today than in the past. Weaver and Wilhoit reported that journalists are mostly influenced ethically by newsroom learning, senior editors, and co-workers.

VALUES, PRINCIPLES, AND LOYALTIES

The first step in determining an ethic for the field is to determine the values, principles, and loyalties at work. A journalist must be able to define these underlying factors in the decision-making process. Ed Lambeth in his book, Committed Journalism, identified the values that are highly regarded by journalists: Newspaper journalists give readers information for their daily lives; information is published to help readers make decisions; information gives meaning to a complex world; newspaper reporters make sure that public and private institutions work fairly and without prejudice; newspapers publish information that help enrich the culture for individuals; finally, newspapers publish information that helps others to distribute goods and services.

These six journalistic values can be distilled, according to Lambeth, to:

1. Knowledgeability,
2. Usefulness,
3. Understanding,
4. Feedback,
5. Education, and
6. Entrepreneurship.

Lambeth also listed the principles that journalists stand by: truth telling, justice, freedom, humaneness, and stewardship. "Most fundamentally, the need is for a habit of accuracy".Truth, beyond all other principles, is the guiding guarantee for ethical journalism.

The principle of justice is related to a reporter's preoccupation with fairness. A story should be complete, relevant, honest, and straightforward. The freedom principle refers to a journalist that is independent both politically and economically.

A journalist should never compromise that independence by "the acceptance of gifts, free or reduced travel, outside employment, certain financial investments, political activity, participation in civic activity, or outside speaking engagements". Humaneness, as Lambeth wrote, is a principle that requires "a journalist to give assistance to another in need".

Finally, the principle of stewardship is closely related to responsibility. A journalist is responsible for "the rights of others, the rights of the public, and the moral health of his own occupation". Vague principles and values are the guiding foundations for the writing of professional ethics codes.

For a photojournalist, the principles detailed in the NPPA "Code of Ethics" roughly follow the principles mentioned by Lambeth. Truth telling, justice, and freedom are principles covered by the NPPA Code when it asserts that "pictures should report truthfully, honestly, and objectively.

" The principle of humaneness is mentioned when photographers are asked to have "sympathy for our common humanity." Finally, the stewardship principle is invoked when photojournalists are told that their "chief thought shall be to lift the level of human ideals and achievement higher than we found it."

Loyalties, as Christians wrote, identify which parties will be influenced by it [a decision to photograph] and which ones we feel especially obligated to support". Loyalties to subjects, readers, society, the organization, the photographer, and the profession, need to be identified and weighed against each other.

If a photographer, for example, is more loyal to him or herself, if he or she values winning contests, receiving peer acknowledgment, or pay raises over loyalty to his or her readers, that photographer is much more likely to have ethical problems. In Approaches to Ethics, Jones et al. recommended that a person with an ethical dilemma first "ascertain the facts, sort and weigh the conflicting principles, apply partially indeterminate principles to the particular circumstances, and then, come to a decision".

Christians et al. used a variation of that ethical inquiry they called the "Potter's Box," named for Harvard Divinity School Professor, Dr. Ralph Potter. The box is used as a model for social ethics. For any situation, first define the circumstances as fully as possible.

News values, principles, and loyalties that pertain to the specific situation are factored into the ethical equation. When all these considerations are within the "box," a course of action becomes more clear. For example, suppose that the ethical dilemma in question is Hartley's first situation, "Klan Rally." A photographer is assigned to cover an anti-Ku Klux Klan demonstration in a city park.

When he arrives, a police officer is speaking to a crowd of newsmen saying it would be a good idea if they left. He says, "Some Klansmen are going to be staging a counter-demonstration and we're afraid the presence of the press will encourage violence." Some of the newsmen leave but the photographer stays.

Violence does erupt and the photographer is later awarded the Pulitzer Prize for his images depicting the fighting. The first step in the "Potter's Box" analysis is to define the ethical question posed by the situation. An ethical question might be: Should a photographer stay at the scene of a demonstration despite his presence possibly inciting violence?

Defined further the question becomes: Should a photographer give up news reporting responsibilities because of the recommendation of a police officc? Defined further still and the ethical issue becomes: truth telling versus law and order. All of the news values mentioned by Lambeth, except for entrepreneurship are invoked.

If the photographer stays, readers will know about those involved with the demonstration. Readers will be able to make decisions about the different sides of the conflict. Understanding of the two sides may help give meaning to each cause. Police officials can be monitored so that justice is served fairly by government officials. The community is educated as the grievances are voiced by its members. In the face of all the values just presented, it is clear that the ethical position for a journalist to take is to stay at the scene to report the news. The next phase in the Christians et al. method is to analyse and weigh the various principles at work. A photojournalist should always tell the truth fairly and objectively.

Following such principles, the clear decision again is to stay and cover the demonstration. Identifying loyalties is the next step. As Christians et al. noted, "ethical principles are crucial in the overall process of reaching a justified conclusion. However, in the pursuit of socially responsible media, clarity over ultimate loyalties is of paramount importance".

A younger photographer's loyalties may be different from a photographer who has been at work for many years. A reader may certainly have a different set of loyalties than a reporter or editor. Loyalties help show why different individuals come to opposite conclusions about the use of a controversial photograph.

What loyalties are at work in the "Klan Rally" situation for a photographer? If loyalty is to the subjects then the photographer would stay at the scene in order to record faithfully the events at the demonstration. Another photographer would leave because participants may be hurt by the increased violence.

If loyalty is to the readers then the photographer would stay at the scene in order to inform them. Another photographer would leave because readers would not like a photographer who causes trouble. If loyalty is to society then the photographer would stay in order to inform a larger public about conditions in the community.

Another photographer would leave out of respect for police authority. If loyalty is to the organization then the photographer would stay to prove that the newspaper is worthy of its watchdog function. Another photographer would leave so as not to cause problems for the newspaper. If loyalty is to the photographer then the photographer would stay because the situation may get violent and result in dramatic pictures.

Another photographer would leave to avoid any legal problems caused by additional violence. If loyalty is to the profession then the photographer would stay and take pictures in a rational, objective and truthful manner. Another photographer would leave to avoid bringing disrespect upon all photojournalists if further violence erupted.

After a decision to stay at the scene has been made, values, principles, and loyalties alone will not tell a photographer how to take the pictures. For that answer, a photojournalist needs to identify the ethical guidelines he or she uses when covering a controversial assignment.

At a potentially violent demonstration, a photographer would probably use a 300mm telephoto lens and take pictures from a distance. Suppose, however, that a photographer is asked to photograph a protest rally for a political cause supported by the photographer. The photographer wants the protesters to look as complimentary as possible.

At the scene, there are 10 protesters out of an expected 500. The photographer has two technical choices: use a wide-angle lens to show how few protesters are present or use a telephoto lens to focus on an individual who carries a sign. With such a technique, the size of the protest group in the photograph will be ambiguous. Photographers are constantly defining reality.

By selecting what stays in the tiny 35mm frame and becomes a picture, the photographer makes a conscious or unconscious decision to edit out a vast majority of the scene. Choices of film, camera, lens, aperture, shutter speed, angle of view, filters, lighting, and cropping can change a photograph's meaning. The reason why the principles of objectivity and truthfulness are so often stressed is because a photographer can easily lose his or her objectivity and not tell the truth.

When Norman Zeisloft was fired for stage managing a sports feature picture, his executive editor, Robert Haiman said, "I believe that a photographer is every bit as much a first-class citizen in this journalistic community as any reporter.

And there is one thing about the journalistic community which is more important than in any other community and that is the obligation to tell the truth, the whole truth and nothing but the truth". Truthfulness is high on any ethical list of principles.

As John Hulteng wrote in his book on media ethics, The Messenger's Motives, "One of the least enviable situations in the debate over what is ethical and what is not in the handling of news photographs is that of the photographer".

A writer can observe a news scene quietly and anonymously and report the facts back in the newsroom. A photographer is uniquely tied to a machine-the camera. There is little opportunity for concealment, nor are hidden techniques desirable.

SIX MAJOR PHILOSOPHIES

Another method used to make and defend controversial decisions is to rely on ethical philosophies that have been established for many years. Six philosophies are discussed here. Along with the six philosophies are quotations from working newspaper photographers that show how each ethical philosophy is supported by different individuals.

The quotations come from a special report in News Photographer magazine titled, "Bibliography of Grief: An analysis and description of tragic situations over the past 15 years".

Although no one philosophy can always explain a person's motivation in supporting or rejecting a picture, generally speaking, a basic knowledge of the six ethical philosophies will help a photographer learn of his or her personal perspective. The Categorical Imperative, Utilitarianism, and Hedonism philosophies are usually used to justify a photographer who takes a controversial picture or for an editor who prints it.

However, the Categorical Imperative and the Utilitarianism approaches are most often at odds with the

Hedonistic, self-centreed philosophy. The Golden Mean philosophy can often be used by a photographer when shooting the assignment or by an editor when deciding how to print the image.

The Veil of Ignorance and Golden Rule philosophies are most likely employed to justify a decision not to take a photograph or print a picture.

CATEGORICAL IMPERATIVE

Immanuel Kant, born in East Prussia in 1724, was a great influence on Western philosophy. Christians et al. noted that Kant's Categorical Imperative means that what is right for one is right for all. Check the underlying principle of your decision and see whether you want it applied universally.

The decision to perform an act must be based on a moral law no less binding than such laws of nature as gravity. "Categorical" here means unconditional, without any question of extenuating circumstances, without any exceptions. Right is right and must be done even under the most extreme conditions.

Lambeth elabouredated on deontological ethics, Kant's emphasis on the nature of an act or a decision rather than the result of such an act or decision. Pure RULE deontology is a form of Kant's philosophy that says there are universal rules that all must follow "regardless of the good produced".

In pure ACT deontology, on the other hand, it is admitted that firm rules or codes are not always possible. With such a belief, a person's instincts become more important in decision making than logical reasons. Mixed act and rule deontology are compromises between the extreme harshness of universal rules and the idea that emotions should guide a decision.

Both mixed act and rule deontology are guided by principle, but the consequences of an act must be considered as well. Two examples of Kant's Categorical Imperative can be found in writings by photojournalists. Mary Lou Foy, former NPPA national secretary, invokes Kant when she admitted, "I think religious services should be off limits for funerals".

For her, a universal rule of not adding grief to family members during a funeral allows her to ban all photographers in all such situations. Although her major concern is not to add additional suffering to a victim's family, a Golden Rule influence, her unequivocal ban on all such photography sides her with the Categorical Imperative philosophy.

Conversely, David Nuss of the Statesman-Journal in Salem, Oregon wrote that a newspaper's role is to cover the news, "and sometimes that involves situations where there is also an issue of taste, judgment, and the right to privacy". For Nuss, the principle of reporting the news is a universal rule that must not be broken, regardless of the consequences.

Utilitarianism

A popular ethical belief used by journalists is the philosophy of Utilitarianism outlined by British philosophers Jeremy Bentham and John Mill. Utilitarianism is the belief that tries to maximize the greatest good for the greatest number of people. A person wants to "maximize value or minimize loss". In Utilitarianism, "various consequences are considered and the impact of the consequences of one action is weighed in relation to the consequences of another course of action". Christians et al. use the Watergate scandal as an example.

Reporting the story was certainly not beneficial to President Nixon, but the "overall consequences were of value to a great many people". Reporters and photographers most likely use Utilitarianism when they justify complaints from readers who object to pictures of gruesome accidents with phrases such as, "People will drive more safely."

A gripping interview with an accident victim is justified with, "Interviews act as a cathartic release for those under stress". Peter Haley of the Journal-American in Bellevue, Washington and Gary Haynes, assistant managing editor of the Philadelphia Inquirer, use Utilitarianism to justify the publishing of gruesome accident photographs.

About a series of drowning pictures Haley wrote, "at least a few parents could be moved by the photo to better train their children in water safety." Haynes wrote of Stan Forman's picture of victims of a fire escape collapse with, "and in some cities [where the photographs were published], codes were quietly reviewed to be certain Boston's tragedy couldn't be repeated locally".

When a drowning victim's photographs were printed in a small-town newspaper, the journalists involved probably used the Utilitarianism philosophy to justify publication after a storm of protest was received by readers. The photographer "pointed out that his photos are under study by the local fire department with an eye toward improving swift-water rescue techniques."

Editors expressed the belief "that the paper's photo coverage has made . . . residents much more mindful of the area's hazards than mere words could have." And the executive editor "plans to promote better relations between the paper and the public with a series of columns he will write explaining how and why certain editorial judgments are made".

Seeing the drowning pictures on the front page of the local newspaper may have upset the victim's family, but from their publication and the controversy that surrounded them, many positive outcomes for many persons occurred.

Hedonism

Hedonism, unfortunately, has gained in popularity in recent years. Hedonism comes from the Greek word for pleasure and is closely related to the philosophies of Nihilism and Narcissism. Aristippus, who died in Athens in 366 B.C., a student of Socrates, was the founder of the ethics of pleasure.

Aristippus believed that persons should "Act to maximize pleasure now and not worry about the future." Aristippus, however, referred to pleasures of the mind-intellectual pleasures. "While he believed that men should dedicate their lives to pleasure, he also believed that they should use good judgment and exercise self-control."

His famous phrase is: I possess, I am not possessed. Modem usage of the Hedonism philosophy, however, has ignored his original intent. Phrases such as, "Eat, drink, and be merry, for tomorrow we die," "Live for today," and "Don't worry-Be happy," are present examples of the Hedonism philosophy.

Dr. George Padgett, assistant professor of communication at Illinois State University, is sure of the motivation for printing graphically violent images. "They were printed," wrote Padgett, "for no other reason than that they were sensational and would sell newspapers-the same reason the supermarket tabloids give their readers a steady diet of Siamese twins and babies with three legs".

Roy Clark, instructor at the Poynter Institute for Media Studies in St. Petersburg, Florida, disagrees with Padgett's explanation. "The real reasons for publication of these photos," wrote Clark, "are not economic, but aesthetic. They involve questions of personal ambition and peer approval. The photographer desires to get his or her best work, a memorable photo, on the front page". Both explanations describe Hedonism as the justifying philosophy.

Golden Mean

Aristotle's Golden Mean philosophy refers to finding a middle ground, a compromise between two extreme points of view or actions. Formulated around the 4th Century B.C. in Greece, taking the middle way does not involve a precisely mathematical average, but is an action that approximately fits that situation at the time.

As Christians et al. wrote, "The mean is not only the right quantity, but at the right time, toward the right people, for the right reason, and the right manner". In a funeral situation, an uncomfortable assignment for a photographer, one extreme action might be for a photographer to walk boldly up to the grieving family during the service, shoot with a wide-angle lens, motor drive, electronic flash, and leave without a thought of adding to the family's discomfort.

The opposite extreme might be a photographer who is so concerned for the family that he or she refuses to take any pictures during the service. Such a photographer might even refuse to go to the site of the service against the wishes of the editor. Although Mary Lou Foy personally believes that all funerals should be off limits to photographers, such news events sometimes need to be covered.

She recommended the Aristotelian point of view when photographs of grieving victims at a funeral need to be taken. She wrote:Photographers must dress as if attending the funeral. When you get the assignment the day before, contact the family or close friend to let them know you are coming. Be early.

If for some reason the family allows you to be up close and you are photographing tears, etc., for heaven's sake, pick your shots and don't unload with a motordrive. Whether or not you get up-close permission, don't forget that the pictures showing sorrow and grief can be made at many places, and often far away.

The Golden Mean most often demands that the photographer find a less obtrusive way of covering the sensitive news event. For an editor who is faced with the decision of how to print a funeral picture, one extreme would be to print the photograph large and on the front page.

The opposite extreme would be to not print the picture. An editor who used the Golden Mean philosophy would most likely decide to print the picture small and on an inside page. The following two philosophies, Veil of Ignorance and Golden Rule, are usually used to argue against the taking and printing a controversial image by photographers, editors, subjects, and readers.

Veil of Ignorance

In his book, A Theory of Justice, John Rawls outlined the Veil of Ignorance philosophy where all members are equal. There are no advantages for any one class of people when all are reduced to their basic position in life. Seeing everyone through a veil, without noticing age, race, sex, and so on maintains "basic respect for all humans . . .".

In practical terms, a photographer tries to imagine what it would be like to be the subject of the photographs. Steele

(1987) noted that "by transferring roles, an individual is forced to consider values and loyalties from perspectives other than his own as a photojournalist".

Rawls' "shoe on the other foot" approach can be found from Jim Gehrz of the Worthington Daily Globe, of Worthington, Minnesota. In his letter to News Photographer magazine titled "How Would I Feel?"

Gehrz wrote, "we are placed in an awkward position where we must make photographs of people who are under great stress. My approach is to ask myself how I would feel if I were the person being photographed? If the answer is unacceptable, I look for a different way to tell the story in my photo".

Golden Rule

The Golden Rule philosophy teaches persons to "love your neighbours as yourself. "From the Judeo-Christian tradition, a photographer should be as humane as possible to try to protect subjects from harm inflicted by photographic coverage. "Love," according to Christians et al., "is personal, dutiful, but never purely legalistic".

Jay Mather, who won a 1979 Pulitzer Prize wrote simply, "Human kindness has always been an effective and impartial editor". Being aware that the different ethical philosophies are the basis for the values, principles, and loyalties upheld by a professional code of ethics will help photographers come to a decision.

The reason thoughtful photographers, editors, subjects, and readers disagree over the same picture is that each person bases their decision on a different philosophy. Those who side with the Categorical Imperative, Utilitarianism, or Hedonism philosophies will never agree with those who base their decisions on the Veil of Ignorance or the Golden Rule philosophies.

Whether you take a picture during a controversial situation or whether you print a controversial image by one of your photographers is often a matter of which major philosophy is your prime concern. A picture of a father grieving over the death of his son killed in a traffic accident touches many philosophical bases. It is a strong, news situation-Categorical Imperative.

It might make people drive more safely-Utilitarianism. It might win an award-Hedonism. It should be published in an inside page-Golden Mean. It might remind you of your own son-Veil of Ignorance. It might add to the father's grief if it is published-Golden Rule. Occasionally, there is blurring between the various philosophies.

You may not want the picture to run large on the front page because it might add to the father's grief-Golden Mean and Golden Rule. You may not want to publish the picture at all. You may think people crying should never be the subject of news photography because such images upset readers-Categorical Imperative and Golden Rule.

You may feel the picture is a good news photo and might make people drive more carefully, but should be used small, and on an inside page so as not to upset readers-Categorical Imperative, Utilitarianism, Golden Mean, and Golden Rule. Throughout this textbook, one of the six philosophies is often attributed to a journalist's motivation.

It is important to understand that there may be other philosophies at work that guide a decision that are unknown to the author. A photojournalist's job is to capture the news-not make it and not run from it. Sometimes, but fortunately not often, that mission runs afoul of the readers' level of sensitivity.

As Jay Mather wrote, "When a reader's visual diet is composed of benign features, routine sports pictures and carefully controlled graphic illustrations, it's easy to see why the sudden confrontation with a hard news photograph promotes such virulent responses".

According to a survey conducted by Beverly Bethune, an associate professor at the University of Georgia, when photographers in a national survey were asked, "What kinds of assignments do news photographers shoot most often?" hard news was at the bottom of the list.

Only 12% of the photographers reported that more than

about a third of their assignments could be called hard news. Nevertheless, news assignments are the ones that cause the most ethical problems. The price of being responsible for the documentation of life in all its gloriously happy and tragically sad moments is that if some people do not like what they see, they will question a photojournalist's moral character.

That reaction, however, is a necessary barometer of a photojournalist's ethics. It is a photographer's moral responsibility that the decision to take pictures is based on sound personal ethics that can be justified to all who disagree. Study hypothetical situations, know the values, principles, and loyalties that are a part of journalistic principles, and be familiar with the six major philosophies. With such a strong foundation, you will be better able to act decisively during a controversial situation.

VICTIMS OF VIOLENCE

Violence and tragedy are staples of American journalism because readers are attracted to gruesome stories and photographs.

"If it bleeds, it leads" is an undesirable rule of thumb. Judges of contests also have a fatal attraction. Pulitzer Prizes are most often awarded to photographers who make pictures of gruesome, dramatic moments. *Milwaukee Journal* editor Sig Gissler summed up the newspaper profession's sometimes Hedonistic philosophy when he admitted, "We have a commercial interest in catastrophe".

Ethical problems arise for photographers and editors because readers are also repulsed by such events. It is as if readers want to know that tragic circumstances take place, but do not want to face the uncomfortable details.

After the publication of a controversial picture that shows, for example, either dead or grieving victims of violence, readers in telephone calls and in letters to the editor, often attack the photographer as being tasteless and adding to the anguish of those involved.

As one writer noted, "The American public has a morbid fascination with violence and tragedy, yet this same public accuses journalists of being insensitive and cynical and of exploiting victims of tragedy".

THE IMMEDIATE IMPACT OF IMAGES

Photographs have long been known to spark more emotional responses than stories. Eugene Goodwin in his book, Groping for Ethics agreed. Goodwin wrote, "Pictures usually have more impact on people than written words. Their capacity to shock exceeds that of language". Other researchers have noted the eye catching ability of newspaper photographs.

Miller wrote, "Photos are among the first news items to catch the reader's eye. A photo may catch the eye of a reader who doesn't read an accompanying story". Blackwood argued that "People who either can't read, or who don't take the time to read many of the stories in newspapers do scan the photographs".

Nora Ephron asserted that disturbing accident images should be printed. "That they disturb readers," Ephron wrote, "is exactly as it should be: that's why photojournalism is often more powerful than written journalism".

When U.S. servicemen were killed in Iran during the 1980 attempt to rescue American hostages, gruesome images of the char-red bodies were transmitted to American newspapers. Ombudsman George Beveridge of the defunct *Washington Star* defended his paper's publication of the photographs by writing, "newspapers were obliged to print them because they gave readers a dimension of understanding of the situation and the people involved that written words could not possibly convey".

For Beveridge, if photographs accurately and dramatically document a news event, even though their content may be gruesome, those pictures should be printed. Beveridge is probably using the Categorical Imperative philosophy. Nevertheless, newspapers received hundreds of calls and letters protesting the use of the images.

A Mississippi newspaper editor tore the pictures up when he saw them because he explained it would have been "the poorest kind of taste to display those ghastly pictures". The editor was most likely guided by the Golden Rule philosophy. Because a photograph can immediately shock, educate, or enlighten a reader, visual impact has long been used by journalists.

The emotional impact of the first war covered by photographs, the Crimean War, was low by today's standards. Roger Fenton, forced to use the slow film and lenses of that day, captured only static portraits and battlefield images. If Fenton's motivation for taking pictures was to educate the public, he was employing a Utilitarian perspective.

Mathew Brady, recognized for his portraits of famous politicians that included President Lincoln, spent his entire family's income to employ photographers to document the Civil War. Brady hoped the pictures would be purchased in galleries for peoples' home photo albums or by the government. If Brady's guiding philosophy, as a businessman, was to make money from the pictures, he used the Hedonistic philosophy.

Americans, however, had grown weary of the wrenching Civil War that divided the nation. Few were interested in static pictures taken with slow film and lenses of battlefield configurations, portraits of soldiers, and bodies mutilated by the arms of destruction.

JACOB RIIS ILLUSTRATES HIS WORDS

Danish immigrant, Jacob Riis, a reporter for the *New York World,* saw what he considered to be inhumane treatment of the nation's poor and homeless by an insensitive government bureaucracy in the later part of the 19th century. He wrote of the dire conditions unfortunate individuals face on the streets of New York for his newspaper.

He became frustrated when, despite favourable reception to his articles, relief for the poor never came. Riis decided that photographs were necessary to show public officials and the general public the horror of the back alleys and the flop houses.

Riis, along with photographers he hired, most notably, Richard Hoe Lawrence, made photographs that brought light (literally magnesium powder that was ignited) to the dank, dark, dingy police stations and saloons. Riis gave public lectures, this time with images mounted on glass slides. The impact of his visual message shaped public opinion and helped make changes. Shortly thereafter, Riis published one of the first books to combine words and pictures in a documentary format, *How the Other Half Lives.*

THE ERA OF SENSATIONALISM

The turn of the century brought the highlight of yellow or "Front Page" style journalism. Visual images played a crucial part in this era known for its sensationalism. Frank Mott, in his history of journalism, noted that the reporting of crime news and disasters with the "lavish use of pictures" was a factor that helped define the yellow journalism period.

Publishers such as William Hearst and Joseph Pulitzer were locked into a bitter circulation struggle. Their use of shocking and gruesome photographs, regularly featured large on their front pages, was imitated by other publishers throughout the country.

The popular belief of the day was that potential newspaper buyers looking for visual amusement, would be attracted to pages filled with photographs. Such a money-oriented, Hedonistic philosophy, contributed to an era where any type of visually stimulating event was fair game for an enterprising photographer. Much of the poor reputation bestowed upon the photojournalism profession was a result of excesses during this time.

Collier magazine photojournalist, Jimmy Hare produced striking images of the Spanish-American War. Fellow reporter, Cecil Carnes wrote that Hare "photographed swollen bodies with bones breaking through the skin; he took pictures of the emancipated living, and of the babies ravaged by disease.

Such images were not used by publishers to educate or explain the war to readers, but to drum up support for a controversial conflict. Joseph Costa of the New York *Daily News,* shocked readers with his sneaked picture of a man whipped in a Baltimore jail for beating his wife.

He later made up for his young recklessness by becoming the first president of the NPPA and teaching photojournalism at universities. Although many of their images were censored by government officials, photographers during World War II produced many dramatic visual documents. A picture cooperative was formed by Acme, Associated Press, International News, and *Life* magazine to cover land and sea battles for use in publications.

Photographers such as Gene Smith and Robert Capa were famous for capturing emotionally charged moments. One photograph that was delayed for several weeks by censors concerned for the public's reaction was published in*Life*. Captioned, "Here lie three Americans" George Strock's shocking picture of the maggot covered bodies of U.S. servicemen face down in the sand of a distant island's beach was the first picture of killed American soldiers published in a U.S. magazine.

Many readers were stunned by the visually graphic image. But Susan Moeller in her chronicle of war photography, *Shooting War,* noted that many soldiers praised the photograph and the accompanying editorial. A lieutenant wrote, "Your Picture of the Week is a terrible thing, but I'm glad that there is one American magazine which had the courage to print it."

A private wrote, "This editorial is the first thing I have read that gives real meaning to our struggle". World War II was the last major conflict in which photographers were on the same side as the government. The Korean and Vietnam Wars produced films and photographs that brought home the terror like never before on a daily basis.

David Douglas Duncan produced sensitive, almost romantic portraits of American servicemen in Korea. Duncan was criticized for his many sanitized views of war by those who thought Americans at home should know the realities of war-that men were dying. Gradually, Duncan came to reject the government's handling of the war and took an anti-war position. Many critics, however, mistook his pro-soldier pictures for a pro-war attitude.

THE DISTURBING IMAGES FROM VIETNAM

Perhaps due to political uncertainty about America's role or a younger crop of photojournalists who were willing to show the worst moments, films and still pictures from the Vietnam War were the most graphically brutal in war-time photographic history.

Many photographs taken during the Vietnam War not only startled, but were responsible for helping to change the American public's opinion against that conflict. In the Spring of 1963, Malcolm Browne of the Associated Press, received a telephone call to come to a public memorial service for Buddhist monks.

Eight people had been killed during a recent demonstration against the South Vietnamese government's crackdown on their religion. The series of pictures he made at that service is unforgettable. In deliberate silence, two monks poured gasoline on a sitting third monk and set the man on fire. Browne made pictures of violent flames that engulfed the protester who never uttered a sound.

Horrified readers in the world's newspapers viewed this series the next day. Eddie Adams' frozen moment of death is another unforgettable instant. In the Winter of 1968, General Nguyen Loan, the chief of police for the city of Saigon, fired his revolver through the temple of a Viet Cong soldier.

The soldier was suspected in the killing of Loan's best friend, a police major, and knifing to death the major's wife and six children. At 1/500th of a second, Adams captured the swift judgment and brutal execution of a policeman's prisoner and sparked additional protest against America's involvement in the war.

According to Time magazine photographer, Bill Pierce, Adams never accepted the Pulitzer Prize money or seldom talks publicly about the image. Huynh Cong "Nick" Ut's terrifying image of young children running toward the camera with open mouths and fire scorched arms held awkwardly away from their sides is all the more horrible when it is known that their injuries were a result of an accidental napalm attack by South Vietnamese forces.

VIOLENT PHOTOGRAPHS OF THE 1960S

During this same turbulent decade, visual images continued to isolate some of the most strikingly terrifying moments in American history. Bob Jackson of the Dallas *Times-Herald* captured the political assassination of Lee Harvey Oswald by the man with the gray hat and the easily concealed revolver, Jack Ruby. Jackson's awful moment is an American icon.

In one picture, it shows the hunched determination of the assassin, the painful gasp of the handcuffed victim, and the shock of helplessness on the face of a policeman. Bill Eppridge and Boris Yaro were both covering Robert Kennedy's campaign speech after the California presidential primary.

For many persons, Kennedy symbolized the hope that America would overcome the shock of a presidential assassination, a seemingly endless and costly foreign war, riots in cities across the country, and finally, the assassination of the leading African-American spokesman, Martin Luther King, two months previously.

Who can forget, amid the technical problems of harsh lighting and the grainy appearance of push-processed film, the image of a caring busboy cradling the head of a man he never met. The loss seen on his face symbolizes all the world's loss. In the Bible belt of America, John Filo, a college student with a borrowed camera, summed up many Americans' anguish over the Vietnam War in one angry photograph.

The National Guard was called to the campus of Kent State University in Ohio to quiet a series of demonstrations against military involvement in Vietnam and Cambodia in 1970. Filo captured the image of Mary Vecchio kneeling over the bloodied body of Jeffery Miller. Vecchio seems to be screaming the hauntingly simple question, "Why?"

Vecchio, a 14-year-old runaway from Florida, was accused by Florida's Governor Claude Kirk of being planted by the Communists. The notoriety brought media attention to her subsequent troubles with the law. It was reported, for example, when she ran away from home again, when she was sent to a juvenile home, and when she was arrested for loitering and marijuana possession.

She later admitted that the picture "destroyed my life". Interestingly, moving films shown to television audiences were made at the same time during the Adams, Ut, Jackson, and other dramatic news events, but it is the powerful stillness of the frozen, decisive moment that lives in the consciousness of all who have seen the photographs.

The pictures are testaments to the power and the sanctity of the still, visual image. Malcolm Mallette wrote that "the electronic image flickers and is gone. The frozen moment remains. It can haunt. It can hurt and hurt again. It can also leave an indelible message about the betterment of society, the end of war, the elimination of hunger, the alleviation of human misery".

THE PUBLIC SUICIDE OF BUDD DWYER

Editors have noticed that when emotionally charged and gruesome pictures come from a local event, readers react the strongest. A mother grieving over a drowned child in Bangladesh will not produce the same level of reactions as an identical subject in a reader's home town.

Pennsylvania State Treasurer, Budd Dwyer had just been convicted of bribery. Journalists from several newspapers, news services, and television stations gathered around a small podium that sat on a table expecting to hear Dwyer announce his resignation from state government. What they heard were the long, rambling last words of a seriously troubled man.

Dwyer pulled out a .357 magnum, long barrel pistol, waved back reporters, stuck the revolver in his mouth, pulled the trigger and ended his torment. His desperate act also created torment with editors around the country who were left with some hard questions: Should any pictures be used? Should more graphic or less graphic pictures be used? Should only one or a complete series of pictures be printed?

On what page should the pictures be displayed? How large should the pictures be? Should colour or black-and-white pictures be used? Journalism researcher Robert Baker found that among the 93 daily newspapers he studied, "Newspapers more than 200 miles away from the victim's hometown were two-and-a-half times as likely to use the 'very graphic' photographs as those within 100 miles". Editors were more likely to use the most gruesome images the further they were from the event.

Robert Kochersberger, another journalism researcher, also looked at the Dwyer suicide photo use. He found a trend toward sensitivity to the publishing of the graphic suicide pictures.

For him, this result may suggest the "abandoning [of I the time-worn patterns of 'Front Page'-style journalism that would have called for using the graphic photos with little second thought".

As evidence of this new sensitivity, Kochersberger cited two editors. "Jess Garber, managing editor of the *Record Herald,* Waynesboro, PA., wrote, 'I believe in the public's right to know but am not sure that carries to seeing a distraught person blowing his brains out' ".

"John Wellington, managing editor of the *Meadville Tribune,* published in Dwyer's home town, wrote'Would anyone with half a whit of common sense want graphic suicide pictures imposed on his or her children? I would not' ".

Apparently, many editors disagreed with Garber and Wellington. Baker's data shows that "very graphic" suicide photographs were used by up to 58% of newspapers in his survey in one of his demographic categories. Editors that used the 'very graphic" images justified their publication with statements such as, "'Photos had tremendous impact as a news story' "and "'We used the photo to show a bizarre news event.

It's not normal for a person to shoot himself at the end of a news conference' ". Once again, opposing philosophies are at work. One group of editors would most likely side with the Veil of Ignorance or Golden Rule philosophies. Another group would probably side with the Categorical Imperative philosophy.

REASONS FOR READER REACTIONS

Some writers fear that readers become callused by the many images of the dead and dying shown in the media. Bill Hodge, past president of the NPPA, recently wrote, "There's a change occurring among our audiences. I see a desensitized viewer and reader that is harder to offend or shock.

They seem to be more immune to-or more interested in-shocking things". Hodge cited such "Trash TV" shows led by Geraldo Rivera and Oprah Winfrey that regularly feature programs that test the public's sensitivity.

There is some concern among professionals that the real culprit in the controversy over gruesome images is not the content, but whether the picture is printed in colour. Readers of the Minneapolis Star Tribune complained about several graphically descriptive pictures that were printed in colour. One caller said, "Colour should be something beautiful."

Another reader complained that an image of a bleeding Arab mayor "needed black and white." Lou Gelfand, ombudsman for the *Star Tribune* reported that former chief photographer, Earl Seubert "says colour is the cause of most of the response.

Some of the pictures ran in black-and-white in an early edition and looked comparatively dull." Colour may be a contributing factor to a reader's reaction, but readers are still moved by dramatic black-and-white content.

Many readers, editors note, complain when a graphically violent picture is published in the morning, rather than the evening paper. For some readers, there is a sacredness about the first meal of the day. A typical response can be found from a Minneapolis reader who admitted, "I can't handle that kind of picture with breakfast".

Another contributing factor to a reader's negative reaction to a controversial photograph is the reader's perception of the respect given to the victim and the family. An image of a photographer at a funeral wearing blue jeans and an open-collared shirt and hovering over a casket with a wide-angle tens for a close-up, gives readers the impression that the photographer has little respect for the subject.

Of course, an editor will seldom print that uncomplimentary portrait. An editor can show disrespect in the eyes of some readers, however, by running a picture extremely large on the front page or with only a brief caption explanation. Readers associate the importance given to a photograph with a story that accompanies it.

When readers objected to a picture of a man killing a calf with a pistol during a mass slaughter of cattle during a protest over the cost of raising beef, Bill Cento of the St. Paul Dispatch and Pioneer Press said, "The story ran across the top of page one, but we ran the picture inside. A mistake, I believe. The words are needed to tell why it was done.

The picture most forcefully tells that it was done". Whenever possible, stories and photographs should be located on the same page. One heartening note: Readers will voice their negative comments about a picture regardless of the victim's race or gender characteristics. Readers seem to be equal opportunity commentators. Many of the most controversial images printed in newspapers in the past 15 years have received reader wrath with subjects who were men, women, African-American, Asian, Caucasian, or Hispanic.

A FAMILY'S TRAGEDY BECOMES PUBLIC

One of the best ways for an editor to learn if readers have grown callused and insensitive is to take note of the calls and letters produced after the printing of a controversial image. When an image offends, an editor knows of it quickly. It is almost reassuring, then, to learn that photographs still have the power to offend readers-particularly an image of a drowned child with distraught family members standing over the body.

The editors of the Bakersfield *Californian,* an 80,000-circulation newspaper, heard loud and clear the anger of readers over a remarkable photograph. The paper received 500 letters, 400 phone calls, 80 subscription cancellations, and one bomb threat. Such a reader reaction is extraordinary given the paper's size. National columnist Bob Greene wrote, "The picture should never have been published; in a way I hope you can understand, it was pornography." For Greene the picture, "epitomized everything that is wrong about what we in this business do".

The controversy at the *Californian* was reminiscent of other disturbing photographs that are printed from time to time and objected to by the nation's newspaper readers. Stan Forman, then with the Boston *Herald-American,* captured a tragic moment with his 135mm lens. A woman and her young niece are frozen by the fast shutter speed in a fall from a faulty fire escape's metal platform. The woman was killed, while the child was saved because she landed on her aunt's body. One critic said the picture was a "tasteless breach of privacy".

Maria Rosas of the *Miami Herald* made a self-admitted shocking photograph of a lifeless, nude Haitian man from a group of 33 who were drowned while trying to reach the safety of Florida. Callers characterized the picture as "vulgar, racist and sensationalistic". Nudity, the fact that the picture was in colour, and that it was used large on the front page were contributing factors in the protest.

From a helicopter's overhead perspective, George Wedding made a striking photograph of the body of 11-year-old Andy Karr lying face-up in the back of an ash-filled pickup truck, a victim of Mt. St. Helen's powerful force. Readers called the image "callous, insensitive, gross, cruel, tacky, in very poor taste, barbaric, unimaginable, and repulsive".

With all three pictures, editors most likely justified them with the Categorical Imperative philosophy-the image described the tragic event like no combination of words ever could. [But utilitarianism could also be evoked by editors since the images educated the public about unsafe fire escapes that should be inspected, dramatically told the results of living conditions in Haiti that led to such desperate acts, and clearly showed the tragic results if the public failed to heed warnings from governmental officials.]

With all three pictures, readers more often objected to them with the Golden Rule philosophy-the images contributed to the victim's family grief or upset readers who would rather not see such tragic events. With a caption head titled, "A family's anguish," there is no doubt that John Harte's photograph of young, lifeless, 5-year-old, Edward Romero, halfway zippered in a dark, plastic body bag with family members crying and a bystander awkwardly reaching for one of the survivors, is a powerful and disturbing image.

Under the outstretched arms and objections from a deputy sheriff, Harte made the picture with a 24mm lens from about 5 feet away. Harte admitted that the family scene was a "get-at-any-cost picture" and the most dramatic moment he had ever photographed. For Harte, his motivation was probably the Categorical Imperative philosophy-a dramatic, human tragedy should always be the subject of pictures.

After a discussion with Harte's weekend duty editor and the managing editor, Robert Bentley, who was called in to make a decision on the photograph, the editors ran the picture on an inside page agreeing with Harte's Categorical Imperative philosophy.

Bentley also employed the Utilitarian approach. One other young boy had drowned on the same day. Clearly the swimming area was a dangerous spot that the editors felt the public needed to know about with Harte's dramatic image.

A storm of protest from readers immediately followed and Bentley changed his position. In a column titled, "What should give way when news values collide with reader sensibilities?" Bentley admitted, "We make mistakes-and this clearly was a big one." Wrote Bentley, "The damage done to the memory of the late Edward Romero and to the offended sensitivities of *Californian* readers cannot be undone.

It can only be followed by sincere apologies and deep company-wide introspection". Bentley now advocated the Golden Rule philosophy, shared by a majority of his readers, to justify his changed position. Not all the letters were negative, however. Connie Hoppe wrote: I was horrified [by Harte's photograph], but I felt the item was newsworthy.

That picture was real-maybe a little more real to me because my own 21/2-year-old son drowned. If maybe just one parent saw that picture of the grieving family and drowning victim and has taken more precautions around pool and beach areas because of it, then that picture may have saved another child's life.

Bill Hodge reported that in the 2 months prior to the boy's death, 14 people had drowned. In the month following the controversy, only 2 drowned. The newspaper and the photographer had to take the wrath of an angry readership who either did not want to be faced with a real tragedy of life or they sincerely were concerned about the rights to privacy for the Romero family. Whatever the rationale, lives were probably saved by the newspaper's coverage.

ETHICS CODES ARGUMENTS

Ethical conduct may be guided by codes established by newspapers and professional organizations, but ethical codes cannot anticipate every situation. Consequently, the language of codes is hopeful, yet vague. For example, the "Code of Ethics" that all members of the NPPA must sign does not specifically mention gruesome situations.

The ethics code does contain phrases such as photographers "should at all times maintain the highest standards of ethical conduct," photojournalism "is worthy of the very best thought and effort," and members should "maintain high standards of ethical conduct."

Some would argue that codes should be ambiguous. Elliott-Boyle wrote that "codes can provide working journalists with statements of minimums and perceived ideals". When a journalist uses highly questionable practices that are outside standard behaviour, the offending reporter can be held accountable.

Others argue, however, that ethics codes should be less idealistic and more specific particularly with regards to the "exploitation of grief." In his 1986 article, George Padgett asserted that vague ethical codes and brief textbook treatment of photojournalism ethical issues do not adequately provide guidelines for dealing with pictures of grieving victims. Without such guidelines, he wrote, regulation by the courts may classify grief pictures as invasions of privacy. "The problem should be addressed," wrote Padgett, "while it is still an ethical rather than a legal issue".

CONDITIONS THAT CAUSE A READER FIRESTORM

When confronting situations and photographs of accident and tragedy victims, journalists are tom between the right to tell the story and the right NOT to tell the story. Arguments by well meaning professional journalists can be made for and against the taking and publishing or the not taking and not publishing of almost any photograph. Curtis MacDougall (197 1) in his visually graphic book, News Pictures Fit to Print Or Are They? argued that news pictures sometimes need to be offensive in order to better educate the public.

He wrote, "If it were in the public interest to offend good taste, I would offend good taste". The problem comes, of course, when journalists disagree on what is in the public's interest.

From the examples just given, it can be generalized that readers are more likely to object to a controversial picture if:

- It was taken by a staff photographer,
- It comes from a local story,
- The image is printed in colour,
- The image is printed in a morning paper,
- The image is printed on the front page,
- It has no story accompaniment,
- It shows people overcome with grief,
- It shows the victim's body,
- The body is physically traumatized,
- The victim is a child, and
- Nudity is involved.

If five or more of these conditions apply, editors should prepare themselves for reader reactions before the firestorm hits. Staff photographers and writers should be selected to help answer phone calls and letters.

Editors should prepare notes for a column that justifies the decision. As many letters to the editor and telephone transcripts as possible should be printed. Readers may not agree, but most will respect the decision if the response to the controversy is prompt and the justification is consistent.

Michael Josephson, president of the Josephson Institute for the Advancement of Ethics, has suggested that editors and ombudsmen write "early warning notes" to readers that a controversial story is about to be printed. The note could describe the reasoning that led editors to print a controversial picture.

Such a practice might head-off public misunderstanding about the intent of printing an image that may be graphically violent or intense. Public Editor Kerry Sipe of the Virginia-Pilot and Ledger-Star wrote a column on the same day a child-abuse story ran.

The paper only received one call from a reader who said the story should not have run. "If he had not written his column, Sipe said, he was sure that he would have received many more".

To better understand what the right course of action is, a journalist should be familiar with the trends prevalent in newspapers and magazines, know what the readers think is acceptable for publication, and have a strong, personal ethical background.

Professional organizations and the literature that is produced by them give journalists a good idea of where photojournalism has been and where it is likely to head. Discussions with a newspaper's ombudsman or editor, who receive many of the complaints, will help to determine the aspects of photographic coverage and publication most objectionable to readers.

Guest lectures or formalized town meetings by journalists with concerned citizens will create a dialogue with readers that will help determine the acceptance level of controversial images. Finally, personal reflection will help balance the sometimes conflicting goals of publishing the news while being sensitive to the feelings of subjects and readers.

A photographer's personal ethics are influenced by many factors: family and religious upbringing, educational opportunities, professional associations, career goals, day-today experiences, and co-workers. Nora Ephron in her book, *Scribble Scribble Notes on the Media,* devoted a chapter to a description and reaction to Stan Forman's fire escape tragedy. Ephron concluded that "I recognize that printing pictures of corpses raises all sorts of problems about taste and titillation and sensationalism; the fact is, however, that people die.

Death happens to be one of life's main events. And it is irresponsible and more than that, inaccurate-for newspapers to fail to show it ". A photojournalist's mission is to report all the news objectively, fairly, and accurately.

The profession can only improve in quality and stature if photographers are mindful of those they see in their viewfinders and those they seldom see, their readers. Decisions, however, should be guided, never ruled, by readers.

Chapter 4

Emotional Intelligence

In the last few decades, researchers have been identifying specific things that make people successful and it's clear that the world's achievers see life and behave in ways that we can learn. They use a set of skills that *we* could loosely call *intelligence* - emotional intelligence. Broadly speaking, our emotional intelligence is our ability to manage ourselves and our relationships.

One study (by Hay/McBer) showed that emotional skills were twice as important as intellectual skills in determining excellence. Many observers say that your intellectual abilities, technical skills, qualifications and experience may get you the job, but your emotional intelliegence will determine how far you are promoted,

Researchers disagree on how much the emotional skills contribute to success, but even the most skeptical we've come across recently, thinks they are probably as valuable as your intellectual and technical skills. You can't do much about your I.Q. but your can certainly increase your E.Q. (Your Emotional Quotient.)

Studies of major organisations in the United States show that the need for emotional intelligence grows with the complexity of the work. For success in the top levels of leadership, emotional skills are virtually the entire difference between outstanding leaders and mediocre ones.

At Media Associates, we prefer to focus on skills rather than emotional intelligence. It's partly so that we don't get distracted by the debate over the definition of intelligence, but mostly because it allows us to concentrate on a range of communication and emotional skills that we know are closely linked with success in business and in life generally. Notice that, with a few exceptions, the list of skills that make up what we could call a kind of intelligence, are relevant to every part of your life. Some are disciplines, such as having initiative and being conscientious. Most are skills you can learn or enhance.

Self-Awareness

For example:

- Knowing your feelings at the moment
- Knowing how those feelings affect your performance
- Having a realistic picture of your abilities
- Having a well-founded self-confidence

Self-Management

For example:

- Having the ability to manage disruptive emotions including handling stressful situations well
- Being open about your mistakes and expecting the same of others
- Being conscientious
- Being adaptable
- Having initiative
- Being optimistic as you strive to perform better

Social Awareness

For example:

- Being able to show empathy
- Giving good service to others
- Being aware of what's going on in your organisation

Relationship Management

For example:

- Developing other people's abilities
- Influencing others (persuasion)
- Communicating effectively
- Managing conflict so that you achieve a win/win outcome

- Leading effectively
- Building bonds with others
- Being an effective catalyst for change

Emotional intelligence predicts exam success. This is the finding of a study into the relationship between emotional intelligence and educational achievement, presented today, 1st November, at The British Psychological Society's Education Section Annual Conference.

At the start of the five year study, 628 Year 7 students were tested on an objective measure of emotional intelligence - the ability to identify, assess, and manage your own and others' emotions. These measures were then compared to each student's English and Science results at Year 9 SAT and again two years later at GCSE.

A significant relationship was found between boys' emotional intelligence and their SAT and GCSE English scores, with boys with higher emotional intelligence scores doing better in these exams. While for girls, a relationship between emotional intelligence and their SAT Science scores was discovered; girls with higher emotional intelligence scores did better in this exam.

Dr Pamela Qualter, from the University of Central Lancashire, said: "IQ does result in better academic test results, but our results suggest that emotional intelligence is another key predictor of academic success. "Further detailed analysis of the results suggests that emotional intelligence may moderate the effects of IQ on academic achievement.

Faced with failure, a student low on IQ but who is emotionally intelligent will be able to manage their emotions surrounding failure, reconcile poor performance and work to improve; a student low on IQ and low emotional intelligence may find failure more difficult to deal with, which undermines their academic motivation."

One implication of this research is that opportunities to develop students' emotional intelligence could be a way to improve their educational achievement. Thus, engagement in current UK educational strategies (SEAL) are likely to be important for children's future academic progress.

The British Psychological Society's Education Section Annual Conference is taking place at Kents Hill Park Conference Centre, Milton Keynes from 31st October to 2nd November 2008.

The term emotional intelligence has been used in academic circles since the late 1980s, but it took American psychologist and journalist, Dr Daniel Goleman, to release his best-selling book Emotional Intelligence for the concept to capture the public's imagination.

Goleman, a former Harvard graduate and behavioural science contributor to the New York Times, has since written a second book, Working with Emotional Intelligence in which he argues that workplace competencies based on emotional intelligence play a far greater role in high performance than do intellect and technical skills.

Moreover, Goleman claims that individuals and companies both benefit from cultivating these capabilities. Drawing on research from some 500 leading businesses, he concludes that emotional intelligence is twice as important as IQ plus technical skill combined. When IQ scores are correlated with how well people perform in their careers, the highest estimate of how much difference IQ accounts for is 25 per cent.

By contrast, says Goleman, emotional intelligence accounts for more than 85 per cent of star performance. What EI is Interest in emotional intelligence in the workplace has grown dramatically in recent years, particularly in America where EI has spawned a movement in schools, home and the community as well as the corporate environment.

A similar level of enthusiasm is evident in Europe and interest is increasing rapidly in Australia, New Zealand and Asia. But what do psychologists really mean by emotional intelligence? Is it just another term for so-called people skills and, if so, why all the hype? Some psychologists describe emotional intelligence as street smarts of sorts.

Goleman defines it as "the capacity for recognising our feelings and those of others, for motivating ourselves, and managing emotions in us and in our relationships". These are soft skills, but he insists there are hard consequences if they are ignored in the corporate world.

To illustrate his point, he cites the example of global consumer products firm that was not assessing emotional competence as part of its recruitment process. Within two years of hiring, some 50 per cent of all division heads left the firm after initial search costs of $4 million.

When the firm started assessing potential candidates for emotional intelligence, only 6 per cent of the division heads left within two years. Why emotions are different While such general attributes, as maturity, commonsense and people skills have long been associated with effective managers and employees, Goleman claims to be among the first to draw on recent scientific research to link emotional intelligence to high performance.

He says that while cognitive and technical skills evolve from only one area of the brain - the neocortex - emotional intelligence involves an integration of several areas of the brain including the higher thinking centres."The thinking brain, which regulates technical skill and cognitive ability, can operate without involving emotions," he says.

In other words, emotionally intelligent behaviour requires all the brain power used for intellect plus more. Our thinking and feeling need to be integrated. "When you are facing a decision, the sense of right or wrong is as important as any other data you might bring to the table," he says. "If it feels right it probably is feelings are fact".

Who needs it? It is generally recognised that managers and leaders need high emotional intelligence because they represent the organisation to the public and they interact with the highest number of people within and outside the organisation. Moreover, they set the tone for employee behaviour and morale.

In a recent paper in the Harvard Business Review titled What Makes a Leader, Goleman argues there are certain competencies within the emotional intelligence framework that are particularly desirable at the corporate executive level. These include self-awareness, self-management including being able to handle our emotions and keep our impulses under control (Bill Clinton take note) achievement drive and empathy.

This last competency is considered essential for leaders who operate in today's diversifying and global marketplace. "Cross-cultural dialogue can easily lead to miscues and misunderstandings," says Goleman. "Empathy is an antidote. People who have it are attuned to subtleties in body language, they hear the message beneath the words being spoken."

Increasing emphasis on matrix structures and cross-functional teams is another reason why empathy is so important. "A team leader must be able to sense and understand the viewpoints of everyone around the table," he says. There is not a single recipe for success in a leadership role. Nor is cloning the means to attaining an emotionally intelligent organisation.

Rather, highly effective leaders can demonstrate quite different competency profiles. What is clear, however, is that successful leaders possess a balance across the four key components: self-awareness, self-management, social awareness and social skills.

TEACHING EI

Are people born with certain levels of emotional intelligence or do they acquire these personal qualities as a result of life's experiences? Goleman claims research and practice clearly demonstrate that emotional intelligence (unlike IQ) can be learned; but not through a how-to-manual or a brief seminar. Nor does he recommend a twist on the popular white-water rafting experience or the executive pow wow in a remote mountain retreat.

"Developing an individual's emotional intelligence (or that of an organisation) requires a different sort of approach," says Goleman who argues that such one-off programs are a waste of money. "American companies are wasting between six and 15 billion dollars a year on development programs in this area which simply do not work.

They have no transfer of learning to on-the-job

performance." Goleman recommends an emphasis on multi-level development and coaching initiatives, rather than one-off workplace programs. The aim is to produce sustained improvements in performance and create an emotionally intelligent organisation. In particular, a business that is more collabouredative and cohesive than its competitors.

Based on his analysis of successful development programs, he advocates using the working environment as the "classroom" for learning. While initial exposure to the concepts of emotional intelligence might take place during an external workshop, and would typically include some assessment of participants, change in behaviour can only be tested in the workplace.

The challenge for organisations is to help managers understand what they need to change and to motivate them to try out new things. For this to be effective, the organisation needs to be supportive and there should be coaching and mentoring available. Often, participants work in mutual support groups to act as sounding boards and advisers for one another.

In other cases external coaches play this role to help individuals monitor their progress against their improvement agenda. Air New Zealand has started such a programme, which focuses more on the internal culture and operating climate to ensure delivery of the brand promise. Air New Zealand believes that it is critical that they integrate EI competencies into all aspects of the management of their people

ASSESSING EI

When it comes to recruiting the best people, it is not surprising that Goleman believes that IQ tests are a poor indicator of career success. He cites a Harvard study on entrance exam scores of people in the business school, the medical school and the law school. In each case entrance exam scores had zero correlation with how the students did in their field. It is relatively simple to assess IQ, and technical skills can be ascertained from past performance and referees reports. Assessing emotional intelligence is not yet quite so easy, though there are several tests available and more in development.

Many of these are reliant on self-assessment, and thus assume possession of one of the crucial emotional intelligence competencies (accurate self-assessment). Others are designed to measure the underlying psychological construct and, as with IQ, depend upon hypothesised or predicted links to performance.

Identification of demonstrated emotional intelligence requires evaluation by a third party, typically involving 360-degree assessment or in-depth interviewing by a skilled practitioner. This latter technique was utilised by the global consumer products company to reduce turnover in senior managers.

Goleman says it is still important to hire technically-minded executives. But these are mainly threshold abilities; they're entry level requirements most executives already have. They may get a person through the door of a company, but abilities like leadership, collabouredation and teamwork, self-confidence and initiative - the emotional intelligence-based abilities - ensure that he or she will thrive.

Chapter 5

Effective Communication, Effective Listening and Understanding People

Active listening is a powerful way of listening and responding to customers, that improves mutual understanding. It is the foundation of effective communication and demonstrates real respect. According to Nancy Kline, author of the book 'Time to Think', when you are listening to someone, much of the quality of what you are hearing is your effect on them.

Giving good attention to people makes them more intelligent. Poor attention makes them stumble over their words and seem stupid. Your attention and your listening is what is important. When we are in conflict, we can sometimes contradict the customer, denying their description of a situation.

This tends to make them defensive and they will either lash out or alternatively, withdraw and say nothing more. However, if they believe that we are really tuned in to their concerns and want to listen, they are more likely to explain in detail what they feel and why.

This in turn gives sales people a much greater chance of being able to develop a win-win solution. Your role in the sales situation alternates between sender and receiver of messages. The very best sales professionals devote a large portion of the sales interview to listening, because sincere listening demonstrates sincere interest.

Ultimately, good listening is the shortest distance between you and more sales; better sales, faster sales. How often has a customer said something that has been misinterpreted by you?

If you accept the view that everyone is unique, then every word has a different meaning to different individuals? What we say can be different to what we actually mean, because we all have to edit our thoughts in order to communicate them in words. We do this by a combination of deletion, distortion and generalisation

Communication involves four steps:

1. Sensing the message and the stimuli that goes with it
2. Interpreting it (to be sure you understand)
3. Evluating it (never judge before you understand)
4. Reacting (either verbally or non-verbally)

That's why it pays to listen with your eyes as well as your ears. Frequently, a gesture, an expression, will reveal as much or more than words. Therefore, effective listeners seek to understand the meaning behind their customers' words. This requires giving the other person full attention and demands conscious practice.

To become excellent at listening, there are three main techniques:

1. *Build high levels of rapport and trust your instincts*: When two people have established high levels of rapport, they unconsciously pick-up on the feelings of each other. At this point the sales person may get an instinct about something the customer 'feels', which is important feedback that is driven from their unconscious mind. Trusting these instincts can sometimes prove to be a challenge for people who work in a corporate, logical environment, yet the ability to 'listen' and act upon these instincts can make the difference between a good listener and a great listener. If for example, you have created rapport and start to feel nervous, then chances are so is your customer. Imagine the impact of asking, "I'm getting a sense that you're feeling nervous about

this, what specific concerns do you have?" will have on your customer.

2. *Demonstrate that you are paying attention:* This really encourages the customer to continue talking and helps put them at ease because they can see that you're interested in what they are saying. Using noncommittal words with a positive voice tone that neither agree or disagree with what is being said, will ensure that the customer remains motivated to want to continue talking. For example, "I see"/ "Uh-huh"/ "That's interesting" are great ways to achieve this. Nodding your head and taking written notes are also effective when demonstrating your interest.
3. *Clarifying your understanding:* Adopting a consultative approach means that it's vital to fully appreciate your prospect's requirements. Even if you think that your prospect has made them very clear, it's good practice to summarise your understanding of them. For example: "So what you're saying is (requirement)." "You obviously value (requirement) as being very important to you." These summaries will strengthen your relationship and demonstrate a genuine desire to really understand what they want. Rephrase their main points at regular intervals and 'play them back' to them. This helps them see if they have said exactly what they wanted to say and to make sure you understand. Put their feelings into words. This will help them evaluate and perhaps modify their statement and it gives further evidence of your understanding.

Understanding what others are trying to communicate to you is essential for building open and strong relationships, whether face to face or by telephone.

More and more organisations are recognising the value of effective communication through effective listening and questioning techniques in increasing productivity and sales. This course is for staff of all levels who wish to enhance their communication skills.

LEARNING OUTCOMES

By the end of the course you will be able to:

- Gain new information through effective questioning techniques
- Pick up on hidden messages
- Listen for feelings as well as meaning and respond to them
- Use techniques to check and build understanding
- Use support to minimise stress
- Increase your confidence when communicating face to face or by telephone

The benefits of good communication:

- Avoiding confusion and misunderstanding
- Reducing frustration, stress and sickness levels
- Capturing new ideas and initiatives facilitating change
- Gaining an understanding of others perspectives
- Meeting customer needs
- Increasing productivity and sales

Good listening skills:

- Empathy - listening for feelings
- Absorbing unpalatable messages
- Appreciation of the other person's point of view
- Listening, not just hearing
- Body language and its impact on communication

Good questioning skills:

- When and how to ask a question
- The purpose of questions
- Techniques to gathering information
- Using information effectively

ACTIVE LISTENING

According to a google web definition, active listening has many different definitions. "Active listening is a way of listening that focuses entirely on what the other person is saying and confirms understanding of both the content of the message and the emotions and feelings underlying the message to ensure that understanding is accurate."

"Communication technique that stimulates open and frank exploration of ideas and feelings and enables trainers to establish trust and rapport with participants. In active listening, the trainer accepts what is being said without making any value judgments, clarifies the ideas or feelings being expressed and reflects these back to the participants."

There are several ways to be an active listener, as demonstrated through this list of "Keys to Effective Listening": Stop working. Stop watching TV. Stop reading. Look at the person. Keep a good distance between you and the speaker. Don't turn away from the speaker. Sit-up straight. Nod your head and make statements such as "uh-uh," "I understand," and "I see what you mean" to show the speaker you truly understand what he/she is saying.

If you don't understand, let the person know that. Don't fake listen! Repeat back phrases to clarify what the person is saying. Act like you are interested and ask questions to show that you are interested in what the person is saying. Don't interrupt the speaker.

According to Thomas Gordon, "active listening involves carefully attending to and demonstrating understanding of what another person says". A teacher can use active listening by nodding their head and then reflecting back to what the student is saying. It is a process of mirroring back what students are trying to say.

No judgment or evaluation is made, but it is important for a teacher to use active listening because it confirms that the teacher is attentive and understand the student's message. In the classroom, active listening is the process of summarizing back to a student his feelings and problem being expressed as the teacher understands them.

Active listening is the most important step in Thomas Gordon's T.E.T. model because it improves communication and allows the teacher to hear what the student is attempting to communicate. Active Listening is a main technique that is used in Cognitive Coaching. It really makes a person feel like they are being heard and understood. You do not agree with the person, but validate by paraphasing what you hear them saying to you. Furthermore, it is a practice that is encouraged to be utilized by applicants at a job interview. The same principles of active listening apply, but "because job interviews are more progressive and fast-paced than leisurely social interactions, it's often necessary to apply a more streamlined version of active listening principles".

In sum, active listening is a skill that good teachers need to develop. Active listeners listen to the person speaking instead of thinking about what they are going to say next. They reiterate what the person is trying to say in an effort to clarify and clear up any misunderstandings.

They seek to understand the person and their needs before their own concerns are heard. ("Seek first to understand, then to be understood"-Covey) Using specific emotions helps to identify how the other person feels and help the two parties come to some kind of "win-win" solution.

APPLICATION IN THE ONLINE CLASSROOM

Active listening as described above is very face to face oriented, if not exclusively. What happens when listening (and speaking) takes place at a distance? Can the varied physical cues discussed above be implemented in a virtual environment? Does the virtual environment lend itself to new forms of active listening?

Recent research indicates that the use of back channeling in the listener-speaker feedback loop improves as technology tools make more and more functionality available. One study from focused on synchronous learning environments and explored the use of audio feedback via microphone (the "uh-huhs") and newer digital backchannels such as IM and text messaging.

The presence of varied backchannels where participants can indicate acceptance or understanding increases the notion that there is someone else out there or a "copresense." As long as the "mechanisms for creating common ground in the enactment of online interactions" are there, we can infer that the environment can support some sort of active listening (or "processing" if the medium is text).

EVIDENCE OF EFFECTIVENESS

Research shows that teaching active listening skills (along with critical listening, note taking and applications for life transfer) can improve students' listening skills and behaviour. Teachers surveyed in this study indicated the majority of students have poor listening skills, while less than half of teachers taught listening skills to their students. Students and teachers alike agreed that listening at school is an important skill.

Students on average are expected to listen in elementary school 57.5% of the time. Clearly, time teaching listening skills is time well spent. Teachers need to model active listening and give children the skills and opportunities to do so. They also need to give students time, experiences and purposes to do so. Once active listening is taught, transfer to other classrooms can occur if that instructor provides an environment for students to do so.

Graves' research, published the month following Engraffia's, looked at ways of teaching active listening to students. This study included first and third grade students in two schools in the same school district in a low to middle income community in central Illinois. To implement a programme of teaching active listening, teachers first need to be trained in active listening.

They then should model it in the classroom and be aware of and monitor whether their students are actively listening. Students can be taught active listening through a variety of required active responses while listening. Habits for giving verbal and non-verbal feedback while listening can be developed.

Students should also practice clarifying what has been said. Listening journals can be quite helpful. The study used journals, standardized tests and KWL charts to assess progress. Students in this study learned that active listening is something you do, not something that just happens.

Not only did the study show that teaching active listening increased student use and understanding of active listening skills, but also indicated "the possibility of the existence of types of listeners". Three categories of active listeners occurred, as during the process of the study many students expressed a liking to certain strategies and frustration with use of others. Students tended to be visual, bodily kinesthetic or verbal.

CRITICS AND THEIR RATIONALE

Signed Life Experiences and Testimonies and Stories

This chapter is a terrific wake up call to teachers, parents, and professional persons. Active Listening is such an important skill. It used to be a natural occurrence in society, where you would actually sit down and have tea and talk one on one on a frequent basis, talk over the fence, have family discussions regularily. I personally am so mentally overloaded with teaching responsibilities, home, and paperwork that my mind is often racing. I have been working on taking a deep breath when the phone rings or someone addresses me. I have attempted to stop Multi-tasking(no emptying the dishwasher when I am on the phone) or thinking of what I have to do when talking with another teacher.

As a computer lab teacher, I think one of the reasons the children love it so much is that they put on their headsets and listen to the prompts, and they are then praised when they make a decision and corrected when they make an error. I think they feel "listened to". I am happy to say that Active Listening is now a part of my daily life. Active listening is really about slowing down and taking the time to value other people and their ideas. In our world of multitasking, we are constantly thinking ahead. As teachers, it is important to stop what we are doing and listen to our students, even if we have to tell them to wait for about a minute, finish up what we are doing and then give them our full attention.

Remember, we are teaching students by example, and if we take the time to listen to their concerns, give them our full attention and listen to what they have to say, hopefully they will do the same when they interact with other people. I find that active listening is sometimes difficult for me when I am interacting with a student especially if they are arguing over a grade or trying to get permission to turn in an assignment late. I am usually trying to think of what I need to say next instead of fully listening to what they have to say. I know this is something I need to work on, but it is sometimes difficult when I am trying to respond to the student with an understanding but firm answer.

Craig Johnson- Active listening is one of the most important skills a person can learn. It involves not only the understanding of what the person has said but also allowing them through your body language etc. to realise that you are actually listening to what they are saying. There is nothing more frustrating then to have someone say repeat that or did you say something.

Teaching students better active listening skills will make them better learners as a whole Bret Helms - Active listening is a very important skill to learn. I spend many class periods a year teaching kids listening skills. I teach a class called quest which spends a lot of time working on these skills.

It is amazing how much the kids will change while you are discussing this topic. The key is to continue the listening skills throughout the year. Someone who becomes a good listener really increases their chances of being successful. Brandon Correa- "I'm sorry, did you say something?" is one of the most demeaning phrases you can say to someone else. I think the key to being a good listener is humility.

If all you think about is yourself, than you won't show any care for what someone else has to say. I think women definitely are better at being good active listeners than men are. They can instinctively tell somehow when you are really listening to them or to the ESPN report on TV. Someone should do a study on how men can just tune people out. It must have to do with the inability to multi-task that hinder the active listening in men.

Rhonda Hall—I think active listening is a great skill. I first learned in depth how to be an active listener in some post graduate courses I took in a counseling programme. It was something I've always remembered and I really try to use that skill, especially with my students. I don't how I would fit teaching that into an already full day.

Ralph Alexander- I was fortunate enough to attend a seminar on listening skills and was fortunate to see how effective listening skills can be. My boss at the time asked(demanded) each of his employees to take a Sunday to attend this seminar he was paying for. Needless to say none of us were very excited about the prospect. I was living in Peoria, Illinois at the time and traveled to Champaign, Il to listen to Dr. Elaine Gregory.

We spent the day practicing listening skills and how to practice practicing listening skills. After the seminar our communication between each other improved and more importantly the communication with the customer improved, thereby increasing our sales dramatically and putting money in the bosses pocket and our own. I can testify to the power of listening closely and well to another person, it can make incredible differences in personal and business relationships. Scott Cebulski- I recall feeling that I had had an epiphany when I used active listening almost unconsciously early in my teaching career. Mostly from a lack of knowing what to say, I remember pausing while talking with a student about a discipline issue privately.

The student saw it immediately as a signal to discuss the underlying causes of the problem and felt more comfortable with me as a result. I unknowingly went from the traditional "I talk — you listen!" stance to one that expressed a concern for the student, a concern that I had but had never been able to express.

It occured too long ago to recall whether the particular instance was better handled as a result, but I definitely remember how it affected the way I was percieved by the student and our future relationship. I felt it was a positive step, and I have become much better at actively listening to my students as a method of understanding discipline problems as a result.

Steve Hetzel- Active listening is about bringing your full self to an enounter with someone else, and committing yourself to them during the time of your interraction. You're there to listen and respond to what they have to say, not to talk about yourself or push your own agenda. You are listening to them under the premise, the mantra, of, "Yes, I am here to listen to what you have to say."

You're not thinking about what you really want to say, or where you have to go, what you have to do, or where you'd rather be, but you're fully committed to that person at that moment. This is not to say that you disregard your own needs, only that you bring them to a level of importance equal to the other person's.

Non-judgement is also key, as is understanding where the person is at with what they're talking about. Ting Hsiao- I think active listening is also important to successful family interactions. Through active listening, teachers are able to understand different family culture, concerns, and priorities, and know how to make positive impact on studenets' learning based not only on students' but also on families' needs.

Through teachers' activie listening, families feel they are welcomed and valued and will be more cooperative with teachers. Jasmine Johnson- I'd never heard of 'active listening' before reading this post, and I wondered what the difference would be between active listening and just plain listening? I definitely think I have a problem with active listening, or listening, and sometimes have a tendency to "tune out" or drift into other thoughts instead of focusing on what someone is saying.

Although I don't believe it has dramatically affected my school performance, I do think that it must have affected it somewhat (although taking notes—no matter what—seems to help). I'd be very interested in taking an active listening class, and I wonder where I might begin to look for some.

In Sociology 480, we are learning how to do research and the different types of research methods. Active listening is such a big step in the research process that you do not realise how much valuable information you gain until you realise this is a strategy to utilize. Just as when you are interviewing someone on your research topic, using active listening is beneficial to draw the person out and get deeper more meaningful information.

This same strategy would be useful when talking with students because you would not be talking at them but rather talking with them and understanding where they are coming from to develop a more meaningful and somewhat more respectful relationship. MJB

Janet Vallowe- It seems like such an easy thing to do when you read a description of active listening. However, in the world of a busy teacher where there never seems to be enough time and we excel at multitasking, this is an aspect of teaching that takes a lot of conscious practice and effort. When a student walks into my classroom I immediately recognize their presence and stop what I am doing.

Many times the student simply has stopped by to say "Hi" or to talk about something. All they are looking for is someone who will listen. After 28 years of teaching, this is something that I still have to consciously think about and do. When I read this post, I immediately thought about how often adults don't listen (actively) to their children.

A lot of children aren't always aware of how valuable and appreciated they are and a lot of this stems from their relationships with adults. Children absolutely love when they know they have the full attention of an adult. Students are more respectful of teachers who *listen* to them. Parents, teachers, and other adults, keep this in mind when you are interacting with young people.

I think active listening is most important for effective communication between children and adults. The younger the children the more difficult because they still have to learn quite a deal to express themselves appropriately.

To be patient and show them through active listening that you care about their problems will help them to learn these skills very well.

When they are adults no one listen to them when they have not learned to communicate and express themselves appropriately. That is why it is so important to take always the time to listen when children want to talk to you . I did not realise how much I did not actively listen until I was confronted by my children.

Also, because of my new awareness I know when someone is really not listening to me. I believe this will be a great tool for both all parts of life. c. yeoman I have noticed since I started working as a teacher how important active listening is. I always thought of myself as a good listener until I experienced the life of a teacher.

Some days my mind is working on several tasks at once. One day a student came into my room to talk about an assignment while I was in the middle of prepping a lab. I kind of rushed through the explanation and the student left. The next day the student turned in the wrong assignment. I clearly recognized my error and have made efforts to always stop what I am doing and give each student my full attention.

It wasn't until my years as an undergrad in college that I actually learned "good" communication skills. My COMS100 class really taught me how to be an active listener and from then on, I have taken those skills with me. I also read an excellent book the summer before I began my professional teaching career on how to effectively communicate with students, though I don't remember the name of it.

Believe me, I would have been lost without that book! Anyway, I use active listening all the time not only when talking to friends about issues they are facing but also with my students. I think my students are surprised when once they have been misbehaving I ask them to go in the hallway and I have a one-on-one discussion with them. I think students are expecting me to yell at them and issue an immediate consequence; however, this really isn't the case at all. Instead, I talk to them and get their input as to why they have been asked to leave the classroom. I ask them if something is bothering them that may be the cause of their misbehaviour or inattentiveness.

Once I have this talk with students, they return back to the classroom and are usually more likely to stay on task from that point on. If not though, the students know there will be a consequence. As a result of our talk, I know their side of the story and they know mine. Active listening is an art! I am a student in the Ed.M. programme and I find that active listening is crucial to the amount of contributions I make in class discussions.

When I feel that the professor is intrigued and that the students in the class are genuinely interested in the subject, I am more apt to share. I found that in undergraduate classes, the professors taught the material with the expectation of little discussion and class participation. Active listening creates an environment where individuals want to share and feel like their thoughts matter.

Craig makes a good point about Active Listening being a very important skill to be learned in life. By paying attention, asking questions and contributing to what someone is saying shows the speaker that what they say matters to you. I try to do this with each of my athletes I coach. My athletes have seemed to gain respect for me, and are more willing to come and talk with me. They know I really care about what they are saying, not just they're putting in time to collect a paycheck.

This also helps with personal relationships. I know my wife really appreciates it when she has had a bad day at work, and while telling me about it, that I participate it he conversation. Let her feel like I am interested in her life and her job. I often find myself very distracted in class. I either can't keep my mind off other things, or I fall asleep. I often wonder if I have ADHD.

One thing that I find helpful is to really try to make eye contact with the teacher as much as possible and sit in the front row. I try to relate the material somehow to my own life, and usually if I think hard enough without becoming distracted, I can. Being an active reader is something that I also need to work on for material that doesn't immediately interest me.

Active Listening sounds like such a simple concept, but it's importance is often overlooked. I look back at my past year of teaching and I am pressed to find examples of times when I was completely focused and concentrated on repsonding to show that I was listening. This is becuase there is constanly so much going on in the classroom, that it is difficult to stop and concentrate on one thing.

However, I look at my like and can tell you the difference it makes when I speak with people who show Active Listening skills. I feel validated and affirmed and confident to share. What a powerful thing it would be if we could provide the same feelings for our students.

Lack of Active Listening skills is what makes working with children with mild autism and Aspergers challenging for me. I can't tell without indication that a person is listening and comprehending. There are times that these students are listening, show no evidence and can answer questions about the topic; this is just a difference in their social skills as part of the condition.

There are other times these same students prove to not be listening. Indications of Active Listening really help the teacher, but there are always those students that can "fake" active listening that are just as, if not more difficult to teach.

This reminds me of a student in one of my college courses in SPED. He was the ultimate Active Listener. He nodded his head during lecture, would just audibly agree with the instructor with a "yes," or "I firmly agree," and felt he needed to interrupt lectures to prove that he was listening. The entire class of 200 was annoyed twice a week for a full hour.

This "excellent" active listener went too far. It was funny when he came to class late for the first time ever. He quickly began nodding, taking notes, agreeing under his breath, and then raised his hand to 'prove' he was listening and make up for being late. We had a guest speaker that day. She was blind.

Yes, he would have known this if he had arrived on time, but he could not have really been listening to her speak about *being blind* since he kept his hand up *the entire time she spoke about being blind* and was showing signs of great frustration at not being called upon. Pretending to be actively listening is a coping skill many master, and others just don't get.

"Verify-Clarify" It is sad that the skills of active listening seem to have been tossed aside as our society changes. I remember as a young boy going to grandma's house and there we would sit in her living room and talk for hours while sampling her fresh baked cookies (which was a great motivation for being there).

And as strange as it may seem, I still remember some of those conversations. We were taught active listening, although it wasn't called active listening at that time. We called it respect; valuing what someone has to say. Since then our society has moved into a media rich world where we are bombarded constantly by every type of media competing for our attention.

Maybe as a way of self-preservation we have been forced to learn the skill of listening without really hearing. Years ago I was taught a concept called "verify-clarify' which I have found to be extremely helpful in active listening. Basically, when listening to a student explain their view on a point, I will take what I have just heard, rephrase it and ask them, "Let me see.

If I understand you correctly you are saying . Is that correct?" This little skill helps me to "verify" that I am understanding what they have stated. Sometimes I can be concentrating so hard on the words that I miss the meaning. This ensures that I am understanding both.

It reassures the person speaking that I am listening and hearing what they have said. It also gives them the opportunity to further "clarify" a point if I did not restate in a form acceptable to the speaker. This little skill has been an excellent skill to help me, in every area of my life, to be a better active listener. I have found the teaching students how to actively listen has improved their ability to take in information as well as respond in seminar/discussion type settings. Conscious thinking to myself that I need to actively listen to something prior to the experience is still something that I try to reinforce myself with beforehand.

ADHD, certain behavioural or emotional disorders, and other conditions can cause issues. It is, however, possible to use interventions/modifications that allow, in most cases, active listening to occur. Active listening is a skill that everyone needs to learn. As teachers, we need to let our students feel that we are listening to them and hearing what they are saying. Also, we need to use active listening with our colleagues. It is important to listen and show you are listening, even if you do not agree.

Students need to be taught active listening skills. In a programme we are currently using called Making Meaning, students talk with other students and use prompts to talk to each other. Some of the prompts are "I heard you say...Did I get that right?" By having students practice this kind of discussion, we promote active listening skills.

Active Listening is definitely something we all need to work on. I can see its usefulness in every aspect of my life (my marriage, with my toddler son, my students, my co-workers, my friends, etc.). Since learning about Active Listening I've been focusing more on using this skill. I was lucky to have the opportunity the other day in my study hall class. I have a student in the middle school that has become socially self-destructive. After yelling at a fellow student I sent her to the hall. She was clearly upset with the other student and with me for reprimanding her by sending her out of the room. When I went out I asked a few simple questions and just listened and summarized.

The student shared some problems she's been having at home, started crying, and sounded remorseful for things she's been doing to her friends. At the end of the conversation I felt really good about knowing WHY the student was behaving the way she was (although I didn't excuse her behaviour).

That was a nice start for me, I need to keep on working though. A common activity in my classroom is to call on students at random during discussions and have them summarize different comments their classmates are making. This forces the students to actively listen to the comments their peers are making, and I then provide them with class rewards (class money, called greenbacks), which are redeemed weekly for participation grades and candy.

Additionally, the students participate in a job interview

unit. The students truly enjoy and are engaged by this unit, which sees them creating resumes, cover letters, and practicing proper job interview techniques in preparation for their future introduction into the workforce.

A human resources employee from a Chicago company visits the classroom and instructs students in the proper ways to actively listen. The practice revolves around such non-verbal communicators as sitting up straight, mimicking the posture of the job interviewer, proper dress, smiling, eye contact, speed, silence, and think time.

Think time occurs when a difficult question is asked and the interviewee must "summarize what [he or she] thinks [the] interviewer wants to know and ask[s] for confirmation before proceeding" (Active Listening for Interview Success). The students are instructed to believe periods of silence are okay, and that simply lets the interviewer know that the questions was truly heard, understood, and that the proper response is being formulated.

Active listening is an important skill that many people lack. After learning more about active listening, I have increased my efforts in having students discuss problems with one another and really listen to each others views. The benefits have been great and I feel that my students are getting along better with each other. Active listening is a skill we must all reflect on to improve our relationships. Hopefully I am modeling this skill for my students.

Active listening has been an asset in several situations with my students. I like how it forces teachers to listen attentively to their students and vice versa. Asking a young child what they heard or understood allows for self reflection and understanding. Once students understand the concepts of active listening they can use this skill in all aspects of their learning.

Even though the majority of us have ears that test in the excellent category for hearing, most of us have not developed the necessary skills or aural skills as the academics call it to be used effectively to listen well. Many experts have tested listening skills through numerous activities focused on how well people remember the information presented. This has been tested in different environments, different time frame and different types of presentations and communications.

The consolidation of results from this myriad of research convinces me that people have very short memory spans. Results have proven that we only remember on average about 50% of the information presented immediately after the presentation. The more time that passes, the less we remember. Research at Florida State University suggests that after 60 days have passed we will only remember a maximum of 25% of the information presented.

In fact, the predominant amount of that memory loss occurs within the first eight hours after listening to the information. Many people may believe that a person's listening ability is directly related to their intellectual ability; smart people listen better. Personally I believe this is a myth. Of course someone with exceptional intelligence may be able to retain more information than someone with a very low IQ.

But For most of us that have average to above average intelligence, our listening abilities are directly related to certain skills that are acquired through experience and training. Keep in mind, being alert, learning to read and being present alone does not automatically increase our listening abilities.

LISTENING IS A UNIQUE ACTIVITY

Listening is different from reading. Listening is about communication, understanding and comprehension. I have known people who are excellent readers that can capture your attention just by the way they form the words that flow through their lips and yet if you ask them to explain exactly what the information means they fall short of expectations. We must be aware of the factors that affect our listening abilities.

These factors include:

- Concentrating on the material at hand – remember we think at a much faster pace than we talk. (average talk = 125 words per minute) We must be careful not to get ahead of ourselves. Since our thoughts are faster we can often get distracted or we begin to sandwich in personal thoughts that may or may not be relevant to the information presented. We also may often wander off with a different line of thought and then hurry back to the listening mode when we feel something is relevant.

- Interest which creates a motivation to learn - Additionally this has a tendency to create opportunity for our wandering thoughts to wander in the direction of anticipating what the presenter is leading up to. This keeps us focused on the material at hand improving the quality of our listening.
- Weighing the evidence -Utilizing our listening and rationalization skills we can focus on weighing the facts presented to determine the validity of the information presented. This also keeps us focused on the material presented thus improving our listening ability.
- Mentally summarizing the points made by actually taking notes reinforces the listening process. Note taking is an essential ingredient to improving our listening abilities. Research has proven that the physical act of writing down information improves our ability to remember and comprehend the information.

EFFECTIVE LISTENING SHOULD SPUR CREATIVITY AND NEW IDEAS

A key technique you can use to improve your listening skills is simply looking for new ideas to utilize in your business or personal life. Ask yourself this question repeatedly throughout the listening process. "How can I apply this (fact – theory – information) to my specific business or challenge?"

Raise your expectations when it comes to what you expect to do with the information that is being presented. Listening to a "motivational speaker" may make you feel good but if you don't come away with some actionable items to work on in your personal environment it is simply a waste of time.

MEMORIZING IS NOT EFFECTIVE LISTENING

You may take pride in getting all the facts and memorizing them considering yourself a good listener. Getting all the facts seems logical to effective listening. However, memorizing all the facts presented in any presentation is often a virtual impossibility for most people. Often we miss critical pieces of information that can often lead to more harm than good.

To be an effective listener we must strive to understand the ideas that are being presented. That is why it is much more effective to ask a listener what he intends to do with the information you presented instead of simply asking them if they understand.

Grasping the idea behind the information being presented is a key skill that must be developed to become an effective listener. If you understand the idea behind the material presented, the facts often follow naturally.

CLEAN THE EMOTIONAL FILTER

Our listening ability is definitely affected by our emotions and the environment we grew up in. Realistically we often tune out when information threatens a preconceived notion, a belief or when we hear something that strikes a painful emotion from our past. We simply turn off our listening skill when what is being said is something we just don't want to hear.

Adversely, we really focus and turn up our listen skill when we hear something that we especially want to hear. Unfortunately, this emotional trait is often taken advantage of by scam artists and "Free Lunch Schemes" you often find on the internet. We have a tendency to believe anything whether it's fact or fiction.

So It is clear that our emotions can act as listening filters. They can both shut out information or they can enhance it. In fact, we must be careful when we begin to hear something that strikes a positive emotion to avoid hearing only what we want to hear.

It is imperative that we clear our minds when listening to prevent our inner emotions from distorting the information being presented both positively or negatively.

That means we should withhold evaluation of the information presented until the presentation is complete and we can rationalize our thought process without emotional influence.

I'll end this chapter with the following tips that may help improve the listening skills in your organization.

Tips to Improve Listening Skills:

- Actually conduct a learning session or seminar devoted to improving listening skills. There are many DVD's and exercises available that can be used to support this learning activity. Mini case studies are also an excellent tool used a breakout session with open discussion.
- Study communication skills as they are an integral part of effective listening.
- Hire a consultant to help your group improve listening and communication skills.
- Create a definitions file for industry terms, acronyms and key phrases specific to your business and planning process.
- Make sure you have a well defined and documented orientation programme for new employees. Create a system to have all employees participate at various times with new employee indoctrination. The most effective way to have someone learn something is to have them teach it.
- Create a session of "Team Role" playing that addresses specific listening challenges.
- Develop a listening critique that can be employed after a specific meeting or session that has been recorded. Have the group actually make suggestions for improvements and identify potential miscommunications as a result of ineffective listening.

SKILLS: GENERATING PROPOSALS

By completing this unit, candidates will be able to multi-skill in audio, text, visual and moving image based media. They will be able to work safely in studios, offices and on location.

Candidates will understand that the success of media products is based on feasible and clear proposals and effective research. They will gain awareness of their own strengths and how to develop further their specific and transferable skills.

KNOWLEDGE, UNDERSTANDING AND SKILLS

Develop basic specific skills to use in text/visual based and audio/audio visual products create a file of work to demonstrate cross media skills:

Two text/visual skills eg:

- Writing copy
- Producing computer graphics
- Word processing
- Taking photographs
- Editing

Two audio skills eg:

- Recording speech/sounds/music
- Mixing sounds
- Editing

Two audio visual skills eg:

- Recording moving images
- Vision mixing
- Designing sets
- Organising lighting
- editing

Skills must include:

- Generating ideas e.g. mood board, storyboard, mind map
- Editing e.g. dubbing music, cropping photographs

Develop basic transferable skills to use in text/visual based and audio/audio visual product. Demonstrate transferable skills which must include:

- Saving, storing and indexing work

- Presenting work showing creativity and good organisation
- Using digital equipment
- The ability to work without supervision
- The ability to follow instructions
- The ability to support other team members
- The ability to meet deadlines

Demonstrate two safe working practices e.g.:

- Lifting heavy objects correctly
- Using cable mats to prevent trips
- Storing sharp/electrical equipment appropriately
- Showing awareness of personal safety when interviewing
- Wearing appropriate clothing
- Present proposals for text/visual and audio/audio visual products.

Make a proposal for one audio/audio visual product and one text/visual product from:

- *Audio:* speech based radio, music based radio, recorded music
- *Audio visual:* films, fictional and factual television programmes
- *Visual:* photography
- *Print:* newspapers, magazines, books
- *Electronic media:* games, websites
- *Advertising:* posters, leaflets, commercials, websites

Proposal includes:

- Contact details
- Title
- Type of product
- Purpose
- Content
- Target audience

Conduct research for text/visual based and audio/audio visual products Research for one audio/audio visual product and one text/visual product into eg:

- Target audience
- Content

- Similar products

Demonstrate one example of primary research and explain its purpose:

- Questionnaires
- Interviews

Demonstrate one example of secondary research and explain its purpose:

- Print products
- Audio visual products
- Internet Explain and present research findings

Review progress in practical skills Evaluate skills in terms of:

- Creativity
- Working accurately
- Use of equipment
- Saving/storing material

IDENTIFY STRONGEST SKILLS, SKILLS THAT NEED DEVELOPING

ASSESSMENT

This unit is centre-assessed and externally moderated. In order to achieve this unit, candidates must collate a portfolio of evidence showing that they can meet all the assessment objectives.

Portfolios of work must be produced independently. They will need to be made available, together with witness statements and any other necessary supporting documentation, to the OCR Visiting Moderator when required.

GUIDANCE ON ASSESSMENT AND EVIDENCE

This unit prepares the candidate for the production work they will do in Unit 3, although some centres may choose to integrate it with some of the optional units. Candidates are not expected to make complete products in this unit when demonstrating their skills.

Tutors may find it useful to introduce this unit at the same time as Unit 1, so that candidates are able to absorb theoretical concepts through practical work. Planning is usually considered to be an important part of pre-production.

However, in this unit, candidates will not necessarily be making one product but possibly parts of lots of products, so for the purposes of this qualification planning has been incorporated into unit 3 in which candidates make a specific media product.

The purpose of Assessment Objectives 1 and 2 is to enable candidates to develop and experiment with a range of basic skills in both print and audio/audio-visual areas. It is important that candidates develop technical, visual and auditory skills and gain competency in using digital equipment across media areas.

Audio skills can be developed and demonstrated through use of radio, music technology or moving image digital technology. Candidates will become aware of how some skills such as teamwork or good presentation of work are useful in all areas. They will then be able to use these skills in other units.

It may help candidates if they carry out some form of initial skills audit at the beginning of the unit and periodically review their own progress as they proceed. These records can then be referred to as part of the review to be carried out for Assessment Objective 5.

Candidates should demonstrate these skills through producing small pieces of evidence, the best of which they should store and index in a work file could be both paper based and electronic or all electronic. A tutor witness statement should be included to support this evidence by confirming what digital equipment was used, what level of support was given, how well the candidates followed instructions and whether they were able to support other team members.

A proforma may form the basis of a witness statement but it must refer to an individual candidate rather than to a group. The witness statement or media products eg photographs may be used to evidence safe working practices. It is expected that most of this work will be individual work though the candidates must have the opportunity at some point to work in a group.

Some media tasks such as writing copy for hard news are solitary tasks; others such as studio filming rely heavily on teamwork. Candidates should have the opportunity to experience both types of work. They need to be able to follow instructions accurately and meet deadlines. For Assessment Objective 3, candidates are expected to make individual proposals for both a new text/visual based product and an audio visual based product.

These products may form a starting point for products made in other units. For example they may make a proposal for a magazine which they intend to make in Unit 3 or Unit 10 and a proposal for a radio advertisement which they intend to make in Unit 4 or Unit 7.

If candidates are working on an integrated project (for example a combined radio and print advertising campaign) they should produce one proposal but this should clearly distinguish between the two products. Making proposals will emphasise to the candidate that the media industry is a business that has to sell its products.

Candidates must realise a proposal is a feasible business idea and must identify who the proposal is from and to whom it is going. Some candidates will want to make up a company name to add to the proposal. It is acceptable for a proforma to be used for the proposal as long as it does not limit the candidate.

The production of proposals requires preliminary research into audience preference and market competition but once the proposal has been developed the research will need to be more specific. For Assessment Objective 4, it will help if candidates' research is focused and narrow (eg how long do magazine readers like articles to be or which colour do readers find most attractive for a title) rather than general and wide (eg what do readers expect to find in a magazine).

The review may take the form of a written or verbal report but it must include feedback from the tutor/teacher or technicians who have supervised the candidate's practical work. Candidates may find it helpful to refer to tutor feedback when referring to their skills.

SIGNPOSTING TO KEY SKILLS

The unit contains opportunities for developing the Key Skill, and possibly for generating portfolio evidence, if teaching and learning is focused on that aim.

Assist with the research of specific requirements of the design brief Research requirements based on the design brief Co-ordinate the art department Liaise with team members to assist the production process Contribute to good working relationships Ensure your own actions reduce risks to health and safety Production Film & TV (Skillset) P5 Identify sources of information and present findings.

RESOURCES

This section provides suggestions of suitable resources. The list is neither prescriptive nor exhaustive, and candidates should be encouraged to gather information from a variety of sources. Some suggested resources are intended for tutor use. The resources in this section were current at the time of print. Develop basic specific skills to use in text/visual based and audio/audio visual products Candidates demonstrate they have developed specific skills in generating and editing material to a basic level possibly with support.

Candidates demonstrate basic specific skills in generating and editing material effectively and confidently. Candidates demonstrate basic specific skills in generating and editing material effectively, confidently and creatively to a high standard without support.

AO2

Develop basic transferable skills to use in text/visual based and audio/audio visual products Candidates demonstrate safe working practices and transferable skills to a basic level possibly with support.

Candidates demonstrate safe working practices and transferable skills effectively without support. Candidates demonstrate safe working practices and transferable skills effectively and creatively to a high level showing initiative.

AO3

Present proposals for text/visual and audio/audio visual products Candidates complete proposal forms for the products, providing only brief details.

Candidates complete proposal forms for the products, providing comprehensive detail. Candidates complete detailed proposal forms and use media terminology correctly.

AO4

Conduct research for text/visual based and audio/audio visual products Candidates carry out general primary and secondary research for the products. They may be unclear on the purpose for carrying out research and its presentation is basic. Candidates carry out relevant primary and secondary research for the products.

They describe the reason for carrying out research and it is well presented. Candidates carry out relevant and detailed primary and secondary research for the products. They explain clearly the reason for carrying out research. The research results are effectively analysed and presented.

AO5

Review progress in practical skills Candidates identify their skills in general terms, eg editing and explain their strongest skills in simplistic terms. Candidates identify skills in general terms, eg editing and justify the identification of their strongest skills.

Candidates review specific skills eg cropping and sizing photographs and justify the identification of their strongest skills and suggest how they might improve their skills Assessment This unit will be centre-assessed and externally moderated. In order to achieve this unit, candidates must collate a portfolio of evidence showing that they can meet all the assessment objectives.

Portfolios of work must be produced independently.

They will need to be made available, together with witness statements and any other necessary supporting documentation, to the OCR Visiting Moderator when required.

GUIDANCE ON ASSESSMENT AND EVIDENCE

Candidates should gain knowledge, understanding and skills through practical tasks so that they can effectively decide where their strengths and interests lie. The focus of this unit is to develop candidates' practical skills. This may help them choose to follow a specific or general pathway within media.

Centres are strongly advised to integrate this unit with others so that the skills developed and the proposals presented may act as starting points for products made in other units. This may be the production work candidates will do in Units 3 and 4 though some centres may choose to integrate it with some of the optional units.

Candidates are not expected to make complete products in this unit when demonstrating their skills. Tutors may find it useful to introduce this unit at the same time as Unit 1, so that candidates are able to absorb theoretical concepts through practical work. Planning is usually considered to be an important part of pre-production.

However, in this unit, candidates will not necessarily be making one product but possibly parts of lots of products, so for the purposes of this qualification planning has been incorporated into unit 3 in which candidates make a specific media product.

The purpose of Assessment Objectives 1 and 2 is to enable candidates to develop and experiment with a range of basic and more complex skills in both text/visual based and audio-visual areas. It is important that candidates develop technical, visual and auditory skills and gain competency in using digital equipment across media areas.

Audio skills can be developed and demonstrated through use of radio, music technology or moving image digital technology. They will become aware of how some skills such as teamwork or good presentation of work are useful in all areas. They will then be able to use these skills in other units.

As different candidates will have different skill levels at the beginning of the unit, it may help if each carries out some form of initial skills audit and then periodically reviews progress as the unit proceeds. These records can then be referred to as part of the evaluation to be carried out for Assessment Objective 5.

Candidates should demonstrate these skills through producing small pieces of evidence, the best of which they should store and index in a work file that could be both paper based and electronic or all electronic. A tutor witness statement should be included to support this evidence by e.g. confirming what digital equipment was used, what leadership qualities were shown, what technical support was given. A proforma may form the basis of a witness statement but it must refer to an individual candidate rather than to a group.

The witness statement or media products e.g. photographs may be used to evidence safe working practices. For Assessment Objectives 1 and 2 candidates could be given a series of small discrete production tasks e.g. writing a feature article, filming a short sequence to include a tracking shot.

They could be given an overarching task that demonstrate a number of skills e.g. producing a 10 second television advert which includes print activities such as storyboarding and writing copy and audio-visual activities such as filming and editing special effects.

It is acceptable for a product such as a web page to be considered as either a text/visual based product or, if it includes animation or video clip, as an audiovisual based product. It is expected that most of this work will be individual work though the candidates must have the opportunity at some point to work in a group.

Some media tasks such as studio filming rely heavily on teamwork whilst writing copy for hard news can be seen as a solitary task. Although some media tasks are completed independently, almost all media employees have to function as part of a team with regular meetings, e.g. the journalist writing hard news needs to liaise with an editor.

Candidates should have the opportunity to experience both types of work. They need to be able to follow instructions accurately, show leadership qualities and meet deadlines. Candidates can observe media teamwork if they visit a television studio as a member of a studio audience. Talks from visiting speakers from the media industries can highlight how job roles operate.

For Assessment Objective 3, candidates are expected individually to make proposals and treatments for both a new text/visual based product and an audio visual based product. They may for example make a proposal for a magazine which they intend to make in Unit 3 or Unit 14 and a proposal for a radio advertisement which they intend to make in Unit 4 or Unit 26 or 27.

If candidates are working on an integrated project (for example a campaign for the release of a piece of music which incorporates a promotional video and a poster campaign) they should produce one proposal but this should clearly distinguish between the two products and offer specific detail, primary and secondary research and treatments for each.

Making proposals and treatments should emphasize to the candidate that the media industry is a business that has to sell its products. Candidates must realise a proposal and treatment is a business idea and should present it as fit for purpose as a commercial document.

It must identify who the proposal and treatment is from and to whom it is going; it should be word processed with clearly presented story boards, drafts and sample copy; and descriptions should be clear and concise whilst also being original and attractive to the commissioning body.

They should also be feasible and legally and ethically appropriate. Some candidates will want to make up a company name to add to the proposal. It is acceptable for a proforma to be used for the proposal as long as it does not limit the candidate.

Some media organisations expect ideas to be submitted

using their submission forms and it is acceptable that if candidates have access to these that they can use them. The research activities related to Assessment Objective 4 will need to be carried out simultaneously with the production of the proposal.

There will need to be preliminary research into audience and the market, and, as the proposal develops, the research should become more focused. It will help candidates if their research is specific (eg which topics attract magazine readers most or which colour do readers find most attractive on magazine front covers) rather than general and wide (e.g. what do readers expect to find in a magazine).

The evaluation may take the form of a written or verbal report but it must include feedback from the tutor/teacher or technicians who have supervised the candidate's practical work. Candidates may find it helpful to refer to tutor feedback and their own skills audits when referring to their skills.

It will be useful for candidates to be able to recognise their strengths so that they can select appropriate roles to work in for Unit 3. Explaining how their skills can be further developed may be addressed in a number of ways e.g. by looking at higher education courses or through making a career plan.

SKILLS: SERVICING

Broadcast writing demands a special set of skills and knowledge from the journalist. Broadcast copy is written to be read out loud by a news reader rather than to be read silently by a news consumer.

The words and sentences must be constructed so they are accurate and clear. They must also complement the pictures, video and audio that accompany a story.

SHORT VIDEOS ON BROADCAST WRITING

For those interested in teaching or learning to write in broadcast style, you should listen to or watch four short video clips about broadcast writing produced by my friend and colleague Mark Harmon, a professor of journalism and electronic media here at UT. They can be found at this Volcasting link. The four clips concern news judgment, attribution, broadcast style and active voice. (All four videos will take less than 10 minutes to watch.) They are well worth the short amount of time it takes to view them.

COURIC TAKES OVER

In the long history of the CBS Evening News, there had been only three permanent anchors: Douglas Edwards, Walter Cronkite and Dan Rather. Now there is a fourth. atie Couric (CBS biography) debuted as the newscast's latest anchor.

Couric is a legitimate journalist who was part of NBC's news team covering the Pentagon and the Gulf War in 1991. For the last 15 years she has been the host of NBC's Today Show, and her work has not been considered to be on the front lines of reporting. Her main job at CBS is not to deliver the news but to deliver an audience (preferably one that is a little younger than the one CBS has).

Here are a few stories and reviews of her first night: New York Times, Washington Post, NPR. News orgs discover web's immediacy. A couple of stories from Romenesko's blog on today show that big time news organizations are discovering the immediacy of the web.

One comes from Westworld, which reports that when the Denver Post stumbled onto a scoop last month about beer magnate Peter Coors being arrested for drunk driving, the Post nailed the story and then put it on the organization's web site – despite some grousing from the traditionalists. These folks thought a story like that should be saved for print first, which was several hours away.

The paper's managing editor said the web would be "our breaking news platform." Then there is the story about CBS streaming its nightly news programme simultaneously with its over-the-air broadcast. This, apparently, has come about only after painstaking negotiations with affiliates. One is tempted to ask: "Where have these folks been for the last 10 years or so?" *(Posted Aug. 17, 2006)*

Off again, on-again. The general manager of the public

radio station in Lexington, Ky., caused a minor flap late last week by announcing that he was pulling Garrison Keillor's Writer's Almanac off WUKY. Tom Godell expressed some dismay at the language that was cropping up in some of the poems that Keillor had read on the programme and fear that his station would be fined by the Federal Communications Commission.

Keillor was certainly no Howard Stern, Godell said, but "the FCC has been so inconsistent, we don't know where we stand."That was Friday. By Saturday Keillor was back. The station received so many phone calls and emails from its listeners that Godell was forced to relent.

One of those who protested was Leonard Press, the founder and long-time director of Kentucky Educational Television who called the cancellation "an overreaction" and said, "This is a man who is one of the premier writers and performers of our time.

I think he's generally recognized for his tastefulness." according to a report in the Cincinnati Post. Godell said he decided to cancel the show after an increasing number of "language advisories" had been sent to produces. Such advisories alert stations to the possibilities of language that might not be suitable to all audiences.

In this case, there were references to the female breast and in one poem to getting "high." While many (including Keillor) are castigating Godell for his decision, we might want to examine whether or not the FCC has created a climate where such fears are legitimate. The heavy-handedness of the FCC should be remembered along with the names of Janet Jackson and Howard Stern.

Put your news on the pod. Podcasting is one of the new terms in online journalism. It simply means putting news and information into an audio MP3 format and making it available to folks who own MP3 players – millions of them. News web sites, particularly broadcast sites where this is a natural, are beginning to use this method to reach those who want to do more than just listen to music on their MP3 players, according to Jonathan Dube, Cyberjournalist.net.

(In addition to the MP3 players, there are lots of cellphones that have MP3 capability.)

Dube cites an article in Digital-Lifestyles.info that says the BBC used this method for extending one of its programs late last year, and the file got 100,000 downloads. The technology and technique are not confined to broadcasters, of course.

Any news outlet can create these files and offer them to an audience that might not otherwise be exposed to its content. (Podcasting comes from Apple's iPod, which dominates the world of MP3 players.)

Update: Cyberjournalist has posted more information on the growing phenomenon of podcasting. As a result of the success of podcasting for the radio show On the Media, WNYC is going to start making another of its shows available as an MP3 download. The WNYC news release announcing this plan says the podcasting of On the Media has added significantly to the show's audience:

"Podcasting is a remarkable boon for local radio broadcasts," added Phil Redo, VP of Station Operations and Strategy. "This easy-to-access, easy-to-use technology allows local programming to transcend the limitations of both traditional radio and online streaming, by allowing users to plug into great programming from far-flung places, anytime, anywhere."

WNYC launched the first podcast of an NPR programme in January 2005 to great success. NPR's On the Media, the station's nationally-broadcast media analysis show, has doubled the amount of listeners it reaches online in just four weeks. OTM's podcast audience now rivals the number of individuals that would enjoy the programme in a mid-sized media market like St. Louis or Kansas City.

CBS and the Bush National Guard memos. The big media story of the week was a report of an internal investigation that CBS News conducted on a story aired in September concerning George W. Bush's service in the National Guard in the 1970s. The report cited memos written by Bush's superior officers showing that Bush has received favourable treatment both in getting into the Guard and during his service there.

The story aired on Sept. 8, 2004, on CBS's 60 Minutes Wednesday just as the presidential campaign was getting intense; it had originally been scheduled to air on Sept. 29. Soon after the show, many people called into question the authenticity of the memos CBS reporters used as the basis for the story.

Initially, CBS and Dan Rather, who reported the segment, defended the story, but they eventually had to back down because the memos had not been properly investigated. CBS suffered a storm of criticism and launched its own internal investigation. The report of that investigation was released this week, and five people from CBS News were fired. (Rather was not one of them.)

The report did not clear up the questions about the authenticity of the memos; nor did it specify who at CBS News made the decision to move the broadcast up by three weeks. A note on format. CBS News put the report on its web site in a PDF format rather than simply having it in HTML.

Consequently, if you wanted to look at the 200-plus page document, you had to download the whole thing onto your computer and then either print it out or try to search through it in Acrobat. Either way, it did not make things easy for the reader.

Breaking in. Want to get into broadcasting? The Poynter Institute (which has a whole section on broadcasting journalism) has a timely article on tips on getting started in broadcast journalism. Here's how it starts:Dig hard, write well, and maybe even sweep a few floors.Broadcast professionals say that's what young journalists should do if they're serious about pursuing a career in the competitive field of news broadcasting.

Television and radio students who want to stand out from the crowd must become enterprising, information-sniffing archaeologists, said Al Tompkins, Poynter's broadcast journalism group leader.

Broadcast professionals say that's what young journalists

should do if they're serious about pursuing a career in the competitive field of news broadcasting. Television and radio students who want to stand out from the crowd must become enterprising, information-sniffing archaeologists, said Al Tompkins, Poynter's broadcast journalism group leader.

Tompkins said that for students to be great storytellers, they must dig up information no one else is looking for, and then produce the package with clarity and cohesiveness. To uncover well-hidden journalistic gems, Tompkins said students need to talk with the people no one else is interviewing.

"If a crowd of journalists is going somewhere, I'd go wherever they are not going," he said. "Break the habit of talking to your friends. Seek out people not like you and learn to listen and not talk." In addition to being a good listener, broadcast students also must be outstanding writers.

"It doesn't hurt to look good, but in the long term it doesn't matter. I've seen too many average-looking and sounding people who are great writers do very well in this business. Mike Wallace and Morley Safer are not pin-ups, but they're fine journalists."Gayle Sierens, veteran co-anchor and reporter for Tampa's WFLA-TV, also said honing writing and editing skills is a top priority.

In addition, she tells budding reporters to "develop a thick, thick skin" and "be yourself." Sierens said students need to work hard while being patient. Getting comfortable in front of the camera or behind a microphone "takes a while and doesn't happen overnight," she said. To get a head start on the competition, Sierens said broadcast-minded students should seek volunteer or internship positions with local stations."Be willing to start small," Sierens said.

"Get your foot in the door and make a nuisance of yourself. Do everything and anything beyond the call of duty. Any shred of experience will only help you." CBS News Radio's Peter King agreed. "The best thing you can do is visit radio stations in your area," said King, a national anchor and reporter. "Visit more than one. Get an internship or part-time job sweeping the floors.

You can learn a lot just by hanging around. Be curious and ask a lot of questions. Don't just ask what; ask why." While a great face may help in TV and a fantastic voice won't hurt in radio, broadcasters agree that it's what's between the ears that counts.

"Good reporters know a little bit about a lot of things," King said. "A good voice helps, but that's not necessarily what's going to keep you going. Being a good human being, having common sense and curiosity – those are the traits that make a good journalist."

SKILLS: NEGOTIATING AND CLOSING

Between 1996 and 2002, the Rhode Island Coalition Against Domestic Violence (RICADV) moved from media obscurity to become the primary information source about domestic violence for Rhode Island reporters. This change was not part of a general trend. During the same seven-year period, most state domestic violence coalitions did not improve their media standing appreciably.

RICADV's success, therefore, merits analysis. This longitudinal study employs both qualitative and quantitative methods to explore how the collective actor, RICADV, working with the university-based collective actor, the Media Research and Action Project (MRAP), strengthened its standing in the Rhode Island media market which ranks in the top quartile of U.S. media markets (43 rd of 200).

Beginning with qualitative approaches, we reconstruct how the collective actor RICADV parleyed growing media standing into expanded media opportunities. We then assess RICADV's media standing quantitatively via a content analysis that measures shifts in RICADV's ability to influence media coverage of domestic violence murders over a seven-year period.

Finally, we tentatively conjecture on the impact of media standing on political standing. In 1996, two collective actors, the statewide Rhode Island Coalition Against Domestic Violence (RICADV) and the university-based Media Research and Action Project (MRAP) * initiated a common project. To further RICADV's mission of ending domestic violence, we wanted to strengthen its media standing, e.g., we wanted Rhode Island reporters to recognize RICADV as an indispensable source for news and background information regarding domestic violence.

RICADV and MRAP saw media standing as a prerequisite for achieving a second objective—to open new opportunities to promote RICADV's framing of domestic violence as a social problem not a private problem, requiring social not individual solutions. This chapter assesses one aspect of our collabouredation—RICADV'S efforts to alter the Rhode Island reporters' representation of domestic violence murders as unpredictable, private tragedies.

Our project's focus on domestic violence murders emerged from our joint work. In spring 1996, a month into our collabouredation, a cluster of three domestic violence murders occurred within a six-week period. First, an elderly man brutally beat his wife to death. Then, a young man killed his girlfriend, his two-year-old, and himself.

Three weeks later, a middle-aged man killed his wife, two children, and himself. Print news presented the murders as inexplicable, private family tragedies. Coverage of the first case stressed the elderly couple's failing health. In the second case reporters quoted a shocked neighbour describing the perpetrator as "a really nice kid.

Things like this don't hap- pen around here supposedly". Print coverage of the third case similarly conveyed shock and denial. The victims were a "model family," insisted their minister. The perpetrator's sister added, "I guess he loved them so much, he just took them with him". RICADV did not influence this 1996 coverage.

While comfortable calling press for a planned event, RICADV then lacked the capacity to leverage an unexpected incident such as a murder into a media opportunity. "We waited by the phone, but no call came," recalled one RICADV staff. To our surprise, the same reporters and media outlets that had covered RICADV education campaigns supportively failed to recognize the murders as domestic violence.

RICADV asked MRAP to analyse news coverage of domestic violence murders systematically; MRAP's preliminary study confirmed that reporters in the Rhode Island media market routinely treated domestic violence murder as an isolated and unforeseeable event—a slasher movie cum morality play in which modern man inexplicably unravels.

Domestic violence murder coverage was sensationalized, decontextualized, and fixated on the perpetrator's motive, findings that replicated those of other studies described below. In 1999, just as MRAP completed our study, a second cluster of three domestic violence murders occurred. By this point, RICADV had strengthened its capacity to respond rapidly to unexpected events.

Its spokespersons, now quoted widely, shifted news accounts of the murders from the previous framing of domestic violence as a private, unpredictable tragedy to the advocates' social framing of domestic violence as a community responsibility. RICADV subsequently published a handbook for journalists summarizing recommendations from survivors, reporters, advocates and MRAP (2000).

When a third cluster of three domestic violence murders occurred in spring 2002, RICADV was even better positioned; it had consolidated its rapid response capacity and strengthened working relations with member groups and a broad network of allies all of whom it rapidly mobilized.

At a packed press conference, Deborah DeBare, Executive Director of RICADV flanked by domestic violence survivors and leading politicians, called for social not private responses to domestic violence. The over-flow audience included film crews, photographers, and reporters from every major news outlet in Rhode Island, candidates for Attorney General, elected officials, law enforcement officers, and domestic violence advocates.

Reporters had labeled the press conference a "must attend" event, and its coverage topped the evening news and the next day's headlines. In contrast to domestic violence advocates' silence in 1996, news accounts in 2002 opened with

RICADV's messages of community responsibility for domestic violence. Reporters high- lighted the testimony of RICADV's domestic violence survivor group, Sisters Overcoming Abusive Relationships (SOAR).

SOAR's Rosa DeCastillo described fleeing with her children barefoot in the snow and urged the audience to "work together to ensure the safety of victims." A friend of Barbara Lombardi, a recent victim, also stressed social responsibility: "Tragically, our present system failed Barbara and should be held accountable—anything less would be an injustice."

RICADV's DeBare then linked these experiences to a major policy initiative; in ten days following the third murder, an RICADV-initiated coalition had crafted a seven-point plan to close gaps in the safety net of domestic violence services. A few months later, the Coalition and its allies shepherded the plan through the Rhode Island legislature. Thus, a seasoned RICADV turned the 2002 cluster of murders into a catalyst for policy change, not only a media opportunity but also a political opportunity.

After the bill's passage, RICADV and MRAP agreed to enter a period of reflection to distill the lessons from RICADV's intentional capacity-building and strategic intervention in the Rhode Island media market. From that reflection, came the study that follows.

Since the founding of Mobilization, social movement theorists have debated whether opportunity is primarily exogenous—a structural opening caused by forces beyond social movements' control—or more negotiable—a strategic tug of war in which unequal contending forces wrestle for advantage amidst shifting historical conditions.

Mapping thirty variables appearing in these debates, Gamson and Meyer warn that opportunity "threatens to become an all-encompassing fudge factor for all the conditions and circumstances that form the context for collective action".

Eight years later, Meyer finds more variables added while previous variables have yet to be "disproved, refined or replaced," a tendency he finds "both completely understandable and frustrating". Since different studies focus on distinct theoretical issues and movements, Meyer continues, "analysts talk past each other".

For instance, studies stressing "big" opportunities (shifts in relatively stable structures and values) do not engage with those focused on "small" opportunities (shifts in more volatile attitudes, policies, and practices). Diverging methodologies further complicate debates; comparative studies of social systems and movements tend to highlight big opportunities, while studies tracking single movements over time, highlight small opportunities.

More fundamentally, theorists begin with divergent definitions of collective action and collective actors. Some focus only on collective acts of protest, others on action in the political arena, while others include cultural and economic dimensions. In defining collective actors, some studies vaguely refer to challengers while others may focus on individual activists, social movement organizations, coalitions, or whole social movements.

Without much uniformity regarding what constitutes collective action or actors, it remains hard to generalize about intentional agency—how collective actors share perceptions, reach common cause, act and reflect together as a collective force: The presumption underneath a political opportunity approach is that the development of movements reflects, responds to, and sometimes alters the realities of politics and policy although most work gives short shrift to how.

Criticizing theorizing that ignores collective actors' intent, Flacks (2005) agrees, It is surprising how rarely the historical studies that constitute the canon of the political opportunity (PO) perspective focus on the ways activists, in the movements being studied, understood and determined their own opportunities. Indeed, how organizers figure out their opportunities, and how movements expand on them is largely unstudied and untheorized.

As yet, he concludes, "the concept of 'political opportunity' provides little help in deciding what opportunities may actually be germane to what sort of mobilizing effort". To ground the debate over the nature of opportunity, Flacks urges that theorists follow the collective actor, a proposal resonant with Morris' (2000) suggestion that theorists study the processes that form and sustain collective actors.

In line with both Flacks and Morris, Alimi (2003, 2004) demonstrates how Palestinian framers in the occupied territories in the years preceding the "first" Intifada utilized both print media and grassroots mobilization to construct a shared Palestinian perception of growing divisions in Israel regarding the continued Israeli occupation.

Alimi argues that this internal Palestinian discourse was a critical component of Palestinians' reassessment of opportunity and that this discourse contributed to Palestinian mobilization; Palestinian organizations' shifting assessments of opportunities catalyzed increasingly overt conflicts with the Israeli state.

We share Alimi's interest in tracking how small opportunities, strategically nurtured by collective actors over time, can expand into bigger opportunities for more permanent structural changes.

This longitudinal study of the Rhode Island Coalition Against Domestic Violence, a statewide organization representing opponents to domestic violence, tracks how they negotiated media opportunities by strengthening their internal communication capacity and broadening relationships. As RICADV negotiated with media outlets to strengthen its media standing, it expanded opportunities to promote its oppositional frame via mainstream news outlets.

MEDIA OPPORTUNITY

Mass media form the "master forum" of our historical period. Yet for social movements, U.S. corporatized mass media markets offer limited access. To gain media standing, actors raising counterhegemonic perspectives as well as actors marginalized by inequalities such as race, class, gender, sexuality, citizenship or age must overcome barriers institutionalized in news gathering routines; pressured to produce fast, interesting stories that avoid legal controversies, journalists gravitate toward sources widely deemed "reliable," and avoid marginalized constituencies.

Sourcing decisions are political; in choosing sources, reporters decided whose accounts count. When accounts count, their sponsors gain visibility and options to press for added power. When accounts do not count, their proponents remain beyond the public eye; they lack credibility and their framings of reality remain marginal.

Individual activists and informal groups can master the skills and resources needed for occasional media appearances. Becoming a routine source in a market-driven mass media system, however, requires the sustainable energy of a collective actor with social and material capital far exceeding that of an individual activist or an informal group.

To sustain a routine working relationship with media outlets, e.g., function as a routine source, a collective actor must invest over time in communication capacity building so that media strategies can enhance political strategies. Movements' often paltry success establishing media capacity and gaining media standing provides anecdotal support for "strong hegemony" approaches that document how modern mass media structures con-strain democratic discourse.

While fully accepting these structural constraints, RICADV and MRAP build their work on weaker hegemony approaches that stress agent-focused opportunities for changing media. In adopting a weaker hegemony model, collective actors strategically assess their options and weigh their resources and networks against the dangers and pressures of structural inequalities.

Raymond Williams calls this reflexive strategizing, "options under pressure". Applying a similar approach to media-movement interactions, weaker hegemony adherent Barker-Plummer calls for a dialogic approach to relations between movements and reporters that can acknowledge collective actors' reflexivity: A dialogic approach looks for two-way influences from any interaction, and it assumes the participants in any interaction can learn about and use the resources of the other— especially if those resources are discursive knowledge resources.

Seeing the media- movement relationship as two-way does not preclude it from being an imbalanced interaction, nor deny that one organization holds more power than the other. A dialogic model comes with no guarantees. . . . But to say that a relationship is difficult, complex, subtle and unbalanced is not to say that its outcomes are inevitable.

Highlighting intentional interactions embedded in historically shaped inequalities, Barker- Plummer's dialogic approach resonates with theorists stressing relationships and coalitions, discourse, power, strategy, reflexivity, and collective processes and infrastructure.

Like Steinberg's historically embedded discourse analyses, Barker-Plummer's dialogic approach recognizes that, at heart, social change involves actors communicating—developing strategies by airing grievances, testing challenges, negotiating conflicts, lobbying allies, evaluating accomplishments, and sharing lessons. As relations deepen and collabouredations widen, the collective actor extends its power, gaining standing in widening circles.

Like Klandermans and Gamson and Meyer, Barker-Plummer calls for longitudinal studies of media opportunity: Movement and media interactions play out over time. Only by studying these interactions across time can we track the influence of one discourse on the other.

Short term studies that declare a critical movement or discourse to have been marginalized and thus to have 'failed' in the short terms, may be missing some of the most important effects.

DOMESTIC VIOLENCE AS AN ISSUE CULTURE

Meyer (2004) flags the value of an "issue-specific conceptualization" of opportunity, an insight of particular importance for the collective actor negotiating media opportunities. Historically rooted framing contests start with the existing issue culture. Domestic violence advocates today build on previous decades of organizing that successfully established domestic violence as a social problem worthy of public and media attention.

While the movement against domestic violence has established public awareness of domestic violence, media coverage does not consistently adopt the movement's framing of the issue—that ending domestic violence requires social intervention. To the contrary, researchers have identified the following recurring problems with existing coverage:

- News suggests victims, at least partially, are responsible for their fate.
- Inscribed as crime news, domestic violence reports focus on the sensational. Reporters revert to predetermined framings such as "tragic love goes awry".
- In an exculpatory search for perpetrator's motive, domestic violence is psychologized and individuated.
- Coverage focuses on perpetrators' motives and victims disappear.
- Coverage obscures social dimensions of domestic violence—ways that society produces and promotes violence against women.

Coverage patterns also vary by beat. A Living Page reporter may describe a new domestic violence shelter sympathetically, yet, re-assigned to the crime beat, may revert to traditional crime reporting lacking substantive insight into underlying issues.

Crime news' common severing of problem from causality undermines efforts to change public policy and consciousness, leaving past and potential victims isolated; atomized victims struggle for protection while the social roots of domestic violence remain obscured.

To address these problems, advocates and researchers have urged:

- Changes in news practices;
- Changes in journalist training;
- Journalistic guidelines regarding domestic violence coverage.

Though practical and compelling, the recommendations

do not address the barriers to change inherent in a market-driven news industry. While some argue that newsgathering practices can change, media critics generally concur that corporate mass media systems bedevil reform efforts unless grounded in strong collective efforts.

Thus, despite their practicality, the reforms proposed above remain a critique. It would take a collective actor to translate the critique into an intervention strategy, to develop the relational ties and networks needed to implement that strategy and distill lessons. In 1996, RICADV decided to attempt such an intervention.

METHODS AND FINDINGS

MRAP's preliminary study found that existing news coverage sensationalized domestic violence murders while framing them as private tragedies. RICADV was eager to replace this individuated framing with its frame conceptualizing domestic violence as a social problem, "everybody's business."

To negotiate wider opportunities for promoting this social frame, RICADV worked to improve its media standing as a routine news sources for reporters, a goal involving internal strengthening and external relation building. Positioning ourselves as theorists and activists working with RICADV, we tracked RICADV's decision making and strategizing, its actions and reflections.

We wanted to explore how intentional collective actors strategize to gain opportunity, an issue on which many studies remain "agnostic".

Conceptualizing the Research

To conduct an actor-centreed, longitudinal study, we needed to resolve questions of scale, scope, and duration, and to identify outcomes that would serve as measures of media standing. Regarding scale, RICADV represented a collective actor working within interacting political and media arenas; as a statewide coalition, RICADV was mandated to work for change in Rhode Island social policy, its political catchment area coinciding with the geographical area covered by the Rhode Island media market.

The research's scope was RICADV's communications work driven by two goals— solidifying media standing and expanding media opportunities in the Rhode Island media market.

To track the development of RICADV's growing communication capacity, we coupled qualitative methods with quantitative content analysis assessing RICADV's shifting influence on domestic violence murder coverage.

Our estimates of duration were informed by previous MRAP research that it took years not months for a social movement organization to become a routine source. Collective actors need to train staff and spokespersons, develop and refine internal and external communications systems, prepare messages and establish standing with reporters as a consistent and reliable source; while added resources can speed some processes, relation-building occurs in real time and the process can not be rushed.

Qualitative Approaches

As do individual activists, collective actors have life histories. To track the collective actor RICADV's growing communication capacity, we broadened life-history methods, which are gernerally understood as: Oral in-depth interviews conducted by a researcher within the framework of a research project.

Thus life histories involve interaction between the interviewer and the interview and involve a scientific intention in the telling of a story. Our collective life history approach involved thirty hours of oral in-depth group interviews with staff, survivors, coalition members, interns etc.

These were transcribed, reviewed by participants, and augmented by archival research, participant observation, and individual interviews.

The resulting collective life history tracks RICADV's conscious efforts to establish good working relationships with journalists (media standing) and, how it turned that standing into new opportunities in its media market.

Qualitative Findings

We began our life history of the Rhode Island Coalition Against Domestic Violence (RICADV) in 1996 when the organization, rooted in the Rhode Island women's movement, crafted a strategic plan to forward its mission of ending domestic violence in Rhode Island.

In winter of 1996, RICADV hired a full-time communications coordinator, Karen Jeffreys, and charged her with developing and overseeing RICADV communications initiatives, including both mass media and grassroots outreach. A seasoned community organizer, Jeffreys took a movement-building approach to communications.

She reasoned that those directly affected by domestic violence—victims and survivors—should be at the heart of setting the movement's directions. Starting there, Jeffreys worked to establish diverse networks of communication and support. "Everyone is a communicator," was our slogan. To ensure group participation, Jeffreys translated MRAP's framing work into a collective process, dubbed as the "media caucus" at RICADV.

Other media systems included a communication plan, media protocols, and a rapid response team at the organizational level. Jeffreys began to build RICADV's communications infrastructure and then worked with staff and members to map a communications strategy resonant with its overall strategy. Jeffreys called what she did "public relations," but her approach was far from the popular understanding of "PR" as sound-bite-driven marketing.

She conceptualized public relations as genuinely relating to one's publics, i.e., creating working relationships with all constituencies relevant for RICADV's mission of ending domestic violence in Rhode Island. Jeffreys also brought to RICADV her existing ties to the Media Research and Action Project (MRAP).

Based on prior experience, MRAP estimated it would take

five to seven years to establish RICADV as a routine source. To establish a baseline of information, the partners began to monitor existing news coverage of domestic violence. RICADV interns combed the news clips to identify reporters covering domestic violence-related beats.

Using the same news clippings, MRAP analysed media framings of domestic violence. At the same time, Jeffreys and other staff with roots in the Black Liberation and feminist movements began to strengthen RICADV's ability to make decisions collectively through solidarity building practices focused on core values and world view, diversity and conflict resolution practices.

With internal capacity to dialog and resolve differences reinforced, RICADV then developed a communications plan, a collective framing process dubbed a media caucus, media trainings and other media systems. As internal and external communications capacity grew, RICADV gained media standing. In 1996, RICADV had not gained access to media coverage when an external crisis—a cluster of three domestic violence murders—occurred.

Three years later in 1999, RICADV could influence media coverage of a similar murder cluster. By 2002, RICADV turned a murder cluster into a media opportunity, and then a political opportunity, a legislative campaign to reform Rhode Island's domestic-violence laws. Furthermore, on a state and national level, RICADV was functioning as a small agency-laden institution supporting other collective actors' media capacity building.

QUANTITATIVE APPROACHES

While increased calls from reporters suggested that RICADV's media standing had grown, we hadn't assessed that growth systematically. To do so, we decided to measure shifts in RICADV's rapid response capacity—its ability to influence unplanned events. The obvious beginning point was RICADV's 1996 decision to intensify communication work. As a closing point, we chose 2002 when RICADV concluded that, within the Rhode Island media market, it had achieved its goal of becoming an indispensable source of news and information regarding domestic violence.

To measure ability to respond quickly to outside, unpredictable events we looked for possible critical discourse moments. We settled on three comparable clusters of domestic violence murders. Each cluster involved three independent domestic violence murder cases that had occurred in a compressed time period—five to seven weeks.

Moreover, the three murder clusters had occurred at three-year intervals at the beginning, middle and end of our proposed study. We measure growth of RICADV's media standing in terms of its capacity to use the critical discourse moment to introduce the domestic violence movement's perspectives via the language and the sources that reporters use.

Study Design and Methods

MRAP's preliminary frame analysis of domestic violence murder coverage, found that coverage stopped framing domestic violence murders as "private family tragedy" or "love gone awry" when the murder was labeled as domestic violence and when domestic violence advocates or experts were quoted.

Based on these findings, RICADV decided to urge reporters to adopt two changes in journalistic practice: first, to use the words, 'domestic violence' if speaking about violence between intimates in order to set context; and second, to downplay or use selectively sources who stress the personal, tragic aspects of domestic violence (family, neighbours, random bystanders).

Instead, RICADV urged reporters to seek sources who discuss domestic violence murder—and its prevention—in its social context. In short, police, domestic violence survivors, advocates, or other experts can frame domestic violence more broadly than family and bystanders.

To analyse RICADV's progress vis-à-vis these changes, we measured the use of domestic violence language and sourcing patterns after three comparable clusters of domestic violence murders. The first cluster in 1996, serves as a baseline occurring before RICADV established systematic communications infrastructure and practices.

The 1999 cluster and the 2002 cluster provide measures at three-year intervals. Sample Selection Using a news-clipping service, we surveyed all weekly and daily papers, in the Rhode Island media market for coverage of any domestic violence murder that occurred between 1996 and 2002.

Crosschecking the sample against Lexis-Nexis, we identified 275 stories addressing the 22 domestic violence murder cases that occurred in Rhode Island between 1996 and 2002. From this sample we selected a subset of murder cases that occurred in comparable conditions; in each case, a cluster of three murder cases in less than two months.

Spaced at three-year intervals, the clusters represent the seven-year time period over which RICADV established a communication staff, strategy and infrastructure. Thus, the clusters permit us to contrast changes in coverage against the incremental growth of RICADV's communication capacity. We treated each cluster of murders as one critical discourse moment.

We focused on murders rather than incidents of domestic violence more generally for several reasons. Use of murders ensured that the issue met news criteria. Murders could be identified irrefutably as domestic violence (as contrasted to domestic violence incidents that are contested by either party). Finally, murder stories represented a clear example of unplanned crisis coverage.

As such, murder stories were a good measure of RICADV's ability to take advantage of an external, unanticipated media opportunity. Moreover, a cluster of murders occurring in close proximity, we hypothesized, might create a media opportunity; reporters might be more open to domestic violence advocates highlighting the murders' common features: in domestic violence murders, usually there is a history of violence, others besides the victim know about it, and existing prevention systems fail.

Our focus on local print media reflects communications scholars' findings that local news provides the most common journalistic venue for domestic violence crimes since they are usually deemed of mostly local interest. National media, covering only the most egregious or unusual domestic violence murder cases, offer a less reliable arena for evaluating coverage patterns.

Our focus on print media grows from Kaniss' finding that local print news outlets serve as kingmakers directly impacting politicians, police and other institutions. Broadcast news, Kaniss finds, generally trails print coverage, the longer print accounts providing raw material for broadcasts' shorter "headline" versions of events.

Coder Training and Content Variables

We trained two teams, each comprised of three coders, to identify both the patterns of sources and the kinds of domestic-violence language used in the newspaper articles. Post- training, intercoder reliability averaged. We compared the reporters' choices of lead and key sources and articles' use of domestic violence language.

Removing advocate/activist sources from the sample, we looked for use of domestic violence language by nonadvocate sources and reporters. This chapter compares media coverage of each of the murder clusters in relation to our two key variables—journalists' choice of language to describe the murders and journalists' choice of sources.

To analyse journalists' choice of language describing domestic violence murders, we first reviewed RICADV press releases for each murder. From these press releases we created a glossary of common phrases used by advocates vis-à-vis the murders. Each news article was then coded for reporters' incorporation of language that corresponded to the advocates' domestic violence message.

Coders documented where and how often the term appeared. Each story was coded three times, each time by an independent coder. A final coding reviewed all cases for consistency, data entry errors, etc. Intercoder reliability exceeded. Positing that journalists use sources to shape the story line, we also studied source patterns.

We coded articles for all quoted sources, identified by relationship to the crime (e.g., police, domestic violence advocate, bystander, victim, victim's family, friend, co-worker; perpetrator; perpetrator's family, friend, coworker, and so on). The police category included court professionals. The advocate category included survivors and all others involved in domestic violence work or activism. We focused this analysis on sources used in lead quotes and key quotes.

CONTENT ANALYSIS: FINDINGS

A comparison of news coverage of the 1996, 1999, and 2002 murder clusters reveals significant changes in reporters' use of domestic violence language and sourcing patterns.

Domestic Violence Language

In news articles covering the first cluster of domestic violence murders, there were only 0.57 references per article to domestic violence, i.e., on average, less than one reference per article. By 1999, news stories, however, were averaging five references to domestic violence per article, roughly a seven-fold increase.

After the publication of the handbook for journalists, subsequent dialogue and relation building, references to domestic Violence rose to ten per article. This doubled the reference per article rate from 1999. Measuring change from the baseline year of 1996, however, 2002 figures represent a sixteen-fold increase.

Sourcing Patterns

To analyse trends in sourcing patterns, we studied shifts in lead source and shifts in key sources. The lead source was the first source cited in the article. No news story covering the 1996 cluster of murders quoted a domestic violence advocate as lead source. The majority of lead sources at this point were police, victim's relations (family, friend, coworker), perpetrator's relations (family, friends, coworkers) and bystanders (the proverbial "man on the street" interview). Police and victim's relations, tied for the most common lead source; 28.6% of the 1996 stories lead with a quote from the police or from victim's family, neighbours, or coworkers. Similarly bystanders and perpetrator's relations split second place at 7.1% and 7% respectively.

By 1999, the situation had changed. In print coverage of the second cluster of murders, advocates rose from invisibility to become reporters' most common lead source; 30.8% of articles quoted an advocate (A) as their lead source. Reporters continued to use police as the lead source but to a lesser extent (P = 19.2%).

Reporters dramatically decreased their use of victim's relations and perpetrator's relations as lead sources; by the second cluster of murders, use of victim's relations (V) had dropped to 7.6% and no perpetrator's relations were quoted. Reporters, however, continued to solicit reactions from random by-passers. (B = 11.5%) 2002 coverage demonstrates further changes.

Advocates and police have remained the two most common lead sources. Reporters' preference for advocates as lead source has continued to rise (40.3%) but reporters' use of police sources has increased as well; in the third cluster of murders reporters cite police as lead source almost as frequently as in 1996 (24.8%). The additional visibility garnered by advocates drew, therefore, not from police but from bystander sources.

A graphical representation of trends in lead source citation can be found. Besides lead sources, we analysed all key sources—sources quoted in the first three or last paragraphs or quoted for at least one paragraph—coding them again by their relationship to the murder. Changes in sourcing patterns for key sources were virtually identical to those cited for lead sources above.

Changes in the Culture

Since advocates routinely use domestic violence language, we expected an increase in use of domestic violence advocates as lead or key sources might result in a concomitant increase in domestic violence language.

This would tell us that domestic violence advocates had become more visible in public discourse but would not mean that other public voices had embraced domestic violence language. To test whether reporters and/or other sources—police, bystanders, victim's families—increased their use of domestic violence language over the six-year period, we created a dummy variable that removed all articles citing advocates as sources.

Using the resulting "nonadvocate" subsample, we conducted an independent sample T-test to determine the means for domestic violence citations when advocates are not quoted. In other words, when advocates are removed from the 1999 sub- sample, reporters average one reference to domestic violence in every four articles. Thus, most domestic violence language in the 1999 clusters—five references per article on average— was attributable to advocate sources.

For the 2002 cluster, however, the mean number of domestic violence citations grew to 5.75 per article—even with advocates removed from the sample. Thus, by 2002, reporters and nonadvocate sources had increased use of domestic violence language ten-fold.

In sum, our findings suggest that by the third cluster of murders in 2002, reporters adopted the newsgathering practices suggested by the Rhode Island Coalition Against Domestic Violence in several critical ways. Articles identifying the murder of intimate part- ners as domestic violence rose. Sources representing domestic violence advocates increased in both relative and absolute terms as did reporters' use of police and other expert sources.

And while reporters continued to use neighbours, family, friends and co-workers as sources judiciously, they curtailed their use of casual bystanders. As a result, bystander and family sources dropped in frequency. In perhaps our most notable finding, even when advocate sources were removed from the sample, reporters and nonadvocate sources had increased their use of domestic violence language ten-fold between 1996 and 2002. Over seven years, Rhode Island domestic violence advocates achieved media standing, moving from obscurity to become routine sources for Rhode Island reporters. RICADV, working with MRAP, strategically negotiated this rise in media standing. When the 1996 murders occurred, RICADV did not have the capacity to respond.

By 1999, RICADV had established a solid communications infrastructure that helped it navigate its media market; its systems facilitated rapid responses to crises and working relationships with reporters were growing. Building on MRAP's initial analysis of domestic violence murder coverage, RICADV opened dialogs with reporters. As RICADV consolidated its communications infrastructure and built relationships, it became a routine source.

Whereas, domestic violence advocates were invisible in newspaper coverage of the 1996 murders, domestic violence advocates were the most prominent sources in the 1999 coverage. As sources changed, frames changed. By 2002, RICADV's efforts in the Rhode Island media market over the previous six years had shifted the public discourse; nonadvocate sources, police for instance, and reporters themselves had begun to adopt domestic violence language.

With broader constituencies framing domestic violence as a social issue, the state's residents and political leaders were readied for the RICADV-led Seven-Point Plan that reformed state policy vis-à-vis domestic violence. The use of domestic violence language by sources other than domestic violence advocates, therefore, suggests a broadened awareness of domestic violence and a culture shift supporting the proposed political change.

RICADV's expanded ability to transform comparable unforeseen events—murders—into media opportunities and ultimately political opportunities suggests that conceptualizing opportunity primarily as external is insufficient.

As Klandermans and others suggest, seen from a longitudinal perspective, the process is more interactive and allows for conscious collective actors to expand their power.

RICADV's intentional decision to develop a media strategy resulted in its hiring skilled staff who developed its internal and external communications capacity.

This helped RICADV take advantage of existing media opportunities. These media opportunities, well utilized, built media standing. Reporters came to trust RICADV, deeming its events "must-attend." As its media standing grew, RICADV's ability to negotiate broader media opportunities grew beyond its original boundaries of the Rhode Island media market. RICADV has already shared its approaches with 37 states.

Its public awareness campaigns have been adopted nationally for three years and it is now working with a national coalition to replicate its communications systems nationally. If RICADV had over-emphasized the very real structural barriers to gaining media standing, it would not have taken its first steps.

If it had under-emphasized the structural barriers, it would not have sustained a seven-year laboured—a sprinter ill-prepared for a test of endurance. Believing that it could make its accounts count, RICADV worked incrementally to strengthen its capacity to respond to unfolding events.

Its ability to navigate the Rhode Island media market helped RICADV deepen its network of relationships with allies and reporters. As RICADV proved useful, reporters' estimation of the group as a valued news source—its media standing—grew.

To the concept of media opportunity, therefore, the concepts of media capacity and media standing add recognition of the advantage of the organizationally stable collective actor over individuals and less formally organized challengers.

A collective actor's media standing is not so easily lost as to be called "volatile," nor are existing hegemonic structures so impermeable that collective actors must wait for opportunity as if it were a state lottery. While individual, isolated challenges to corporate mass media rarely succeed, a collective actor operating strategically and reflexively over time can accrue media standing if it builds sustainable communication infrastructure and relations suited its media market(s).

This study also suggests the importance of locating structural challenges at local, state, or national levels depending on the collective actor's level of development. In our case, a statewide collective actor successfully breached structural barriers in a state-level media market.

Had RICADV, as a state-level collective actor new to media organizing simply entered the national media fray without attention to analyzing market structures or its resources, they would have found the barriers facing them insurmountable. Breaking structural critiques of the corporate-dominated media arena into its component markets makes local, state, and regional challenges viable.

Replicated, challenges in individual media markets provide the infrastructure to sustain a national challenge. Thus, our work moves us to define opportunity not as residing in structure or agency but in historical conjunctures—strategic fits that allow the intentional collective actor to craft a challenge to relations of domination suited to its resources and historical position.

While in our case, the right fit was a regional challenge in a regional market by a regional actor, the question of scale is historically variable. In the early stages of a social movement, smaller collective actors working on a limited scale may dominate. If theorists ignore how these early stages accrue to catalyze political sea changes, the theories they manufacture may miss how collective actors identify strategic opportunities appropriate for their historical moment.

They may present institutionalized power as impenetrable rather than understanding that social relations and processes are vulnerable to challenge and change over time. We have noted that by 2002, RICADV used the third cluster of domestic violence murders not only as a media opportunity, but to launch a successful political initiative, the Seven Point Plan.

As political leaders look to the media to reach their

constituents, media opportunity becomes inextricably linked to political opportunity. While here we emphasize media opportunity, political opportunity forms the ever-present background that, like an M.D. Escher drawing, shifts to the foreground with the blink of an eye.

Since RICADV's 2002 media strategy represented one of many strategies used to pass the Seven-Point Plan—legislative lobbying, grassroots mobilizing, coalition-building—we hesitate to conjecture too broadly regarding the impact of media standing on political opportunity apart from a full analysis of the campaign.

Social movements and their participating collective actors start with seemingly impossible goals—to create macro shifts in social structures. By organizing strategically with support from agency-laden institutions, collective actors gain tensile strength over time—despite pressure from existing structural arrangements, they find opportunities and turn them into bigger ones. For an intentional, reflexive strategic actor, a little meeting on creaky chairs in a musty, echoing church basement can represent an increase in opportunity; its participant's respected allies.

In challenging hegemony lived, in learning and growing from experiences even on a small scale, a collective actor creates tantalizing tastes of counter- hegemony lived. Critical to the collective actor's growth is the formation of a strategy and infrastructure that will guide and support action over time; intentional actors, social movement organizations channel the limited resources of many to mount focused challenges to existing structures.

The reflective collective actor grows as it reflects on its experience, a process in which theorists may be useful. This chapter represents the collabouredative reflections of RICADV and MRAP working within a one media market to nurture internal and external communication capacity and leverage that growth into broader media standing and opportunity. That reporters bestowed media standing on RICADV fits our historical times.

In the wake of the civil rights movement and other

counter-hegemonic movements and now, with the rising tide of conservative mobilizations, reporters recognize social movement organizations as recurring players in American life. U.S. residents today may not be startled to hear their nation labeled a "social movement society".

The 1996 launching of Mobilization signaled a parallel emergence of social movement studies as an institutionalized field of social science. Ironically, social movement theorists may work with social movements less than reporters.

While reporters recognize social movements as permanent features of American society, social movement theorist remain relatively isolated from activists, an isolation all the more troubling because activist-theorist collabouredations might provided insights into outstanding theoretical tangles. To illustrate the opportunities such collabouredations present, we offer our experience. In the coming decade of Mobilization, this opportunity beckons all takers.

Chapter 6

Rights to Privacy

When victims of violence and their families, through no fault of their own, are suddenly thrust into the harsh light of public scrutiny, they often bitterly complain. Their private life is suddenly the subject of front-page pictures and articles. Readers are quick to react when they feel a journalist has crossed the line and intruded into a subject's personal moment of grief. Anne Seymour, public affairs director for the National Victim Centre in Fort Worth said, "Any time there is a yellow line, some journalists in the interest of news will cross over". Public officials and celebrities also feel that journalists sometimes cross that yellow journalism line in covering their everyday activities. Television actress, Roseanne Barr, who frequently advocates her and her family's right to privacy, told a story on the "Oprah Winfrey Show" that illustrates this point. Her mother saw a television camera, Barr said, coming through the window of her home. Barr's mother was forced to lie on the floor to avoid being videotaped.

The judicial system in America has recognize that private and public persons have different legal rights when it comes to privacy. Privacy laws, as can be imagined, are much stricter for private citizens not involved in a news story than for public celebrities who sometimes invite media attention.

Journalists need to be aware of the laws that are concerned with privacy and trespass. But ethical behaviour should not be guided by what is strictly legal.

PRIVACY IS AN EARLY ISSUE

Historically, invasion of privacy issues are linked with

candid photography. Limitations with the type of camera, lenses, and film in the early days of photography prevented many of the candid moments that are commonplace today. Once cameras became hand-held and lenses and film became faster, amateur and professional photographers were able to make pictures that previously were impossible.

Early news photographers were forced to use bulky cameras that limited the type of picture possible. Candid pictures were simply not possible when subjects quickly spotted a photographer. The photographs of Paul Martin and Jacques-Henri Lartique stand out as wonderful exceptions. They captured many candid moments among 19th-century citizens.

Typical subjects of Martin's candid style were Victoria-era children playing in public parks, women enjoying the surf during holidays, and men working along the busy streets of London. It was rare when a photographer could capture a spontaneous news event.

More likely, subjects in news and feature assignments were carefully composed by the photographer to create a static or stereotyped look. As Wilson Hicks, author of *Words and Pictures* wrote, "Instead of picture consciousness, it was a time of camera consciousness. Practically everybody looked at the camera. . . . When the photographer entered a situation of movement involving people, life stopped dead in its tracks and orientated itself to the camera".

The successful documentary photographers during the early years of newspaper photojournalism were the ones who could make pictures that did not have a highly manipulated look. Jacob Riis and Lewis Hine were photographers who used the equipment of their day-large, bulky cameras with slow film and lenses.

Although their photographs, for the most part, showed individuals and groups looking into the camera's lens, their pictures are classic documentary statements because of the lack of manipulation by the photographers. It is a rare occurrence to find images by Riis or Hine that show subjects unaware of the camera's presence.

Lewis Hine, of Oshkosh, Wisconsin, worked in a factory for long hours during the day when he was a boy. Consequently, his photographs of children suffering for many hours at low pay and with dangerously, fast-moving machines were vivid and disturbing. Child laboured laws were passed to protect children, a direct result of his photographs.

GEORGE EASTMAN'S AMATEUR CRAZE

The invention of a faster dry plate film meant that medium-sized and smaller, handheld -cameras could be used. Such cameras allowed amateur and professional photographers to make pictures of unsuspecting subjects. George Eastman came up with a camera he dubbed, the Kodak. The Kodak slogan was, "You push the button-and we do the rest."

The camera was small, easy to use, and contained 100 pictures on a dry gelatin roll. When the snapshot shooter had exhausted the roll, the camera was mailed to Rochester, New York where the film was processed, printed, and returned to the owner with the camera and a fresh roll of exposures.

Amateur photographers immediately took snapshots of practically anything that moved with the little Kodaks and other cameras. No one was considered safe as unsuspecting strangers clicked off exposures. The camera craze that began in the 1880s was an international epidemic that prompted retaliation by those upset with photographers taking candid pictures of people without permission.

The *New York Times* "likened the snapshot craze with an outbreak of cholera that had becomc a I national scourge' ". A popular poem, a parody of the Kodak slogan was,

Picturesque landscape,
Babbling brook,
Maid in a hammock
Reading a book;
Man with a Kodak
In secret prepared
To picture the maid,
As she sits unawares.

Her two strapping brothers
Were chancing to pass;
Saw the man with the Kodak
And also the lass.
They rolled up their sleeves
Threw off hat, coat and vest
The man pressed the button
And they did the rest!

Vigilante associations were formed to protect the honour of unsuspecting women. A brick thrown through a camera's lens was advocated as a possible remedy. The *Chicago Tribune* wrote in an editorial that "something must be done, and will be done, soon.

A jury would not convict a man who violently destroyed the camera of an impudent photographer guilty of a constructive assault upon modest women". A photographer intent on capturing people in embarrassing or compromising situations was despised by a great many people.

Although anti-photography bills were never introduced in America, Victorian London photographers required free official permits to take pictures in parks. Restrictions often included "Persons and groups of persons on Sundays . [with] hand cameras" and without tripods. Germany passed a statute prohibiting photography without permission in 1907.

Of newspaper and magazine photographers who put small cameras to use, Bill Jay in his article, "The Photographer as Aggressor," wrote, "As any impartial observer will admit, no aspect of a life was too private, no tragedy too harrowing, no sorrow too personal, no event too intimate to be witnessed and recorded by the ubiquitous photographer".

Small, hand-held professional cameras, particularly those made by the Leica company, made it possible for photographers to take high quality pictures of people in low-light situations without a subject's knowledge or consent. Two early prolific and respected users of the small cameras were Paul Wolff and Erich Salomon.

Wolff became known for his feature pictures where he, according to Hicks, showed that a picture could be made out of any subject. Salomon, a lawyer who took up photography to earn a living after the loss of his family's fortune, made unposed pictures of presidents and statesmen during meetings and public functions.

Salomon's images are beautifully composed candid moments of hard-talking politicians caressed by the gentle glow of available light. His photographs were published in several illustrated German publications and became a model for candid pictures for future generations of news photographers.

Salomon's photographic career was tragically cut short when he was captured and executed by the Nazis. Privacy violations would not became an issue if it were not for editors who were willing to publish the revealing, hidden moments. Magazine and newspaper editors once the halftone process became relatively inexpensive and aesthetically acceptable, were eager to fill their pages with photographs that were used, admittedly, to sell more copies.

Hicks summed up the philosophy of the editors of the day with, "Get the picture-nothing else mattered". This was the era of the scoop. Competition was so fierce that photographers would go to great lengths to beat a rival photographer. One of the best known freelance newspaper photographers, Arthur Fellig, gained his reputation for taking pictures of accident and murder victims no one else had. Fellig's motto was, "F/8 and be there." Professionally known as "Weegee," a variation of the popular table entertainment, "Ouija," Fellig, aided by police informants, arrived at news events often before the police.

THE COURTS BAN CAMERAS

The era culminated with the trial of Bruno Hauptmann for the kidnapping and murder of aviator, Charles Lindbergh's baby. Over 700 reporters and 125 photographers covered the sensational events of the trial. Although photographs were allowed in the courtroom before the trial, during recesses, and after the trial, there were many abuses by competitive-crazed photographers.

After the trial, the American Bar Association issued the 35th canon of Professional and Judicial Ethics. Most states adopted Canon 35 to ban photographers from their courtrooms. Before the ruling, a judge could independently decide whether to ban news photographers.

In the 1950s, Joseph Costa and the NPPA lobbied to appeal the states' ruling. Slowly, acceptance for photographers' presence in the courtroom grew. Florida's cameras-in-the-courtroom model, approved by the Florida Supreme Court, was tested successfully during the Ronnie Zamora trial in 1978.

In another Florida case, the Supreme Court in 1981 upheld the conviction of two Miami Beach police officers for burglarizing a restaurant. Officers Noel Chandler and Robert Granger felt that they were denied a fair trial by the presence of television and still photojournalists in the courtroom.

The Supreme Court allowed individual states to decide how to regulate the coverage of trials. Florida, as with many other states, does not require permission from all participants for photo news coverage, but restrictions were imposed.

"Only one television camera and only one still photographer are allowed in the courtroom at one time. Equipment must be put in one place; photographers/camera persons cannot come and go in the middle of the proceeding, and no artificial light is allowed."

Other states have opened up their courtrooms to photographers. Federal trials are still off limits for cameras. As opposed to the small, 35mm camera, the bulky 4X5 press cameras were seldom used for candid images. The press camera was simply a hand-held version of the view camera that had to be set on a tripod.

The camera only held one 4 X 5-inch negative holder with two sheets of film at a time. The negative holders were awkward to manage. There was no through-the-lens or rangefinder mechanism to aid focusing. After each exposure a new flash bulb had to be inserted into the flash unit while an unexposed film holder had to be inserted in the back of the camera.

Despite the availability of small, hand-held cameras, a 1951 survey of 61 newspapers with circulation of over 100,000 showed that 97% of the staff photographers used the 4X5 press cameras. Arthur Geiselman of the York, Pennsylvania Gazette and Daily was attacked by a crowd at the scene of a child's drowning. "The 4 X 5 is not the camera for this kind of spot news coverage," wrote Geiselman. "1 believe if I had had a 35 millimeter camera I could have avoided trouble. The clumsy, black box is too much in evidence at a time when a camera should be inconspicuous". The subjects of the press cameras, were for the most part, aware of the photographer's presence, unless the subject was greatly preoccupied.

Privacy problems arose when editors chose to use sensational pictures on their front pages. In an era of yellow journalism, photographs contributed greatly to the public's repulsion of news photography as a profession. Photojournalists were labeled as mindless ambulance chasers without a thought for the subjects of the images.

As one writer noted, photographers were considered "reporters with their brains knocked out". Such a characterization was misleading because reporters also wrote stories that contributed to the sensational era. Photographers did produce moving photographic documents with large, press cameras, however.

The Farm Security Administration (FSA) was a governmental agency set up by the Roosevelt administration to document the weather and economic affects upon people during "The Great Depression." Led by Harvard economics professor Roy Stryker, the photographic unit of the FSA included such household names as Walker Evans, Dorothea Lange, Russell Lee, Carl Mydans, and Arthur Rothstein.

One of the most memorable images of all time came from the FSA collection. Dorothea Lange made "The Migrant Mother," a sad, roadside close-up of a destitute mother with a faraway look and her shy children. Unfortunately, the mother in the portrait, Florence Thompson, complained that Lange received fame for the picture while she lived in relative poverty.

Nevertheless, when Mrs. Thompson suffered a stroke and her family could not pay her medical expenses, people around the country donated over $15,000. Many wrote that they were touched by Lange's photograph. Newspaper photographers eventually replaced their 4X5 cameras with more easily manipulated 35mm cameras.

Consequently, photojournalism reporting gained respect as many more photojournalists were more inclined to photograph people as they really were rather than stage direct a subject's actions. Private moments that involved social problems were now the subject of photographers. Picture magazines such as the London *Post* and America's *Life* and *Look* ushered in what many considered to be the "Golden Age of Photojournalism."

Gene Smith, Margaret Bourke-White, Alfred Eisenstaedt, Leonard McCombe, and Bill Eppridge are some of the photographers that worked for the picture magazines. Eisenstaedt's Time's Square celebration kiss between two strangers, a soldier and a nurse, beautifully shows the joy the world felt that World War 11 was at an end.

The picture, however, has been embroiled in controversy as up to 10 sailors have claimed to be the man in the famous picture. The ultimate goal of the claims made by the soldiers is a percentage of the profits Time, Inc. has made throughout the years for the sale of the image.

Smith made classic picture stories of individuals: a country doctor and a nurse mid-wife are two of his favourite stories. McCombe produced one of the first "A Day in the Life" stories with his coverage of a young woman from a small town working in New York City. Bill Eppridge produced one of the most dramatic picture stories in the history of *Life* magazine.

Headlined, "We are animals in a world no one knows," Eppridge and a reporter, James Mills, produced a sensitive and shocking portrait of a young, educated couple forced into prostitution and robbery to feed their $100 a day heroin addiction. Eppridge and Mills received permission to intrude into their daily lives without paying their subjects.

ROBERT FRANK AND MAGAZINE PHOTOGRAPHY

Many photographers established a style of photography that was unique to the 35mm film medium. Their images were usually of people in bars or on the street who were unaware of the camera's presence. Inspired by the writings of "beat" novelist, Jack Kerouac, Robert Frank is best known for his gritty portrait of America contained in his book, *The Americans*.

Frank spent more than a year "on the road" through a Guggenheim grant. He made pictures that showed a side of America that contrasted greatly with the pretty picture postcard scenes that typically "documented" America at that time. Although his photographs were severely criticized by photography experts, Frank inspired future generations of photographers who realized that the subjects for photography were not limited to traditional, postcard views.

Magazine photographs developed a more casual visual style as many of the "street photographers" freelanced for the magazines. Magazine images are usually more graphically complicated than straight-forward news photographs because readers spend more time viewing an image in a weekly or monthly magazine.

Curiously, magazine images of hard news subjects can be much more graphically violent and threatening to an ordinary person's privacy without the typical reader uproar found with similar images published in a newspaper. Readers have a more protective, almost personal commitment to their hometown newspaper.

Nevertheless, newspaper photographers started to imitate the candid shooting style seen in the magazines. When that style is used for spot news situations in newspapers, subjects and readers sometimes object that their privacy has been violated. *News Photographer* magazine has printed several articles that detail the right to privacy of a photographer's subject. In an article titled, "'Inside Story' Inside Photos," a television programme hosted by the former state department spokesman for President Carter, Hodding Carter, featured a discussion of controversial images.

Editors and photographers in the programme generally agreed that a newspaper's mission is to sometimes make people uncomfortable. Although it is unfortunate that people complain when their anonymity is taken away when their picture is published, Hal Buell of the Associated Press remarked that if newspapers do not print pictures that upset people once in awhile, "Don't we stand a chance of the reader losing his credibility in the newspaper?"

Some critics complain that deadline pressures and competitiveness are responsible for journalists sometimes trampling on the privacy of others. Zuckerman noted that "News organizations, driven by intense competition, rarely let concern for a victim's privacy get in the way of a scoop".

HILDA BRIDGES SUES FOR HER PRIVACY

A woman in Florida did more than complain about the loss of her privacy. She sued the newspaper for millions of dollars. Hilda Bridges was kidnapped by her estranged husband, Clyde Bridges and forced to remove all of her clothes. He thought that his wife would be unwilling to escape if she were nude. When police surrounded the apartment building, Bridges killed himself. Behind police lines, Scott Maclay of the *Cocoa Today* newspaper was waiting with a 300mm lens.

The photograph Maclay made shows a frightened woman, disrobed, but partially covered by a dishtowel, running with a police official who's face shows deep concern with his hand firmly grasping the woman's shoulder. After several hours of consultation with various editors, Maclay's picture of Hilda Bridges' rescue ran large on the front page. The newspaper's editor said that the picture "best capsulated the dramatic and tragic events".

Some readers later complained that the picture of the scantily clad woman was published to sell additional copies of the newspaper and for no other reason. Bridges claimed that her privacy had been invaded because she was naked. She testified that the photograph made her want to "crawl away, hoping nobody would see me."

A lower court awarded the woman $10,000. On appeal, the decision was overturned. The key in court cases seems to hinge on the conduct of the news photographer or the news medium. "If the conduct is so extreme, so 'beyond all possible bounds of decency' . . . then one may be found guilty of intentional infliction of emotional distress".

The court in the appeal said that the picture "revealed little more than some bathing suits seen on the beaches. The published photograph is more a depiction of grief, fright, and emotional tension than it is an appeal to other sensual appetites." Furthermore, the court said, "Because the story and photograph may be embarrassing or distressful to the plaintiff does not mean the newspaper cannot publish what is otherwise newsworthy".

CELEBRITY PHOTOGRAPHS

A classic example of a photographer overstepping the bounds of decency was Ron Galella. Galella had one passion in his life-to photograph Jackie Onassis and her family. It was a lucrative passion. He once earned over $20,000 a year just for his pictures of Onassis. But Galella was no "one shot wonder."

He followed Onassis and her family wherever he could. Galella was seen taking pictures of her while hiding "behind a coat rack in a restaurant, jumping out from behind bushes into the path of her children, and flicking a camera strap at Onassis while grunting, 'Glad to see me back, aren't you Jackie?" Galella even disguised himself as a Greek sailor and made pictures of Onassis sunbathing in the nude on the island of Scorpios. The pictures were later published in *Hustler* magazine.

Galella claimed he was simply exercising his right as a journalist under the First Amendment. In two courtroom decisions, (he simply ignored the first decision that ordered he stay at least 25 feet from Onassis) the court said he was guilty of "acts of extremely outrageous conduct." To avoid a possible 6-year prison term and a fine of $120,000, Galella signed an agreement to "never again aim a camera at Mrs.

Onassis or her children". Thousands of dollars and careers can be made by photographing famous people either doing extraordinary or quite ordinary actions. Readers seem to enjoy seeing famous people in ordinary situations given the popularity of the publications that use the images and the high prices editors pay to photographers for their pictures. Pictures that show the windblown skirts of a queen, the bikini look of a pregnant princess, and a president slipping down a plane's steps have earned large paychecks for the photographers.

The foreign and national press have a tremendous interest in star-studded photographs as the popularity of personality publications and "infotainment" television programs attest. Photojournalist Ross Baughman suggests that pictures of famous people undergoing ordinary activities need to be taken. Such pictures "can play an important role in democratizing royalty or in letting the public know these people are only human like the rest of us".

The intense competition among photographers to come up with unique angles of famous people has led to some obvious excesses. Six helicopters filled with photographers flew over the wedding of movie stars Michael Fox and Tracy Pollan. Recently, photographers have drawn criticism from the public and their colleagues by confronting a famous person until a reaction is visually demonstrated.

Comedian Eddie Murphy was recently badgered by a photographer until he angrily reacted. The photographer then took the unflattering portrait of Murphy. Other celebrities such as Cher, Sean Penn, Meryl Streep, and the bodyguards for Prince have all had recent confrontations with overzealous photographers with some resulting in criminal action.

Louisiana State University journalism instructor Whitney Mundt said, "The furtive manner in which paparazzi operate in order to track down famous individuals is inherently unethical." Mundt suggested that photojournalists should not photograph famous people simply because they have familiar faces, but wait until they are involved in a situation that has "intrinsic news value".

A photographer who saw Zsa Zsa Gabor walking her dog would avoid taking her picture, according to Mundt's standard. A photographer, however, who saw Gabor slapping a Beverly Hills policeman would take the photograph. Such a standard, according to Mundt, "would have photojournalism which is no longer exploitive, and would no longer endanger the credibility of the press."

The trend in that direction may have started with the publisher of The People newspaper in London who fired his editor for printing pictures of 7-year-old Prince William urinating in a public park. Athough photographers have been criticized for their over-zealous candid coverage of the rich and famous, studio portraits of stars, for the most part, are carefully controlled public relations pictures.

Jim Marshall, a photographer represented in the book, Rolling Stone The Photographs, criticized the magazine for accepting the strict photographic demands of stars and their representatives. "The stakes are much higher now," Marshall explained, "and with that kind of money at stake, everybody is very edgy about everything. Now we're seeing only what the artists and their managers want us to see. I think we are the lesser for it".

FOUR AREAS OF PRIVACY LAW

A quarterly publication of the Reporters Committee for Freedom of the Press titled, "Photographers' Guide to Privacy," is helpful in sorting out the areas of privacy law that affect news photographers. Privacy law is divided into four areas:

- Unreasonable intrusion into the seclusion of another,
- Public disclosure of private facts,
- Placing a person in a false light in the public eye, and
- Misappropriation of a name or likeness for commercial gain.

UNREASONABLE INTRUSION

Consent is the most important factor when dealing with

unreasonable intrusion or public disclosure of private facts. Generally, anything that can be seen in plain, public view can be photographed. Pictures in private places require permission. A photographer must be sure that the person who gives permission has the authority to grant the request.

Some states will not accept the authority of a police or fire official or a landlord for a photographer to enter a private home. Written consent is preferred over oral consent. The Galella case was certainly an example of unreasonable intrusion on public property. The Lindbergh case was another.

DISCLOSURE OF PRIVATE FACTS

Trespass laws require that photojournalists have the permission of an owner of a property before access can be gained. However, court rulings have sent mixed messages. A tenant at an alleged substandard apartment complex in Philadelphia gave permission to a television crew to enter the property. The landlord sued, but loss the case. Permission from a tenant is acceptable.

A Kansas film crew lost its case when it was shown they used deceitful methods to obtain permission to film a nonpublic area of a restaurant. Misrepresentation is not acceptable. A Florida newspaper photographer was found not guilty of trespassing after obtaining permission from police and fire officials to photograph the body remains of a young girl killed in a fire.

Permission from police officials is acceptable. However, that same Florida Supreme Court upheld a lower court decision in the case of a television crew who obtained permission from police officials to enter a private home that was part of a drug raid. States have different laws for journalists and trespassing.

Editors should put together a package with the newspaper's legal representatives for all journalists on their staff telling them the trespassing laws that apply in their state.

FALSE LIGHT

Dr. Michael Sherer of the University of Nebraska

explained the concept of false light. "Generally speaking," Sherer wrote, "a photojournalist can be found guilty of false light invasion of privacy if a person's image is placed before the public in an untrue setting or situation".

For there to be a false light decision against a photographer, the image must be highly offensive to a reasonable person, the photographer must have known that the image was false, or the photographer acted "with 'reckless disregard' (in other words, did not care) about whether the information was true or not".

The publication of a "stoutish" woman was ruled acceptable as the court noted, "There is no occasion for law to intervene in every case where someone's feelings are hurt." Filming by a camera crew of a man holding hands with a woman who was not his wife was ruled "not an act of extremely outrageous conduct." A person accidentally identified falsely in a caption does not constitute outrageous conduct. However, the publisher of *Cinema-X* magazine was cited for a "misidentified . . . photograph of a nude woman in a section of the magazine featuring I aspiring erotic actors and actresses' ".

MISAPPROPRIATION

The fourth area of trouble for a photojournalist in a privacy case is using a person's image for monetary gain without that person's permission. Clarence Arrington sued the *New York Times* for a picture it printed on the cover of its Sunday magazine illustrating an article, "Making It in the Black Middle Class."

Arrington's "suit for invasion of constitutional and common law right to privacy was dismissed, but his complaint based on the sale of the photograph was upheld in the New York Court of Appeals." The newspaper could not be sued because of the First Amendment protection, but CPI and the freelance photographer, Gianfranco Gorgoni, could have a claim against them.

Unfortunately, the case was settled out of court without a ruling that might have protected picture agencies and freelance photographers. A photographer may have the right to photograph anyone in public, but problems will occur when that image is published and is used to represent a class of individuals without that person's consent. Freelance photographers need to be especially careful.

One of the main reasons magazine editors and picture agency managers require releases from freelance photographers are to protect them from lawsuits by subjects. When covering a news event, courts have ruled that photographers do not have to conform to rigid rules required for a subject's consent.

Nevertheless, news media organizations are sometimes sued by individuals who argue that because the newspaper makes money, their violation of privacy case is valid. Most of these cases go in favour of the news organization on appeal because of the newsworthiness of the images. Freelance photographers, as Sherer noted, "need to pay special attention to the appropriation concept. There have been cases in which the selling of a photograph without the permission of those in the image had been held to be an appropriation of the person's likeness".

THE WHERE AND WHEN OF PICTURE TAKING

Because many readers react strongly to pictures that seem to violate the privacy of others, it is important to be clear on the legal and ethical issues surrounding the right to privacy.

An editorial writer in a 1907 edition of The Independent commented, "As regards photography in public it may be laid as a fundamental principle that one has a right to photograph anything that he has the right to look at".

Such a declaration is not true for today's more complicated society, however. Ken Kobre in his textbook, *Photojournalism The Professionals' Approach* listed where and when a photojournalist can take pictures:

WHERE AND WHEN PICTURES CAN BE TAKEN

Public Area:

- Street (Anytime)

- Sidewalk (Anytime)
- Airport (Anytime)
- Beach (Anytime)
- Park (Anytime)
- Zoo (Anytime)
- Train station (Anytime)
- Bus station (Anytime)

In Public School:

- Preschool (Anytime)
- Grade school (Anytime)
- High school (Anytime)
- Univ. campus (Anytime)
- Class in session (Permission)

In Public Area—With Restrictions:

- Police headquarters (Restricted)
- Govt. buildings (Restricted)
- Courtroom (Permission)
- Prison (Permission)
- Legislative chambers (Permission)

In Medical Facilities:

- Hospital (Permission)
- Rehab. centre (Permission)
- Emergency van (Permission)
- Mental health centre (Permission)
- Doctor's office (Permission)
- Clinic (Permission)

Private but Open-to-the-Public:

- Movie theater lobby (If No Objections)
- Business office (If No Objections)
- Hotel lobby (If No Objections)
- Restaurant (If No Objections)
- Casino (Restricted)
- Museum (Restricted)

Shooting from Public Street into Private Area:

- Window of home (Anytime)
- Porch (Anytime)
- Lawn (Anytime)

In Private:

- Home (If No Objections)
- Porch (If No Objections)
- Lawn (If No Objections)
- Apartment (If No Objections)
- Hotel room (If No Objections)
- Car (If No Objections)

If photographers persist in harassing their subjects, courts can further limit their actions in public and with famous persons.

If courts can limit the actions of photographers making images of famous individuals, there may come a time when injured and grieving subjects are ruled off limits by sympathetic courtroom decisions as was done in some countries during the early years of photography.

Legal rights should not be the guiding principles for ethical consideration. What is legally acceptable is not always the right action to take. Staff photographer Sherry Bockwinkel of the Bellevue, Washington *Journal-Gazette* photographed a photojournalist who learned a lesson about the ethics of privacy.

During a rope-descending performance, a Japanese acrobat fell to his death. A television videographer moved close to the scene as attempts were made to help the dancer. Suddenly a spectator angrily pushed him back.

Although the news event occurred on a public sidewalk in downtown Seattle, managing editor, Jan Brandt wrote that the videographer "had moved into a sensitive area. Bockwinkel defines it as personal space, others call it invading privacy. His presence had become an intrusion seen and felt by those close to the scene and the feeling spilled over onto other photographers".

A photographer must be aware of the privacy laws that apply to his or her jurisdiction, but that photographer must also realise that credibility, a highly valued principle, might be lost if a publicly grieving or famous person is unduly harassed.

Chapter 7

Picture Manipulations

Photojournalism has a long and cherished tradition of truthfulness. The impact of the visual image on a viewer comes directly from the belief that the "camera never lies." As a machine, the camera faithfully and unemotionally records a moment in time. But a machine is only as truthful as the hands that guide it. John Szarkowski, director of photography for the Museum of Modem Art in New York, explained that when truthfulness and visual impact are combined in a powerful picture, such an image can shock the public. But that public trust, however, can also be manipulated.

The faking of photographs, either through stage direction by the photographer or through picture manipulations, also has a long tradition. Photographers and editors learned early in photography's history that economic and political gains can be made by photographic manipulations because of a naive and trusting public.

Even Pulitzer Prize winning images, photographs that have been hailed as beautiful, humanistic documents filled with sorrow, hope, or joy, have been questioned because of rumors of manipulation. The media have been criticized for showing so many gruesome images that the public has hardened toward violent injustices.

There is growing concern that new technological advances that allow easy and undetectable picture manipulation cause the public to be unconcerned about the truthful content of photographs as well. With the acceptance of television "docu-dramas" that show fiction within a factual framework, it is not surprising that news organizations have used Hollywood techniques to create facts.

When pyramids are moved and moons are enlarged for cover pictures of well-respected photojournalism publications, the public grows cynical and mistrustful of journalism. The Hedonism philosophy is taken to its most exaggerated point when business, not telling the truth, is the prime concern.

Howard Chapnick eloquently summed up the dangers to journalism with such manipulations. "Credibility. Responsibility. These words give us the right to call photography a profession rather than a business. Not maintaining that credibility will diminish our journalistic impact and self-respect, and the importance of photography as communication".

With all the other ethical issues photojournalists should be concerned about, picture manipulation, especially through the use of computers, is a topic journalists are most concerned about. The threat to credibility is irreversible if the public starts to mistrust the integrity of the news photograph.

HIPPOLYTE BAYARD AND THE FIRST FAKED PHOTOGRAPH

Early photographic history is filled with artists-turned-photographers who set up situations with models and backdrops and made elabouredate compositions from several negatives. Although he is seldom given credit, Frenchman Hippolyte Bayard discovered a useful photographic process independent of Daguerre and Fox Talbot in 1839. Frustrated by the lack of recognition, Bayard made the first faked picture and caption combination in 1840.

He made a photograph of himself posed as a corpse and wrote on the back of the print, "The Government, which has supported A Daguerre more than is necessary, declared itself unable to do anything for M. Bayard, and the unhappy man threw himself into the water in despair." Two years later, the Societe d'Encouragement pour I'Industrie Nationale gave Bayard a prize of 3,000 francs.

In 1857, Oscar Rejlander produced a picture with a

documentary quality. Captioned, "Street urchins tossing chestnuts," the photograph shows a young boy in ragged clothes, delightfully looking up at a chestnut he has presumably just tossed into the air.

But stopping a moving object in mid-air was a technical feat impossible with the slow film and lenses in use at that time. Rejlander produced the effect through the use of a fine thread. In that same year, he also made the controversial, "The Two Ways of Life," an elabouredate story of a young man's decision to follow the good or evil way of life. Thirty separate negatives were combined to produce the single image.

Another artist-photographer who produced composite pictures was Henry Robinson. From five separate negatives, Robinson created the enormously popular, "Fading Away." In a stage-like setup, the image shows a young woman on her deathbed accompanied by grieving family members in various poses.

Cliff Edom noted that "Both composite pictures were criticized by a minority group for 'misrepresenting the truth' ". The criticism apparently moved Rejlander to denounce the process. In a letter to Robinson he wrote, "I am tired of photograph-for-the-public, particularly composite photos, for there can be no gain and there is no honour, only cavil and misrepresentation".

Portrait photography was enormously popular among the middle class, but picture patrons complained that the images showed all their facial peculiarities. Consequently, photographers of the day regularly softened wrinkles and removed facial blemishes with elabouredate techniques.

One of the earliest portrait photographers was Frenchman, Gaspard Felix Tournachon, or Nadar as he was professionally named. Although Nadar employed "six retouchers of negatives; and three artists for retouching the positive prints," he personally found the custom of retouching photographs to be "detestable and costly". The photographic materials of the 1840s and 1850s were not overly sensitive to green and extremely sensitive to blue. Consequently, prints of nature scenes were often disappointing as a landscape was either a silhouette with clouds appearing in the sky, or the landscape was exposed correctly or the sky was printed white.

To satisfy the public's thirst for photographs that contained a well-exposed landscape and sky, photographers usually reduced the sky with cyanide of potassium or painted on the sky with India ink. As Gernsheim noted, "By the first method dark rain clouds were obtained, by the second, white cumulus clouds."

Double exposure techniques were sometimes used to bring land and sky into exposure harmony. Some photographers by the 1880s even traded or sold favourite cloud negatives to other photographers "with incongruous results: a dramatic cumulus cloud might serve for an Alpine scene, an English cathedral, and the Pyramids".

CIVIL WAR MANIPULATIONS

By the time of the Civil War, photography was well established as one of the most influential mediums in the world. Mathew Brady, a respected portrait photographer with galleries in Washington, DC and New York, established the first picture agency to cover the war. He hired brave photographers and equipped them with all the necessary tools of the trade to ride in horse-drawn portable darkrooms and make pictures of the war.

Most of the pictures Brady's photographers took were in the form of tintypes, cheaply made images printed on metal or inexpensive images called, "cartes de visite." The soldiers sent the images to their loved ones back home. Many of the battle scenes and portraits, credited to Brady, are valued documentary images in the Library of Congress. But Brady made few photographs during the Civil War.

When pictures were sent to him from the cannonball covered battlefields by his staff photographers, he quickly attached the credit line, "Photograph by Brady." Brady hoped to increase the likelihood of picture sales if people thought he made the images.

Brady thought he would make a fortune with the documentary pictures from the war. But the public, grown weary of a costly war, were not interested in paying for the images. Brady died practically penniless. Other unethical picture manipulations during the Civil War have been discovered by researchers. William Frassanito located two stereocard views attributed to Brady taken after the first battle of Bull Run in July 186 1. One view shows a group of standing, kneeling, and firing soldiers.

The second picture titled, "Confederate Dead on Matthews Hill," shows the same group of soldiers lying on the ground, presumably killed. Frassanito disputed the authenticity of these scenes because Brady fled with the Union Army shortly after the battle and one man in the picture is dressed in a heavy overcoat, a strange wardrobe choice for July. "Someone apparently told the soldiers to pretend they were fighting in the one view," wrote Frassanito, "and then instructed them to pretend they were dead in the other".

In an article titled, "The Case of the Rearranged Corpse," Frederic Ray, art director for *Civil War Times* magazine, detailed a more famous manipulation. A photographer under Brady's employ, Alexander Gardner, is credited with a series of pictures he made of 18-year-old Pvt. Andrew Hoge of the 4th Virginia Infantry in Gettysburg. Hoge was stationed in a sniper's nest behind a barricade of rocks. The photograph captioned, "Home of a Rebel Sharpshooter," in Gardner's book, *Gardner's Photographic Sketch Book of the War,* shows the dead sniper lying on his back, his face turned toward the camera, and his rifle propped up against one of the rocks.

The image would have remained a striking photographic document if it were not for another picture by Gardner that shows the same soldier in a different location. This photograph is a closer view of the young man still lying on his back, but his face is turned away from the camera and his rifle lies on the ground by his side. Apparently, the frustration with using slow films and lenses that made it impossible to photograph action during the heat of a battle, caused Gardner to create his own dramatic pictures.

Ray wrote that Gardner "was guilty of at least a misdemeanor as a photographic historian" and concluded that his ethical transgressions were "nothing serious". But when a photographer is shown to fake a picture, all of his work is put into question. Again, the issue is credibility. Stefan Lorant found an early photographic fake when he was investigating pictures for a book about Abraham Lincoln. Lorant was the art director for the London Picture Post magazine, the inspiration for *Life* and *Look* magazines.

He discovered that the popular close-up portrait of Lincoln seen on the $5 bill was sandwiched atop the body of Southern statesman, John Calhoun by a darkroom technician. The result was a classic full-length portrait of the former president. The North and the South were once again united. Entrepreneurs at the time were eager to make money from Lincoln's assassination.

But in their haste, the President's famous mole appeared on the wrong side of his face. Nevertheless, the full-length view of Lincoln is a popular portrait. Mathew Brady and his staff were responsible for one last photographic fake that involved the Civil War. General Sherman and his staff came to the Brady studio to have their group portrait made after the War. However, General Blair, an important member of Sherman's staff, could not attend the photo shoot. Nevertheless, the group picture was taken.

At a later date, a head and shoulders picture of Blair was made. The image of his head was then attached to the group picture with his name already imprinted. Lucky for Brady that Blair did not suddenly die between the two portrait sittings. Although never accused of faking a picture, documentary photographer and writer, Jacob Riis, did use a manipulation technique that was successfully accomplished by Mathew Brady.

Because Riis was not a trained photographer, he often hired them to accompany him on his nightly journeys through New York's seedy underworld. The popular story is that Riis could not rely on his photographers because they either would not show up for scheduled appointments or became frightened by the rough characters they were asked to photograph.

Riis was forced to learn photography and took the pictures that were used in his lectures and for his book, *How the Other Half Lives*. But one of his most famous photographs, "Bandit's Roost," was actually taken by Richard Hoe Lawrence. How many other photographs Riis took credit for, but were actually the work of Lawrence or another amateur photographer, Henry Pifford, is not known.

ENGRAVING AND HALFTONE MANIPULATIONS

Stephen Horgan in 1873 is credited with inventing the halftone printing process that replaced the artistic renderings of the engraved images with real pictures that were captured "from nature." The first photograph printed with the new technique, captioned, "A Scene in Shantytown, New York" showed crumbling buildings and piles of dirt from an obvious poor section of town.

The image printed in 1880 by the New York *Daily Graphic*, was not meant to be an illustration of the newspaper's commitment to correcting dire social problems within the city of New York, but was simply part of a set of various printing techniques that were demonstrated by the newspaper. The Horgan invention was considered too expensive and difficult to use. F. E. Ives improved the process in 1890 to a technique that is still in use today.

It took several years before the halftone process caught on because publishers had a large investment with engravers, many disliked the quality of printed photographs, and editors and artists had more control over engraved images. Once publishers started using photographs, however, engraving technology was abandoned.

As Estelle Jussim wrote in *The Eyes of Time: Photojournalism in America*, the turn of the century began an era when readers were "impressed more by the fact that a photograph could finally be made to appear in a newspaper or magazine than by the content of that picture. It was an era deluged by the products of the press and manipulated by warring publishers who displayed few ethical concerns.

Photojoumalistic images would be perceived as visual

fact, but were actually more often propaganda and pure sensationalism". Faked pictures, as Jussim wrote, "became a frequent accompaniment to hyped stories". Robert Taft noted in his book, *Photography and the American Scene,* that "by the time the faked photograph is reproduced in halftone, it is impossible to detect the forgers from the print alone".

Art directors who regularly ordered the manipulation of engravings saw nothing ethically wrong with manipulating photographs. Stage-managed and composite photographic techniques were common contrivances by the turn of the century. The highly theatrical photographs were usually made by painters new to the photographic medium. Typical of the genre was the early work of painter-turned-photographer, Edward Steichen.

In 1902 he made a striking portrait of the artist, Rodin with his famous piece, "Le Penseur." The 11 portrait of the artist and the sculpture were exposed on separate negatives and combined into a single print". Later in his career, Steichen is most known for creating one of the most successful photojournalism exhibitions in the world, "The Family of Man."

Worried over real estate prices and population declines, Gladys Hansen, in her recent book, *Denial of Disaster,* showed evidence that many of the photographs made during the 1906 earthquake in San Francisco were re-touched. City officials authorized artists to alter photographs to minimize the appearance of damage from the earthquake.

It was assumed at the time that prospective settlers to San Francisco would understand damage from a great fire, but would not move to the area if the full fury of the earthquake was publicized. Susan Moeller wrote that many pictures taken by war photographers covering the Spanish-American War in Cuba were posed. Fighting scenes were re-enacted and bodies were moved for better compositions.

Some creative photographers even re-enacted famous battle scenes in New Jersey backyards and bathtubs. During World War I, many photographs were manipulated for propaganda purposes. For example, newspapers showed faked photographs of Kaiser Wilhelm of Germany cutting off the hands of babies.

In *Making People Disappear,* Alain Jaubert, chronicled numerous photographic abuses by mostly totalitarian regimes. Through retouching, blocking, cutouts, recentreing, and effacement techniques, historical pictures have been altered to reflect a political leader's version of the truth.

For example, the photograph that showed the 1917 attack by revolutionary soldiers on the Winter Palace in Russia was actually a re-enactment during a daylight street celebration three years later. The actual attack occur-red in almost total darkness. The famous photograph was darkened and the windows of the Palace "were painted white to give the illusion of a building seen at night and lighted from within".

SPIRIT PHOTOGRAPHY

A curious and little-mentioned photographic genre, spirit photography, supposedly captured the likeness of the spirit of a deceased person. Spirit photography, an outgrowth of the Spiritualism religious movement, was proven by photographic experts, including the famous magician and escape artist, Harry Houdini, to be double exposure fakes.

Unsophisticated to the technical considerations of photography and wanting to believe in the truth of the photograph, people paid money to spiritual mediums and believed the results.

Usually a psychic medium would make, an appointment with a customer and ask for a picture of the deceased. This portrait, it was told, was necessary in order to communicate more easily with the dead loved one. The spirit photographer would expose part of a negative plate with the image. Using that same negative during a portrait sitting, the photographer simply developed the image and showed the print to the amazed and grateful customer.

Houdini traveled the world exposing the tricks mediums used to dupe their customers. There were hundreds of ways the spirit photographers used to manipulate negatives to produce spirits on film and Houdini usually caught them all.

He often traveled with Arthur Conan Doyle, of the Sherlock Holmes stories, to debate the truthfulness of the spirit photographs.

Curiously, Doyle, an amateur photographer, was one of the most strident advocates of spirit photography in the world. With large prints and stories from mediums, Doyle would spread the gospel of ghosts. He usually opened his lectures with, "Tonight I propose to put before you some pictures and photographs which will illustrate.

The physical results which come from psychic knowledge" (from the "Opening of the Photographic Lecture," Humanities Research Centre, Austin, TX, Doyle collection). As more people became technically sophisticated about photography, spirit photographs soon faded into thin air.

The "Yellow Journalism" era, fueled by the intense competition between Joseph Pulitzer, publisher of the *New York Tribune* and William Hearst, publisher of the *New York Journal,* created a readership that demanded dramatic and sensational stories in their newspapers.

In a time when ethical considerations gave way to economic interests, editors and photographers were willing to obliged their publishers. Ken Kobre in his textbook, *Photojournalism: The Professionals' Approach,* credited editor Emile Gavreau and assistant art director Harry Grogin of the New York Evening Graphic with creating a faked news picture.

The technique called a composograph, used 20 separate negatives to fake a sensational divorce trial after photographers were ejected from the courtroom by the judge. Newspaper staff personnel posed as trial participants for the picture. Although the Graphic admitted in tiny print that the composographs were faked, the sensational images were enormously popular among readers.

Photographers were recruited to satisfy the visual needs of the newspapers. "Competition for the low-paying, exhausting [photographer] jobs was fierce," wrote Claude Cookman, a photography historian. Joseph Costa, NPPA's first president, admitted that the heightened sense of competition fostered many unethical acts besides faked images.

Some photographers put ear wax on lenses, exposed negatives, and stole negative holders from other photographers. "Sabotage was standard practice," said Costa, "and no photographer with any street savvy at all would ever let his camera bag or equipment out of his sight".

As William Strothers, readers' representative for *The San Diego Union* wrote, sometimes those camera bags contained more than camera equipment.

"There are stories of some long-ago reporter-photographers covering the police beat who used to carry teddy bears in their cars. When they sped to the scene of an accident involving a child, the toy would be employed to add poignancy to the photograph.

It also was common practice for photographers to pose participants in news events to get good pictures". In 1943, *New York Journal* photographer Harry Coleman admitted in his book, *Give Us a Little Smile, Baby,* that he would dress up a body at the morgue with a shirt and tie and prop it up for a seemingly life-like portrait of the deceased subject.

At the scene of a homicide, Coleman would also describe the victim to a fellow photographer over the telephone who would "dig up a real photograph of, say, John L. Sullivan, remove his ferocious mustache, paint a General Grant beard across his massive chin, and send it to the engravers as a legitimate picture of an unidentified body in a foul murder".

In a reaction to the many manipulated pictures by news photographers, Kent Cooper, an executive for the Associated Press wrote the following:

This is a personal appeal for a new approach to pictures of people taken individually or in groups. I earnestly ask that you put a premium on the natural, unposed pictures of people. Obviously you cannot pose spontaneous shots without being deceitful. It is just as deceitful for a photographer to make a man or woman to look some way or act some way that is unnatural.

C.William Horrell noted in a survey of newspaper photographers that "a need was expressed for more natural and truthful photographic reports, a kind of report which could be achieved through greater use of unposed subjects being photographed with existing light". By the 1950s, the manipulation of subjects was widely condemned by professionals. However, abuses still occurred.

APRIL FOOL'S AND POLITICAL FAKES

April Fool photographic fakes were popular in newspapers during the first half of this century. Curtis MacDougall in his book, *Hoaxes,* detailed several instances where newspapers published such images as giant sea creatures, Viking ships, and a man supposedly flying by his own lung power.

The Madison, Wisconsin *Capital-Times* went so far as to publish a photographic composite of the capitol dome collapsing in 1933 that needlessly alarmed hundreds of people. Photography editor Cliff Yeich recently revised the April Fool joke for his newspaper, the Reading, Pennsylvania *Eagle-Times.* Yeich used double printing techniques to show the Concorde SST aircraft landing at the Reading airport, an oil tanker cruising down the Schuykill River, and two children playing with a giant wishbone from a 750-pound turkey.

Although popular with many readers, such examples of fun with photography do not belong in a newspaper. A photographer who employs such trickery might be tempted to use the technique for news events. Yeich, for example, after a recent rain storm, created the look of flooded conditions on Reading's main street with a mirror.

Another wet day at a horse racing track resulted in a picture of a faked motorboat ride on the oval course. The pictures were not printed on April Fool's day. Curiously, April Fool's day hoaxes can still be found on college campuses. Many university newspapers have April Fool's editions that lampoon campus issues and personalities in faked stories and pictures.

More serious fakes involved political subjects. A 1928

campaign picture of Herbert Hoover and his running mate was faked because Hoover refused to pose with the vice-presidential candidate, Charles Curtis. *Life* magazine revealed a composite photograph, produced by a rival politician, of a Maryland Democrat running for office that looked like he was conferring with a Communist leader.

The image was actually the result of two separate photographs. The image was widely distributed among the electorate. The Democrat lost the election.

FLOYD COLLINS' FAKED CAPTION

Truth was again a victim during journalism's most sensational era. Floyd Collins was a man who wanted to build his own amusement park. In 1925, he became trapped while exploring Sand Cave a few miles from the famous, Mammoth Cave in rural Kentucky. For 17 days, rescue workers attempted to free Collins, but without success.

He died from starvation. Fifty reporters on the scene turned Collins into a national martyr. Over 20,000 people from 16 states jammed into the area after reading the newspaper articles. In the movie, *Ace in the Hole,* Billy Wilder critically presented the side-show atmosphere surrounding the hole in the ground.

Competition was intense among journalists on the scene to get interviews and pictures no other newspaper had. William Eckenberg, a photographer for the New York Times, learned that a farmer had a picture of Collins taken 10 days earlier while inside another cave.

Eckenberg found the picture, made a copy and sent it to New York. The picture was used by many papers across the country. Some papers, including the *Chicago Daily Tribune,* accurately described the circumstances surrounding the picture's history. Many other newspapers, however, perhaps to heighten interest in the image, used the picture without an explanation. A team of journalism historians were also fooled by the picture.

In *America's Front Page News 1690-1970,* a caption under a reproduction of the front page of the New York, *The World* reads, "The haunting picture of explorer Floyd Collins, peering from the Kentucky cave in which he was wedged for 17 days, appeared on the day he was found dead of exhaustion and starvation".

MANIPULATIONS BY CROPPING

Cropping out significant elements of a picture in order to produce a misleading image has been used for various motivations by photographers. President Franklin Roosevelt, stricken with polio and confined to a wheelchair, was photographed with close-ups by sympathetic photographers who did not want to show the public the full extent of his feeble condition.

Likewise, photographs of Governor George Wallace, after he was paralyzed from an assassination attempt, were cropped for the same reason. An infamous example of creative cropping occurred during Senator Joseph McCarthy's hearing on Communists in the government. To imply that Secretary of the Army Robert T. Stevens had a close relationship with an enlisted man, Private G. David Schine, a picture of the two was closely cropped omitting a third man in the photograph, Air Force Colonel Jack T. Bradley.

CHARGES OF MANIPULATION CLOUD FAMOUS PICTURES

Perhaps most troubling to the reputation of photojournalists and their photographs are reports that well-known and deeply moving pictures have been stage directed by the photographers. Three famous photographs, Robert Capa's moment of death of a Republican soldier during the Spanish Civil War, Arthur Rothstein's skull on parched South Dakota land, and Joe Rosenthal's raising of the American flag over Iwo Jima, have all been reported to be photographic manipulations. These three images have a cloud of uncertainty that surrounds each photographer's reputation.

ROBERT CAPA'S 'MOMENT OF DEATH'

Published in *Life* magazine in 1937, Capa's photograph

shows in one instant the sudden and lonely death of an anonymous soldier. The picture shocked readers with its sudden impact. Never before had the public witnessed in such graphic horror a soldier's moment of death.

After an offhandedly made remark by the teasing Capa and weak evidence that the killed soldier appeared alive in subsequent images in Capa's contact sheet, rumors spread that the picture was either a result of Capa simply shooting blindly and capturing the shot by chance or stage managed for the camera.

Luck often helps experienced photographers. Bob Jackson who took the Oswald murder picture and Eddie Adams who captured the Viet Cong soldier's assassination were startled by the sound of a gunshot and pressed their shutter buttons. Photographic reflexes, a result of years of experience, plus a little luck can produce extraordinary photographs.

Robert Capa was never the kind of photographer who needed to set up his subjects. Capa, who's motto was, "If your pictures aren't good, you aren't close enough," would have been dismissed had the moment-of-death photograph been the only picture in his portfolio. However, Capa produced many war-time photographs throughout his career.

Another famous picture of Capa's is the grainy and blurred image, caused by a lab assistant's high drying temperature, of a soldier crawling in the shallow waters of Normandy during the D-Day invasion.

He photographed in Spain, China, Israel, and finally in Vietnam, where he was killed when he stepped on a land mine. Capa consistently produced images with strong emotional impact and high technical expertise. He was not a photographer who needed to fake a photograph in order to enhance his career.

ARTHUR ROTHSTEIN'S SKULLS

Arthur Rothstein, a documentary photographer for the Farm Security Administration (FSA) during the American Dust Bowl era, made photographs of a steer's skull on grassy and parched land.

When the different backgrounds were discovered, the skull was labeled a prop by Republican politicians who used the Rothstein pictures to attack the credibility of all the FSA photographs and particularly the Democratic administration.

The Democrats, it was argued, were using the photographs to make environmental conditions look worse than they actually were in order to pass controversial legislation through Congress. Rothstein was accused of traveling around the country with his suitcase, his camera, and his skull.

Although he only moved the skull 10 feet, Rothstein would be the first to admit that it was wrong of him. He regretted the controversy for the rest of his career. Rothstein produced several memorable photographic documents including the classic Dust Bowl photograph of a father hurrying toward shelter through a dust storm with his two young sons trailing behind.

He received more than 50 photography awards and wrote several books on the subject of photojournalism and documentary photography. Given such a reputation, it is difficult to imagine him packing a skull with his clothes and camera.

JOE ROSENTHAL'S FLAG

An Associated Press photographer, 33-year-old Joe Rosenthal, made three photographs atop Suribachi, a Japanese observation post on the island of Iwo Jima in 1945. His first picture became the most reproduced photograph in history and won for him a Pulitzer Prize.

His second picture, although similar to the first, did not capture a dramatic moment and was forgotten by history. His third photograph became the source of accusations that the first photograph had been set up. The first picture is the image most remembered.

It shows six soldiers erecting a large, American flag on a long diagonally slanted flagpole. The soldiers seem to be straining, as they had strained to capture the mountain from the Japanese, to fly the banner of the United States. This large flag, however, was not the first American flag to fly over Suribachi.

Staff Sgt. Louis Lowery, a Marine photographer, who beat Rosenthal to the top by several hours, recorded the first flag-raising ceremony that used a small flag. On his way up to the top, Rosenthal saw a Marine carrying a much larger flag.

The raising of that larger flag was recorded on film by a motion picture cameraman and by Rosenthal with his Speed Graphic press camera.

After the raising of the flag, Rosenthal made a group picture of 18 soldiers smiling and waving for the camera. Although the flag-raising ceremony was re-enacted, it was the Marines who were responsible for the decision-not Rosenthal.

The confusion over the authenticity of the famous photograph resulted from Rosenthal's casual response to a correspondent 9 days later in Guam. Congratulations poured in from newspapers across America about the picture. A writer happened to ask if the picture was posed. Thinking that he meant the third photograph, Rosenthal admitted that it had been set up.

Speaking later of the famous picture, he rightly argued that "had I posed the shot, I would, of course, have ruined it. I would have made them turn their heads so that they could be identified for AP members throughout the country".

Nevertheless, when the picture was first offered to the editors of *Life* magazine, it was rejected because it looked too perfect. As one writer noted, "*Life* was all for making movie stars look glamorous and frequently staged photos, but this was hard news, and they wanted to be careful."

After the photograph was used throughout the world as a symbol of America's victories, the picture was printed in *Life*. Incidentally, Mt. Suribachi was soon recaptured by the Japanese. Many of the Marines who were photographed by Rosenthal were numbered as casualties.

Writing of the Rosenthal icon, picture editor Harold Evans, in his book *Pictures on a Page,* noted that "no genius could have posed the picture if he had spent a year in a studio with lights and a wind machine". Lucky for photojournalism, Rosenthal did not carry a wind machine to the top of Iwo Jima.

MANIPULATIONS BY TRADITIONAL TECHNIQUES

In the present era of ethical awareness, some photographers have learned the hard way that giving stage-managed, manipulated prints or misrepresented subjects to editors without explanations is ethically wrong. Professor Jim Gordon of Bowling Green State University, Ohio and editor of *News Photographer* magazine detailed the firing of Norman Zeisloft.

NORMAN ZEISLOFT'S FEET

A 17-year veteran of the St. Petersburg *Times* and *Evening Independent,* Zeisloft was assigned to cover a baseball tournament. As baseball games often go, sports action was hard to find. He spotted three fans in the stands and said that it would be 11 cute if you had 'Yea, Eckerd' written on the bottom of your feet."

One young man agreed and Zeisloft started to write. A photographer for a competing newspaper took a picture of him writing on the bottom of the fan's foot and later put it up on his photography lab's bulletin board as a joke.

Zeisloft's pen would not write on the man's dirty sole so he returned to shooting the game. In the meantime, the man in the stands washed his feet, wrote the message on his foot and called Zeisloft over. He took the picture. Zeisloft gave the image to his editor without a word about the stage-managed situation. Two days later it was printed in the *Evening Independent.*

Someone sent the picture of Zeisloft writing on the bottom of the fan's foot to Norman Isaacs, who served as chairman of the Pulitzer jury for commentary and was chairman of the National News Council in New York. Isaacs sent the picture to Gene Patterson who was Isaacs' close friend and president and editor of the St. Petersburg newspapers.

Patterson was also chairman of the Pulitzer Prize Board

who had recently voted against awarding the Pulitzer to *Washington Post* reporter, Janet Cooke. (Cooke had admitted that a story she wrote of a little boy surrounded by drug dealers was actually fiction. Her scandal was an embarrassment for the *Washington Post* and the Pulitzer Prize Board.) Zeisloft was fired.

At his administrative appeal, he explained, "we set up pictures for society and club news, recipe contest winners, ribbon-cutting and ground-breaking ceremonies, award shots and enterprise features." Zeisloft, at 61 years old, may have been influenced by the stage managing techniques that photographers had used several years earlier because of their bulky cameras.

Even Gene Smith, *Life* magazine's premier picture story producer, has admitted, "If I really felt that it was absolutely essential to the truth of the story, I would not hesitate to pose the subjects". Another famous *Life* magazine photographer, Margaret Bourke White, regularly posed her documentary subjects in order to get better compositions and emotional impact in her photographs.

Posing is close to the ethical line. Writing on a foot to create a more interesting picture is over the edge. Executive editor, Robert Haiman made the decision to fire Zeisloft. His explanation should be tacked to the bulletin board of every newsroom in the country.

"It seems to me," Haiman said, the worst thing from the standpoint of the photographic community is for editors to have that condescending attitude, well, you know, he's only a photographer. I'm told that there are still some editors in this country who regard photographers as second-class citizens in the newsroom.

I don't happen to buy that. I believe that a photographer is every bit as much a first-class citizen in this journalistic community as any reporter. And there is one thing about the journalistic community which is more important in it than in any other community.

And that is the obligation to tell the truth, the whole truth and nothing but the truth. There is simply no room for people who don't tell the truth. (p. 34) Zeisloft's defence of his picture is the words of a past generation of press photographers.

"It was just a whimsical thing, just for a little joke," he said. "It was just a little picture to make people smile rather than an old accident scene". Norman Zeisloft's sin was not realizing that the ethics of stage-managed pictures had changed.

OTHER SUBJECT AND PICTURE MANIPULATIONS

Other photographers have lost or been suspended from their jobs when editors were not told of a print or subject manipulation. Eric Demme, a freelance photographer for United Press International (UPI), was fired for a double printing manipulation.

A picture of a jet airplane in one photograph was combined with a chicken wing restaurant's sign. The sign read, "Air traffic controllers dont [sic] affect our wings" and referred to the national air traffic controller strike of 1981.

When the composite was discovered, UPI ordered a "mandatory kill" on the picture. All editors were instructed to destroy the picture. Demme explained that because staffers helped him produce the image, he expected "a slap on the hand." "It [the photograph] doesn't involve people," said Demme. "Why not?"

A panda bear "in his last remaining natural habitat" was found to have been photographed in a 2-acre pen at a research centre in China's Wuyipeng province. Contract photographer for Geo magazine, Timm Rautert, was fired. *Geo* managing editor, David Maxey said that the experience "will make us more vigilant in the future.

Embarrassing though this message is, there's no substitute in journalism for candor". The Sunday newspaper magazine, *Parade,* illustrated a cover story on teenage prostitution with three pictures purported to be actual scenes of women soliciting themselves for money. Under the headline, "Kids For Sale," one of the pictures from New York City was taken by Pulitzer Prize winning photographer, Eddie Adams.

Professionals became concerned when it was discovered later that Adams' 11 prostitute" was actually a paid model. A disclaimer, identifying the woman in the picture as a model, had been "dropped." Adams admitted that stories concerning children require the use of models because of problems with obtaining parental permission.

Magazines set up cover pictures, Adams explained, "to draw attention to the story, to illustrate a point. Newspapers have even more instances with it with set-up feature pictures". Nevertheless, if models are used to illustrate a news editorial picture, the readers should be told.

Eddie Motes of the Anniston, Alabama *Star* was looking for a weather feature picture after a rainstorm produced flooded conditions. He asked Angie Shockley, a community centre employee, to walk with an umbrella through ankle-deep water so that he could make pictures of her.

Shockley suddenly disappeared as she stepped into a ditch hidden by the flood waters. Paul Kennedy had been watching the photography session and immediately jumped into the culvert to save Shockley. A group of basketball players and the Anniston Rescue Squad were needed to rescue Kennedy who had become trapped against the culvert. Meanwhile, Shockley had been sucked through the 50-foot drain and was unhurt on the other side.

Kennedy was treated and released at a local hospital. In one assignment, Motes had created human interest feature and spot news pictures. Motes reported that his editor did not hold him responsible for the accident. But in letters to *News Photographer* magazine, photojournalists around the country let Motes know what they thought of him setting up a situation that almost turned into tragedy.

Typical of the responses was Jason Grow's letter. "Motes' situation clearly illustrates the danger of explicitly, or implicitly, encouraging someone to perform for the sake of the camera. Eddie Motes was damn lucky that neither Shockley nor Paul Kennedy were killed. Maybe through this near-tragedy we all may re-evaluate what it is we are doing when we put our cameras to our eyes".

Pulitzer Prize photographer for the Detroit *Free Press,* Manny Crisostomo was suspended for 3 days after it was learned he "bought a Sony Walkman and a sausage from a crack addict referred to as Tim in a story." Crisostomo "feared the addict might become violent if he wasn't given any money".

For *Life* magazine in 1965, Bill Eppridge photographed a young couple addicted to heroin. Eppridge admitted that the couple asked for money, but he explained "that if we paid them, the story could no longer be valid".Crisostomo and a reporter gave money and then drove the addicts to where they could buy more crack.

The large, lead picture in the layout of the addicts smoking crack was taken inside the reporter's car. In an article in *News Photographer* magazine, Crisostomo admitted that "Integrity is everything. Reputations are hard to come by, but easy to lose.

When confronted with a serious ethical question, I can't go it alone. My editors have to know what's going on. And if it comes down to a choice between compromising my ethics or dropping the story, I'll drop the story". Credibility is severely damaged when reporters set up a situation or provide money and transportation for subjects to purchase illegal drugs.

When the Tokyo newspaper, *Asahi Shimbun,* sent a photographer to document the environmental problems with a coral reef, he carved his initials in the reef for the picture when he could not find enough damage. The newspaper received 6,000 phone calls and 2,000 letters in I month when the alteration was learned by the public.

The photographer was fired. But the Japanese did not stop with the photographer's punishment. As William Strothers wrote, "Another photographer involved was suspended, the salaries of the executive editor and three other editors were cut, and the managing editor and photo editor were demoted. Finally, the president of the newspaper resigned". The Japanese really know how to get the message across.

COLOUR AS A CULPRIT

The spread of colour photography for magazines and newspapers has been blamed for the trend toward the increased use of set ups and illustration assignments. John Coffeen of the *Tampa Tribune,* noted that because of the lighting techniques necessary to take good colour pictures, many photographers have returned to the posed shooting style, popular in the 1950s while on location and in the studio.

When newspapers bought new colour presses, studio shots increased "because it was a chance to show off what we could do with the new presses," according to Coffeen. When colour photography is well printed it attracts more readers and advertisers to the newspaper. Editors felt that colour slide materials would be best for colour reproduction on the presses.

Slide exposures have to be right on the mark and that sometimes requires the use of fill-in flash and set up techniques. Many newspapers have purchased computer-controlled picture scanners that make colour separations.

Consequently, photography staffs have been able to change to more forgiving negative colour films that can be used under adverse technical conditions. Editors have also steered away from meaningless sunset and sailboat pictures and use photojournalism photographs that happen to be in colour. Nevertheless, *USA Today,* with its pages filled with colourful, tiny head and shoulder portraits, has been a model for many newspapers around the country.

Photographers continue to get assignments for food, fashion, and editorial illustrations where they use highly manipulative techniques common to advertising photographers and then are expected to be straight documentary photojournalists when they cover any other assignment.

Concern runs high among professionals about the increased use of the illustration assignment. The judges for the Pictures of the Year (POY)/47 competition, sponsored by NPPA and the University of Missouri, have eliminated the editorial illustration category from the competition.

The contest instructions state, "Given the growing popularity of set-up and contrived pictures and the threat to photographic credibility posed by computer manipulation of images POY will, in the future, focus entirely on documentary work". The POY judges will also prefer photo reportage over photo illustration in every category.

COMPUTER MANIPULATIONS

In national surveys sent to photographers, editors, and educators, as if guided by a single voice, all exclaim the same concern: The most serious threat to the integrity and credibility of photojournalism images is computer manipulation. Why is there such a concern for a technique that is simply a technological step up from photo retouching by hand?

To simulate colour in early daguerreotypes and tintypes, photo retouchers, with brushes and inks added rouge to cheeks and cyan to dresses. Before the halftone invention, engravers regularly "improved" a photograph's content and composition.

Wedding portrait photographers regularly remove unwanted warts and wrinkles. Advertising art directors customarily combine parts of pictures, change colours, and create fantasy images to attract customers. But people are well aware, and knowingly suspend their belief, when it comes to portrait and advertising photographic images.

The concern comes when computer retouching is used for untouchable images—photojournalism photographs. Imagine a newspaper that's masthead motto is, "April Fool's Day-Every Day." Like the little boy who cried wolf in the fairytale, magazine and newspaper readers would eventually turn their backs on the media out of mistrust.

Hal Buell of the Associated Press said, "I don't think your ethics can be any better or any worse using electronic methods than they are using the classical methods. Ethics is in the mind. It is not in the tools you use". There are two approaches that one can take about the use of computer technology: absolute or relaxed.

Either computer manipulation should never be performed for news/editorial images, or changes are allowed. Robert Gilka, former director of photography for *National Geographic* magazine, articulated the absolute viewpoint. Gilka said that manipulating images is "like limited nuclear war.

There ain't none". Jack Com, director of photography for the *Chicago Tribune* said manipulations are "ethically, morally and journalistically horrible". Michael Evans, editor of graphics and photography at the Atlanta *Journal and Constitution* and former White House "photo opportunity" photographer for the Reagan administration, has a more relaxed opinion.

Evans cited W. Eugene Smith's work as an example of "emphatically accurate photos" that are nevertheless manipulated. Evans wrote that "Through burning, dodging, bleaching, negative-sandwiching, double-printing and a veritable arsenal of other brilliant special effects, Gene Smith produced prints that dazzled a photographically unsophisticated world that literally thirsted for images".

A famous portrait of Dr. Albert Schweitzer by Smith was a composite print from two images because the main negative was technically flawed due to fogging. Even the famous photograph, "The Migrant Mother" by Dorothea Lange was retouched to eliminate a "ghostly thumb" in a comer of her composition.

The first time many learned that a new age in photo retouching had dawned were the reports of cable mogul Ted Turner using computerized colourization techniques on classic, black-and-white movies. The motive was profit-it was hoped viewers would be more attracted to the colour versions. The list of computer and set up abuses grows daily at an alarming rate.

Most of the computer enhancements have occurred on the covers of various magazines. *National Geographic* magazine, long known for its reputation of photojournalism excellence, used a computer digitizer on two occasions.

On a cover story of Egypt, the Great Pyramids of Giza in a horizontal picture by Gordon Gahen were squeezed together to fit the magazine's vertical format. Editors for a picture story on Poland used a photograph by Bruno Barby for the cover and the special supplement that combined an expression on a man's face in one frame with a complete view of his hat in another picture.

Tom Kennedy, who became the director of photography at *National Geographic* after the covers were manipulated, recently stated that "We no longer use that technology to manipulate elements in a photo simply to achieve a more compelling graphic effect.

We regarded that afterwards as a mistake, and we wouldn't repeat that mistake today". The photojournalism compilations in the *A Day in the Life* books of America, Australia, Canada, and California all had cover pictures manipulated by computer technology.

The horseman, hill, and tree on the cover of *A Day in the Life of America* were moved closer together enlarging the moon. The photograph was originally a horizontal. The objects in the picture were moved to fit the cover's vertical format. Dandelions behind a boy and a girl on the cover of *A Day in the Life of Canada* were turned into green grass.

An inch of water was added to the top of the cover picture to include the title, *A Day in the Life of Australia.* The top of a surfboard was created for the cover picture of *A Day in the Life of California.* The short-lived and experimental magazine, *Picture Week* fused two different photographs in tabloid magazine style of Nancy Reagan and Raisa Gorbachev to portray a misleading attitude of friendliness.

A cover picture for *Rolling Stone* magazine was altered with the computer. The gun and shoulder holster were removed from "Miami Vice" actor Don Johnson because editor Jan Wenner is an ardent foe of handguns. *Popular Science* magazine used the computer to combine an airplane in one picture with the background of another.

Television interviewer Oprah Winfrey's head was spliced on top of Ann-Margret's body for a *TV Guide* cover. To illustrate Rob Lowe's troubles with videotape, Atlanta magazine used a model holding a video camera and Lowe's smiling face in a computerized cover composite. Shiela Reaves reported that a cover picture of planes flying over the Chrysler building in New York City for the Conde Nash Traveller was a composite from three separate negatives.

A former art director for *Better Homes and Gardens* admitted that "45 of the 48 covers from 1984 to 1988 were digitally manipulated, primarily because the magazine often uses inside photos for its cover". For the examples just given, readers were not told that the covers had been altered with a computer.

Editors argue that the cover photograph can be altered in order to achieve maximum impact because the image is designed to attract a potential buyer just like an advertisement. Sean Callahan, former editor of *American Photographer* magazine feels that covers are sales tools that are used to attract browsing newsstand buyers.

"There is tremendous competition in that kind of environment and so you have to do something to get [buyers'] attention," Callahan said. Co-director David Cohen of A Day in the Life of America said, "I don't know if it's right or wrong. All I know is it sells the book better".

Creator and photographer for the *A Day in the Life* series, Rick Smolan said, "We are very proud of the fact that we were able to use this technology to make the covers more dramatic and more impressive". In a later interview, Smolan altered his position.

"At some point the audience deserves to know," Smolan said, "whether or not [the cover picture] is something you caught on the fly or something either you created in the darkroom or created by setting it up". What if a newspaper editor decides that the front page or a section front is a sales tool that should be used to attract more readers?

Such a philosophy would send computer retouchers; scrambling to make front-page news photographs as visually dramatic as possible. *Arizona Republic's* art director, Howard Finberg sees the danger of eager editors who might "clean up photographs as they might clean up grammar in a quote." "I know who runs the newspaper and it's not the photographers," Finberg asserted. "It's the editor who has no visual literacy at all" who makes the retouching decisions. Such editorial decisions have crept into the news photography divisions of newspapers. The *St. Louis Post-Dispatch* used a computer to remove a can of Diet Coke from a picture taken of a Pulitzer Prize winning photographer.

The Hartford Courant (CT) used a computer to show readers what the downtown skyline would look like with a new skyscraper. The *Asbury Park Press (NJ)* ran an illustration that confused readers. For a health and fitness story, computer artists combined a picture of a cow eating hay with a studio set up of a salad.

The *Orange County Register (CA)* changed a smog-filled sky into cloudless blue for an outdoor Olympics photograph and still won a Pulitzer Prize in 1984 for its coverage. Backshop personnel for the *Register* also mistakenly changed the colour in a news picture. When vandals dyed a swimming pool red, the production staff, unaware of the news story, thought the water should be blue and used the computer accordingly.

Publishers spend millions on computer retouching systems that may pressure art directors to show some results. However, most newspaper editorial departments have adopted policies for the use of the computer. Since the Coke can incident, the motto at the *St. Louis Post-Dispatch* is "If you don't do it in the darkroom, don't do it in the system."

But despite the best of intentions, abuses still occur. *Chicago Tribune* associate design director, Judie Anderson, says, "We do not do anything to alter a photograph unless it's absolutely necessary." Nevertheless, she admits, "If there are blemishes on somebody's skin that do detract, then we may do something". Hopefully, Anderson will not put Oprah Winfrey's head on that person's body.

In 1981, Sony was the first company to introduce a film-less camera, the Mavica. Because the image quality was low, most experts viewed the camera as an expensive toy. Since 1981 however, improvements have been made. The ProMavica camera with a 2-inch, reusable floppy disk can record 25 frames of still video images and time-compressed FM audio sounds at a higher degree of quality.

Nikon, Canon, and Kodak also have still video cameras with transmission and computer-recording devices that can send images via telephone lines to a photo editor's computer terminal. Scitex, Crosfield, and Hell are leading manufacturers of digital retouching and pre-press electronic scanning devices used by newspaper and magazine art directors.

Reproduction quality and price are barriers to widespread acceptance of the new technology. A computerized image is composed of tiny dots, called pixels or picture elements. A high quality video image typically contains approximately 380,000 pixels. Kodak has manufactured a floppy disk that can record 1.4 million pixels. With high definition television (HDTV) systems, the pixel count can be raised to 2.2 million.

But computer technology is far behind traditional film resolution standards. Typically, a medium resolution film product contains over 18 million pixels. The computer storage capability necessary for saving pictures increases enormously in direct proportion to the resolution.

Optical disk technology has the capability to record high resolution video images at the fraction of the cost of traditional floppy disk recording devices. There is little doubt that by the new century, photographers and editors will commonly use still video cameras and computer terminals to record, manipulate, and save images.

There is an increasing trend in using television images for newspaper reproduction. When only television cameras have recorded an important news event, Polaroid and other print technologies can capture a video image with a "Frame Grabber" for use in a publication. Newspaper publishers may sign licensing agreements with cable operators to use still images captured with this technology.

Although the quality of the reproduced picture is not as high as with traditional film products, the images are certainly good enough to print. Why send photographers to an important news or sporting event when an editor can "grab" pictures off a television screen? On October 6, 1989, the NPPA published the first issue of *The Electronic Times*, an all-electronic newspaper. Digital and video cameras recorded images that were manipulated using computer scanner and pagination systems. The Associated Press recently announced its plan to supply member newspapers with picture receiving and editing computer stations.

Students at the Rochester Institute of Technology produce a totally electronic publication, *E. s. p. r. i. t.* Electronic cameras, video, film and print scanners, and electronic darkroom software are available for students in the electronic still photography programme run by Associate Professor, Douglas Ford Rea. Darkrooms will soon turn into lightrooms as photographers move out into the newsrooms.

TELEVISION MANIPULATIONS

Television news organizations, on the 50th year since the introduction of the medium at the New York's World Fair, are not immune to simulation criticism. NBC's "Unsolved Mysteries" and "Yesterday, Today and Tomorrow"; CBS' "Saturday Evening with Connie Chung"; and Fox Broadcasting's "America's Most Wanted" and "A Current Affair" are programs that have all mixed real news with re-enactments of events.

The loudest opposition to news simulations came when ABC's "World News Tonight" aired a re-enacted segment depicting Felix Bloch, the U.S. diplomat under investigation for spying, handing a briefcase filled with secrets to an enemy agent. Sam Donaldson, a senior correspondent for ABC, told the Associated Press that viewers could be easily mislead by the film to believe "that they had actually seen the event. [But] they didn't.

They didn't see that at all." Peter Jennings apologized for the failure of ABC to properly and promptly label the film as a simulation with, "We're sorry if anyone was mislead and we'll try to see that it doesn't happen again". Because of the criticism, some changes have been announced by news executives.

Roone Arledge, president of ABC News said that since the Bloch simulation, anything done out of the ordinary must receive the approval of the president or his assistant. However, ABC's "20/20" later used a re-enacted scene that was screened by executives, of a private detective rummaging through a garbage can looking for evidence.

Arledge defended the film with, "It didn't confuse anyone. Everyone knew we weren't actually there when he was first going through the garbage." Arledge then admitted, "I don't know if I would have it done that way, though". NBC announced that it would "stop its use of controversial news re-creations and shift the only one of its programs that uses the technique from the news to the entertainment division".

Subject manipulations are an unfortunate necessity for television videographers. Photojournalists and reporters are faced with demanding deadlines often exasperated by the trend toward live newscasts by local stations.

Professional video cameras need a tripod for static pictures. Additional lighting is often required for high quality illumination. Vans that contain a satellite link with the newsroom sometimes need a specially trained technician to operate the elabouredate broadcasting system.

Most on-the-air broadcasts show interviews between reporters and a subject. Consequently, technical and subject constraints combine to produce a televised report that is at best, not spontaneous and at worse, rehearsed. Videographers can compare themselves to the press photographers of the 1940s and 1950s who also produced set up images due to their technological constraints.

With the advent of small, handheld, high quality video cameras, television reports may become more candid as happened with newspaper and magazine photography with the introduction of handheld still cameras.

FUTURE THREATS TO CREDIBILITY

In an article for *American Photographer,* Dr. Willi Heimsohm, described a scenario in which editors played with history with their computer. Heimsohm detailed a faked assassination, made possible through computer technology, of Colonel Muammar Kaddafi of Libya for a fictitious publication.

The hypothetical situation, although far-fetched, can be considered the ultimate fear of professionals. The re-creation is reminiscent of a quote from George Orwell's, 1984: "There were the huge printing shops with their sub-editors, their typography experts, and their elabouredately equipped studios for the faking of photographs".

Photographs, particularly those used as accurate and trustworthy accounts of a significant event by respected publications, are our best hedge against the threat of devious editors and special interest groups who want to change truth and history. If the manipulation of photographs is accepted for any image, the public will naturally doubt all photographs and text within the publication.

At the very least, readers should be informed that an editorial image has been altered. For example, Jim Dooley, photo editor/chief for *Newsday,* was careful to let the readers know that a fashion feature picture was a "photo-illustration with a caption that said a model with clothes".

Such a disclaimer does not always help a reader understand a complicated computer procedure. Nancy Tobin, the design director for the *Asbury Park Press,* explained that the cow and salad illustration was labeled, "composite photo illustration, but some people were left scratching their heads".

With the price of digitizing equipment getting so low that editors for corporation newsletters can afford to manipulate images, the temptation to combine pictures without readers being notified will be great. Because of the new technologies, photographers may have limited input over the use of their pictures.

The digital transmission of images, recently demonstrated during the Olympic games and national political conventions, allows a photographer to instantly send a digitized colour negative directly to the computer terminal of the photography editor across a city or across the world via telephone transmission. Although telephone transmission of photographic images has been a common practice for many years, the photographer has always been able to print the picture the way he or she thought it should look. The photo editor was only able to crop the picture to fit into the space on the newspaper's page.

When the picture is sent to a computer, the photo editor can crop, but also dodge, bum, correct the colour, eliminate distracting elements, flop, and combine images from separate photographs. Editors are even capable of sharpening blurred or out-of-focus pictures.

When computer-digitized transmissions become common, staff photographers may have as much say over picture selection and use as freelance photographers or television videographers who frequently transmit live images via satellites without an opportunity to edit their work.

Such a trend would conflict with *Houston Post* staff photographer Craig Hartley (1983), who wrote that the "photojournalist must be responsible for his or her actions in the field and at the publication". It would be difficult for a photographer to discuss a controversial image with an editor over the telephone.

Beverly Bethune, in a national survey of photographers, reported that newspaper photojournalists listed "input into photo use, layout, etc." as a major factor that defined job satisfaction.

"Photographers," wrote Bethune, "who said they have a strong voice in making photo decisions that affected their work as it appeared in their papers were generally more satisfied overall than photographers with voices less strong. They are happier, then, when they have a say in how their work is used". Computer transmission technology could take away that job satisfaction requirement.

Freelance photographers have been the first group affected by computer technology. A picture agency, The Image Bank, offers their best-selling transparencies on videodisc to their clients throughout the world. Jim Mostyn, president of The Image Bank/Chicago, predicted that "within the next 10 years, all photography will be viewed and transmitted electronically."

As detailed in *Photomethods,* "special software offers image masking capabilities which enable clients to combine elements from many different photographs to form one image". A photographer's style, established over a lifetime of experience, will be lost once pictures are fabricated on a computer.

Furthermore, if for example, 30% of one picture and 70% of a picture from another photographer are used to make a third image, how is payment divided between the two shooters? Does the art director/computer operator get a percentage? How are copyrights for the created image assigned?

As much as it is possible, photographers should be consulted if a news picture is controversial. When discussion is not possible, written guidelines for such use, strictly adhered to by the editor, would be appropriate. After all is said and done, the photojournalist is still left with the question, should all forms of subject and picture manipulations be banned, or are exceptions acceptable?

For many writers, the choice is simple. J. D. Lasica features editor and columnist for the Sacramento Bee wrote in an article titled, "Photographs that Lie," that "the 1980s may be the last decade in which photos could be considered evidence of anything."

Director of photography for the *Sacramento Bee,* George Wedding, also warned, "The photograph as we know it, as a record of fact, may no longer in fact be that in three or five years". Brian Steffans, a graphics photography editor at the *Los Angeles Times* pointed out, "You've got to rely on people's ethics.

That's not much different from relying on the reporter's words. You don't cheat just because the technology is available". In a column titled, "Troubles with re-creating news," William Strothers wrote that "There is no substitute for truth.

Viewers and readers expect that when we give them the

news we are telling the truth as best as we can determine it. We may not always get it right, but we try. We can't make up for lack of truth by re-enacting the event the way we think it ought to be". Finally, John Long, of the *Hartford Courant* and former president of the NPPA, wrote:

Each day when you step out onto the street, remember that you have been granted a sacred trust to be truthful. You have the responsibility to produce only honest images. You have no right to set up pictures; you have no right to stage the news; you have no right to distort the facts.

Your fellow citizens trust you. If you destroy the credibility of your work, even in small ways, it destroys the credibility of your newspaper or TV station in the eyes of the people you are covering. As demonstrated by the many examples in this chapter, photographic truth is an elusive, often subjective, concept. Generally speaking, whenever the Hedonistic philosophy is put into play, the truthfulness of an image suffers.

Personal presumptions about how a subject's story should be told, concerns for clean, photographic compositions, deadline pressure panic, unreasonable demands from an editor, layout efficiency, a cover picture's eye-catching ability, and political, religious or personal beliefs can all demean the credibility of the photograph, the photographer, and the publication. Let a truth based on sound, journalism principles be your guiding philosophy. When an objective truth is put first, photographs and the stories behind them can be easily defended and are a source for humanistic concern and inspiration.

Chapter 8

Issues of Concern

Ethical concerns are more common conversational topics among news personnel than in past years. A discussion of ethics among journalists moves photographers from a mob of "animals" who are only concerned for their next contest-winning picture to a fraternity of professionals who deeply care about their rights as journalists and the public they serve.

There are several miscellaneous issues that photojournalists regularly face that do not fit into the neat and ordered categories of victims of violence, rights to privacy, and picture manipulations. Nevertheless, when a photographer is confronted with one of them, the ethical problems the issues pose can be equally troubling for photographers and editors.

In responses to surveys, telephone interviews, and within the pages of *News Photographer*, photojournalists bring up at least 20 issues that occasionally cause them trouble. The topics in no particular order are as follows:

- Police/press relations,
- Job-related stress,
- Proper dress,
- Helping or taking a picture,
- Objectivity,
- The use of hidden cameras,
- Office politics,
- Accepting gifts,
- Nude subjects,
- Deadline pressures,
- Photo packs and pools,

- Obeying minor traffic laws,
- Encouraging violence with presence,
- Misrepresentation,
- Contest pressure,
- Comical, obscene, or offensive subjects,
- Inaccurate caption information,
- Children shown not playing safely,
- Covering hazardous assignments, and
- Context-excluded images.

At first glance, the 20 miscellaneous issues do not seem to be related. But they can be divided into three areas: organizational, photographer, and reader concerns.

ORGANIZATIONAL CONCERNS

The pressure to produce attention-grabbing, award-winning, and technically pleasing pictures on a daily basis causes a whole host of problems between editors and photographers. When a newspaper organization emphasizes photography contests as a way to give raises and promotions, but does not give photographers time to adequately work on assignments, the mix can lead to ethical troubles.

The combination of contests and deadline pressures can lead photographers to take unethical actions they might not attempt at a more relaxed organization. The use of hidden cameras and other misrepresentation techniques might be justified. A photographer might remain a cool, detached, objective journalist who is happy to let a situation become visually dramatic and not help a subject in physical trouble.

Other, less objective photographers may encourage subjects to become more violent during a demonstration so that dramatic pictures can be taken. The photojournalists might rush to the scene of a news event and break minor traffic laws.

Such an action might cause trouble between the photographer and the police resulting in film confiscation and arrest. Trying to get a competitive edge over another photographer may actually result, when many photographers cover the same event in a photo pack, in all shooters using the same lens and camera angle. Creativity suffers when every photographer is afraid of missing what some other photographer may have.

Trying to get a picture in a hurry, a photographer might inaccurately report names and other facts for the caption. Finally, shooting for contest wins while being pressured by editors to produce those images quickly, results in strained relationships in the office and even stress-related illnesses. In order to take pictures of young, tired children working with dangerous machinery in factories, Lewis Hine at the turn of the century, regularly misrepresented himself.

He would tell the foreman of a factory that he was working for the company and needed to take pictures within the plant. Other times, he would simply hide his bulky view camera under a large overcoat and sneak into the factory. He justified his actions with the Utilitarianism philosophy. Although it may be wrong to falsely represent himself, the greater injustice was the exploitation of children.

More recently, journalists have used the same philosophy to justify their questionable actions. A famous misrepresentation/hidden camera case is the Mirage Tavern story by the *Chicago Sun-Times*. Photographers hid in a secret compartment above a bathroom and photographed reporters giving bribes to corrupt city inspection officials.

Pamela Zekman, the principal reporter for the project, does not support such techniques in a private home, but thinks "it to be an acceptable technique in a public place, like the Mirage". Freelance photographer, J. Ross Baughman's Pulitzer Prize winning photographs of Rhodesian soldiers torturing their victims were withdrawn from the Overseas Press Club (OPQ competition because of "so many unresolved questions about their authenticity."

Baughman, who has infiltrated Nazi and Ku Klux Klan groups in the United States "had worn a Rhodesian soldier's uniform, carried a gun and joined a Rhodesian cavalry patrol for two weeks in order to get the pictures." John Durniak, picture editor for *Time* magazine and a member of the OPC stated that "the jury felt the pictures had been posed" .

When a photographer misrepresents him or herself and becomes a participant to violent actions, credibility should be severely questioned. Persons would change their actions, especially if they were involved in a criminal activity, if they knew a photographer was capturing their movements. Therefore, the use of long and hidden lenses is sometimes justified.

Former president of NPPA, Bill Sanders admitted that if "a city official was using city trucks and work crews for personal jobs" it would be acceptable to use hidden cameras in public places. Editors and photographers need to weigh the public's right to know against the paper's need for credible news practices that can be defended.

A Minneapolis *Star Tribune* reader criticized photographer Stormi Greener for taking a picture of a mother spanking her child that was part of a story on a family near "the edge of serious abuse" of their children. "Greener," the reader wrote, "could have helped her wash a dish, bathe a child, buy groceries for the week.

The mother needed some help not the documentation of her treatment of those poor kids on film." Greener admitted that she could have easily helped the family by giving money to the mother. "But our story," Greener explained, "was not about a journalist coming to the aid of the family. My job was to take an honest look at a family in a struggle. I was guilt-ridden and frustrated with the ethics that I had to live with, [but] the first rule of journalism is to divorce yourself from your subject and do nothing but document and record" Would Greener have dropped her objectivity principle if the mother was severely beating her child? Greener asserted that had the mother abused the child, she would have intervened.

The principle of objectivity is valued among the journalism profession. But taken to its extreme can result in the loss of a subject's life when help could have easily been rendered. Bill Murphy of the *Oregon Journal* tried his best to be a compassionate journalist. While trying to convince a man not to leap from a bridge, Murphy also took pictures. Unfortunately, he was unsuccessful in his attempts to convince the man not to jump. The man leaped to his death. Murphy was severely criticized by readers who asked why he took pictures instead of helping. Despite admitting that "I did all I could," he was in agony over his decision.

CECIL ANDREWS PROTESTS UNEMPLOYMENT

Greener and Murphy know there are limits to a journalist's strict interpretation of the objectivity principle. Two television news journalists did not set such limits. The two recorded on videotape an obviously distraught man who set himself on fire.

They hid behind the principle of objectivity to justify capturing a dramatic piece of news film that their station did not even put on the air. Cecil Andrews was an unemployed roofer in the small town of Jacksonville, Alabama. He called the TV station late in the evening and said he would set himself on fire to protest unemployment in America.

Ron Simmons and his part-time assistant, Gary Harris, who thought Andrews sounded intoxicated, made several calls to the police warning them about Andrews and where to meet him. Andrews, Simmons, and Harris met in a dark, downtown park. Simmons was concerned that he could not see any police officials.

If they were hiding in the bushes, he thought he could signal them by turning on his camera light. But when he did, Andrews squeezed charcoal lighter fluid on his pants leg, made several attempts with matches to light the spot, and eventually started a small flame.

For over 30 seconds, the camera crew let the flame grow higher before an attempt was made to put out the fire. By that time, the fire was out of control. Andrews started running across the park, his body a terrifying ball of flame. Luckily, a volunteer fireman with an extinguisher was there to save Andrews' life.

Andrews survived with severe injuries. He later filed a $4 million suit against the television news crew. On national television news shows, special reports, and on front pages of newspapers across the country, the story was reported-not the story of Cecil Andrews protesting unemployment, but the story of two journalists who watched a man trying to kill himself.

Typical of the response from the media was a *Time* magazine story that called the camera crew's actions a "gruesome result of lapses in communication and judgment." The situation brings to mind Malcolm Browne's coverage of a Buddhist monk who set himself on fire to protest the Diem regime's crackdown on his religion. Newspaper editorial writers at the time "maintained that the newsmen should have intervened."

The media is often criticized for contributing to the violence they cover. Journalists noticed that Iranian students outside the American Embassy in Tehran during the hostage crisis in 1979 only yelled their insults against America when the red lights of the television cameras were lit.

The police chief of Jacksonville, Alabama summed up the popular opinion when he told the Associated Press that "I'm not trying to condemn the news media but it's a fact when you have lights and cameras that people are going to perform for the cameras". Cecil Andrews would not have set himself on fire if no news personnel had shown up at the park.

He orchestrated the photo opportunity, like any public relations person, to promote his cause. Andrews knew that the television reporters would be interested in a dramatic, eye-catching visual demonstration. One reason protest marchers for any issue carry signs is because they know that media personnel like to see highly visual slogans written on signs.

Two questions remain: If a journalist knows he or she is being manipulated by a subject, should the event be covered? and, Once a decision to cover the event is made, should a journalist step in to help a subject in physical trouble? It seems unlikely that journalism will ever come to a point when it can resist being manipulated by subjects. Press conferences and White House photo opportunities are scheduled all the time to allow reporters access to governmental officials.

Local organizers of craft and art fairs make it easy for

photographers to cover their charitable events by giving information and schedules to editorial staffs. But during a demonstration, photographers can make sure that their presence does not contribute to the violence.

A thoughtful photojournalist should watch the demonstrators closely, perhaps from a far vantage point, As more journalists with their cameras arrive at the scene, does the intensity level of the protesters seem to grow? Does a demonstrator ask to have his or her picture taken? If the protest occurs at night, do the protesters react to a camera's flash or a video camera's light?

These are some questions you can ask yourself to help determine if the media's presence and not the issue is creating news. Unfortunately, when protesters and police are battling, no matter the contributing factors, it is a major news story that should be covered. Knowing what is and what is not news becomes extremely important in these situations.

The arrest of many protesters is clearly news. The self-immolation of a possibly drunk individual is not news. But the fact that two videographers taped a man trying to kill himself instead of preventing the act, is news. *News Photographer* magazine often reports stories of journalists putting away their cameras and helping people in trouble. Ed Bradley of CBS rushed to rescue refugees from Vietnam off the coast of Malaysia.

Reporter Christine Wolff of the *Bradenton Herald* (FL) physically prevented a man from jumping off a bridge until state troopers arrived. Arriving at the scene of a serious car crash before emergency personnel, Cramer Gallimore of the Fayetteville, North Carolina *Observer-Times,* stopped the bleeding from a head wound of one of the drivers before he made pictures. At another assignment, Gallimore rushed into a burning apartment building to save the life of a hysterical woman.

Photographer John Doman and writer Chuck Laszewski of the St. Paul, Minnesota *Pioneer Press* saved a woman from possible drowning. Doman used his portable radio to call the police for help. Jeff Greenfield on ABC's "Nightline" programme feels that journalists should always help a subject "where you as an individual have a direct possibility of stopping a life-threatening piece of behaviour.

Put down your pad and pencil, put down the camera; save the life. You can get the story later, if indeed there is a story". One of the largest index sections in the NPPA directory is a list of stories in *News Photographer* on relationships between the press and the police. From 1978, over 45 articles have been published about the issue.

Problems with the police typically result from overly anxious police officers, during an emotionally charged situation, who do not understand the reporting rights of journalists. Sometimes, however, a photographer exasperates the situation with an impolite or cavalier attitude. One of the primary principles for journalists is the monitoring function.

Reporters observe government officials to make sure individual rights are not violated. But when those officials do not want to be monitored, problems can result. Alec Costerus, a freelance photographer for the *Boston Globe,* AP, and UPI, was driving to his parents home in Marion, Massachusetts late one night.

He saw a police car with its blue lights flashing and decided to stop. Costerus observed two teenagers suspected of driving while intoxicated being beaten up by the police officers. Costerus identified himself and started taking pictures. He was immediately arrested and charged with interfering with a police officer.

Costerus was acquitted and he was eventually awarded $24,000 in damages, but that is not the important issue. From his case, guidelines were established by the Marion police department that stated "the mere presence of a photographer or reporter at an accident, crime or disaster scene, and the mere taking of pictures relative to the incident do not, in themselves, constitute unlawful interference with police activity and should not be restricted".

NPPA and Mark Hertzberg, regional director and photographer for the Racine, Wisconsin *Journal-Times,* drafted guidelines for police/press relations in 1981. The guidelines are meant to be "incorporated into a [police] department's training manual".

Despite NPPA's best wishes, photographers usually do not have good relationships with police personnel. Seminars and lectures explaining the roles of each group are helpful to create better understanding. Photographers should respect the difficult jobs police officials have. That respect starts with obeying traffic and trespass laws. Photographers are divided on the issue.

In a national survey, a photographer said that "Breaking any kind of law should be extremely unethical, although we all fudge a little bit on the accelerator. I will not park illegally as television vans do. But what do you do when you need close access and there is no parking?"

A director of photography has a direct answer, "I feel very strongly that especially with regards to traffic laws all journalists should be accountable and not feel above the law". At a news scene, photojournalists should be especially careful not to unduly upset victims or their families. Many problems with the police are a result of a photographer trying to get too close to a distressed subject.

A police officer will often try to protect such an individual. Whenever possible, use long, telephoto lenses. Speak simply, directly, and politely to any police officer who asks you questions. If an officer gives you trouble, try to speak to his or her superior or save the issue for a later meeting with police officials after emotions have cooled. Remember that you may be right, but it is hard to take pictures while handcuffed.

PACK AND POOL PHOTOJOURNALISM

Deadline and competitive pressures are blamed for contributing to pack journalism. Writers and photographers must produce meaningful stories and photographs within a narrowly defined time frame. As a result, journalists often ban together into a media mob so that no event, no matter how trivial, will be missed. The media was criticized for its coverage of the 1988 presidential campaign because journalists concentrated on photo opportunities orchestrated by campaign handlers instead of under-the-surface issues.

Journalists need to break from the pack and find stories and pictures that are not a part of a handler's plan. The main story is not always what the candidate looks like when speaking to a crowd. Photographers need to observe quickly developing human interest moments that only occur outside the special press section next to the candidate's podium. Remember the maxim: Only hacks travel in packs.

When access to an assignment is unusually limited, photographers often find themselves members of a pool with reporters and videographers. In a photo pool, a photographer is allowed access to an important news event with the understanding that the pictures produced will be shared openly with other news organizations. The U.S. government was severely criticized by members of the journalism community when it barred reporters and photojournalist's access during the invasion of Grenada.

Consequently, photo pools were established during the invasion of Panama. The day following hurricane Hugo's rampage across South Carolina in 1989, Tom Fowler of the South Carolina Educational Television network provided news footage taken by a videographer in a government helicopter at courtesy credit to any news organization who wanted it.

Because access to the South Carolina beaches by journalists was severely limited, the photo pool gave the public vital visual information that would otherwise been unknown. Photojournalists, especially freelance photographers' need to be sure that members of a pool are selected fairly. Although a pool of photographers were selected, a rescue picture of a man trapped in his car for 4 days after the 1989 earthquake in San Francisco was taken by one of the rescue workers. The picture was used in several newspapers, despite objections from members of the pool.

THE NEED FOR ACCURATE CAPTIONS

The verbal information that photographers gather during

an assignment is as crucial to the reporting process as taking pictures. Facts, whether verbal or visual, need to be absolutely accurate. When a photographer misspells a person's name or juggles the order of participants in a group portrait by mistake, the result can be embarrassing, but not serious.

But if a major fact is wrong, the result can be devastating. Photographs of the family of teacher-in-space, Christa McAuliffe were mislabeled in the captions. Three photographers thought they were taking pictures of the family reacting to the shuttle's explosion. The pictures all show what could easily be interpreted as a family reacting to an extremely stressful moment-the death of their loved one. There is open-mouth screaming, crying, and hugging among the family members.

The subjects in the pictures, however, are simply animatedly reacting to the shuttle's lift-off. Jim Cole, an AP stringer, summed up the feelings of the photographers involved in the caption controversy. "Obviously this mistake has caused me considerable and personal anguish. While it will always be my loss, I hope photographers and editors will be able to profit from my experience".

Either as a result of deadline pressure that prevented a thorough investigation of the facts or heat-of-the-moment concentration that ignored important details, photographers must be sure that they remain calm and accurate reporters.

PRESSURE FROM CONTESTS

Contests are often blamed for contributing to an atmosphere of hectic competition among staff photographers. Competition can be healthy. It encourages all involved to produce their best work. But when competition is combined with an emphasis on contests, unethical actions can sometimes result.

In a national survey of 157 newspaper editors, "most newspapers had policies, usually informal, that encourages prize seeking." It was also found that most editors encourage their reporters to enter contests. As with competition, contests can be positive. Photographers in another national survey generally agreed that contests can improve a shooter's output. "We're probably the only profession with such an emphasis on awards.

However, it does allow us to measure ourselves and our work against others in the rest of the country," wrote one photographer. Another photojournalist wrote that contests "improve the quality of photos by providing good examples to younger shooters." A third photographer made the point that "In many ways competition helps improve quality over the years, but photographing grief is usually done simply to get a clip winner".

Another valuable function of contests is that the winners are published in *News Photographer* and other magazines, along with the stories behind them. The problem with contests is that their results are often inconsistent.

Judging is often subjective with few but the winners satisfied. Judges select contest winners for a variety of reasons. Most picture prizes, it is hoped, are given on the basis of good journalism. But judges sometimes let personal likes and dislikes, personality conflicts among judges, and simple fatigue sway results.

Although the size of the picture and the reproduction quality of tearsheets are overlooked in competitions, judges do not always follow that mandate. Judges in the Pictures of the Year contest are typically asked to select winners out of over 36,000 photographs and tearsheets.

It is an exhausting task. Good pictures sometimes fall through the cracks. When a photography staff emphasizes contests as raise and promotion requirements, the politics within the department can become critical. Friction between photographers and editors often results when photographs are cropped, used small, and on an inside page despite a photographer's recommendations.

Photographers know that a larger size will influence some contest judges. Photographers will complain when other staff members get better assignments. Instead of sharing information and helping one another, photographers become secretive and jealous. Editors should never require photographers to enter contests. Likewise, raises and promotions should be decided on the contribution the photographer has made to the community by a consistent body of solid photojournalism. Editors, those who are familiar with a photographer's work, should make crucial career decisions and not judges who view only a small sample.

An ideal competition would be a monthly clip contest in which first, second, and third places are chosen for the assignment categories by judges outside the photographers' region. A monthly publication would immediately publish the judges' results and comments.

Technical and background information from the photographers would also be included. No points would be awarded as no end-of-the-year winner would be selected. Such a contest would award a photographer's effort, let others know what content is most respected by members of the profession, and relieve much of the stress associated with traditional contests.

STRESSFUL ASSIGNMENTS TAKE THEIR TOLL

Too many deadlines, contests, and gruesome assignments can be dangerous to a photographer's mental and physical health. Photojournalism is a highly stressful profession. Besides the everyday life stresses that all must face, photojournalists must also deal with picture demands from editors and writers, technical decisions that determine proper exposure and coverage, assignment schedules that are sometimes vague or conflict with other events, and subjects that are uncooperative, grieving, or dead.

Within a few years on the job, a photojournalist learns all the ways people die-drowning, car and plane crashes, murders, and many mind numbing accidents. And as with others who witness such dreadful events-police, fire and ambulance workers, nurses, and doctors-post-traumatic stress disorder (PTSD) or "battle fatigue" effects photojournalists as well. When a victim is a small child or a person the photographer knows or can relate to, the impact can be devastating.

A newspaper writer described the personality of emergency rescue workers. The description could easily fit most photographers:

Emergency-service workers tend to be perfectionists; they have an eye for detail and enjoy taking risks. Typically highly dedicated, they want to set things right and hate to take no for an answer. They often develop a false sense of security-they have always tolerated the pressure, and assume they always will.

Those suffering from PTSD "may become depressed, refuse help, hallucinate, quit jobs and families, even kill themselves". A stressed photographer may also turn to alcohol and drugs as short-term relief.

Dr. Jeffery Mitchell, a University of Maryland psychologist, travels around the country setting up programs in local communities to help "paramedics, firefighters, and police officers cope with tragedies they see". Newspaper organizations need to recognize that PTSD is a condition that can be treated if diagnosed early enough.

Photography editors must know how to recognize a staff photographer who exhibits symptoms of stress-related illnesses. Journalists should be included in group discussions for rescue workers that would not only help those who participate, but would foster appreciation of the problems both journalists and rescue personnel face.

Editors need to give their photographers adequate time to complete assignments. Picture story deadlines, for example, need to be realistic. An in-depth lifestyle story cannot be accomplished in a few hours. If a photographer has a problem brought on by stress or any other factor, editors need to seek compassionate help for that valued employee.

Photographers need to be included early in discussions with editors and writers about stories. Photographers are often told to produce meaningful pictures in a few hours while a writer has been working on a series of articles for several months. Photographers need to realise that their whole world does not revolve around equipment and subject concerns.

Strong personal relationships and interests unrelated to

news photography make photographers more interesting, caring, and relaxed people. If a photographer feels the stress that the many pressures can apply, he or she should never hesitate to talk it over with a friend, colleague, or editor and seek professional help.

PHOTOGRAPHER CONCERNS

COVERING DANGEROUS ASSIGNMENTS

Photographers are sometimes asked to cover assignments that can be hazardous to their health.

Without proper training and safety equipment, photographers can be injured covering accident scenes where "unstable and reactive materials, corrosives, liquid, gas and solid flammable materials, toxic materials, explosives and radioactive materials" are present.

Photographers can also be injured covering a demonstration that turns into a violent riot. Michael Green of the *Detroit News* gave advice to photojournalists covering dangerous assignments. "It's important to stop and think before going in to [a hazardous area]," Green warns. "It's also one time you might want to listen to the cops or authorities when they tell you not to stand some place or enter certain areas".

At an NPPA convention, Greg Lewis, a professor of journalism gave tips for covering an assignment that involves hazardous materials:

- When you first arrive at the scene, check with a police or fire commander for information about the hazardous materials;
- Use a long lens;
- Stay uphill and up wind; do not walk through or touch any liquid; green, yellow, or orange smoke indicates a chemical source; do not inhale smoke;
- Toxic vapors can be odorless and tasteless; because of the danger of explosion from internal sparking, motor drives, flashes, and radio gear should not be carried to a flammable liquids fire;

- Assume hazardous materials are involved at any industrial site; and
- If contaminated, seek immediate decontamination.

Time magazine photographer, Bill Pierce, has covered combat zones in troubled areas throughout the world. Pierce has had many photojournalist friends killed and wounded photographing wars. His advice can be applied to newspaper photographers covering violent events in their own communities.

- Wear a flak jacket all the time;
- Minimize equipment for quick movement;
- Rravel in pairs;
- Know the language of the people you photograph;
- Take pictures that show the cost on lives after the firing has stopped; and
- Have clear, journalistic reasons why the violence should be documented.

Editors have a responsibility for the safety of their personnel. Safety concerns start with proper ventilation and handling of photographic materials.

Jim Jennings of the Lexington, Kentucky *Herald-Leader* said that covering the news should not "take precedence over the safety of their personnel." An editor must never put photographers "into a situation that is even remotely life-threatening".

PERSONAL APPEARANCE AS AN ISSUE

For most assignments, dress and personal grooming is a matter of taste and professionalism and not a matter of ethics. But a photographer's ethics may be questioned if his or her appearance is inappropriate for an assignment. In a national survey, photographers were asked to voice their opinions about attending an assignment while improperly dressed.

One photographer wrote, "You may come to work dressed for a sporting event and then be called to go on a different assignment. As long as your clothes are clean and not tacky you should be able to cover almost any assignment."

Another respondent wrote, "If I wanted to wear a tie I'd

work in a bank!" A third photographer said, "Oftentimes the scheduling of assignments precludes changing clothes. However, dressing appropriately for the assignment at hand is as important as other ethical concerns".

The appearance issue was hotly debated in the late 1970s when the television show, "Lou Grant" was aired. Daryl Anderson played the sloppily dressed and unshaven, "Animal." Many news photographers objected to his appearance, but producers said that his character was based on real, West Coast photojournalists.

Rich Clarkson, the former director of photography at *National Geographic,* said that photojournalists "dress and behave so poorly that they increasingly face restrictions in covering major news events." Photographers, Clarkson asserted, are roped off in out-of-the-way locations during sporting events, out-of-sight of television cameras and fans, because of their appearance.

A photographer's appearance is never so critical as when a funeral is covered. Those on the scene judge a photographer's concern for the family by what the photographer wears. Obviously, cut-off blue jeans and a T-shirt is inappropriate attire, but photographers have been known to cover such events wearing not much more. Photographers should have a coat and a tie or a nice blouse and a skirt in their car in case they are needed for an unexpected assignment.

Mark Hertzberg wrote that "Dress is an important part of the way the public perceives us and in their acceptance of us in times of stress. I think many of us can dress better day-to-day without having to wear a three-piece suit". During a sensitive assignment, if a photographer is dressed neatly with a tie or skirt, the awkward job of taking pictures is made a little easier.

Accepting free gifts from subjects can cause a reporter to lose his or her credibility. How can a photographer be an objective recorder of facts if money or gifts are changed hands? Richard Oppel, editor of the *Charlotte Observer'* (NC) recalled that when he was a young Associated Press reporter covering the Florida legislature, the press corps "accepted electric razors as gifts from Gov. Haydon Bums." Oppel said that "Even the sole woman correspondent got a lady Remington".

Subjects sometimes hand out small gifts or amounts of money in the hope of buying loyalty or favouritism. Seldom is a gift given as a simple act of friendship. Journalists need to recognize the practice for what it is and not succumb to the temptation.

A press junket, a trip organized by a corporation to show correspondents a new operation, can amount to a gift of thousands of dollars.

The Observer, like many newspapers across the country, do not allow their reporters to accept anything for free from any source. Just as newspapers should pay for a movie critic's ticket and a food critic's meal, if a story is worth covering, the paper should pick up the entire tab for any writers or photographers.

One photographer said that "The gifts we are allowed to receive must not exceed $5 in value." A director of photography at a newspaper admitted that "if after the work has been published, a subject wants to offer something out of friendship, I will make a trade, offering prints."

Photo sales is a common practice with newspaper photographers, but they should be handled by a business manager and not the individual photographers. Another director of photography said simply, "Company policy is we accept nothing".

Television journalist, Linda Ellerbee was severely criticized by journalism professionals for accepting a large amount of money to participate in a series of television commercials for a coffee producer.

Making paid, public endorsements for any product damages a journalist's credibility.

As Loren Ghiglione, president of the American Society of Newspaper Editors said, "the public demands higher and higher standards from public officials, and journalists are feeling that too".

READER CONCERNS

NUDE OR EMBARRASSING IMAGES

Just as with gruesomely violent images that editors place on their front pages, embarrassing or obscene behaviour by subjects caught with a camera, can produce a flood of mail from readers who object to the pictures. Editors need to be sensitive to the taste of readers, but not be guided exclusively by those changing standards.

Many editorial decisions are based on a publication's readership. London's Fleet street newspapers have a reputation for printing pictures of scantily clad, beach-strolling women. The New York *Daily News* often prints the same subject in its tabloid. Editors print these images because their readers expect to see them.

Many readers would complain if the pictures were omitted. The same kind of pictures found within the vertical fold-out of *Playboy* magazine would never be considered by an editor of a "family-oriented" newspaper.

A college newspaper sometimes covers subjects that are not covered because of the acceptance level of readers. When running nude through college campuses, streaking, was popular in the late 1970s, college photographers regularly covered the over-exposed subjects. The *Daily Collegian,* the student newspaper for Pennsylvania State University, printed a bare-chested winner of a wet T-shirt contest. Kathleen Pavelko, columnist for the *Collegian,* wrote that the picture was printed not because of its nudity, "but as a student phenomenon and a possible trend on American college campuses.

The contest was a slice of student life". Hal Buell of the Associated Press admits that nudity is a delicate subject with readers. "We will not carry full frontal views of nude men or women except in a most extreme case," wrote Buell. "We will transmit pictures of bare bosoms when such pictures are pertinent to the story."

A bare-chested protester during the 1972 political convention in Miami, a topless woman on a beach in

Denmark, and an opera soprano disrobing at the end of her aria are examples of AP wire transmissions. Yet most editors filed the pictures in a desk drawer rather than print the images in their community newspapers.

Don Black could not get his pictures published by his newspaper because editors were worried about shocking their readers. Black made pictures that showed a father delivering his own son. His pictures later ran in *People* magazine. Some newspapers stay away from pictures that show famous people looking silly or embarrassed.

Many papers would not print pictures of President Ford who was caught tripping on several occasions by photographers. When presidential candidate, Edmund Muskie cried during a campaign, some editors did not print the picture. When President Reagan wiggled his fingers during a White House news photographers banquet, Rich Lipski of United Press International captured the gesture that many editors did not print.

One-finger gestures give editors more problems than Reagan's wriggling hands. Vice President Nelson Rockefeller was pictured by Don Black "giving the finger to Binghamton, N. Y. hecklers" in 1976. Harry Thernal of the Wilmington, Delaware *Morning News-Journal,* recalled that editors were concerned that if Rockefeller's picture was published, children might "think it's all right to copy the gestures".

Thernal was involved with another obscene gesture controversy at his newspaper. Ernest Parsons, a convicted double murderer, raised both of his middle fingers of his chained hands for Ronald Cortes' camera. The picture ran on the front page of the *Morning News-Journal.* Themal wrote that "The phone was already ringing as I stepped into the office.

It didn't stop ringing for hours as caller after caller complained about the picture's being published on the front page." A man said that the picture was "absolutely tasteless. I found it embarrassing when my 7-year-old son brought in the paper and turned it to this picture. I've lost all respect for the newspaper." Another man said, "You shouldn't be glorifying an individual convicted of murder."

As an answer to the readers' wrath, editor Donald Brandt said that "the gesture is not as obscene as the crime of which Parsons was found guilty the photo made an eloquent statement about the obscenity of the crime." Managing editor, Norm Lockman said that the picture "showed Parsons utter contempt for society. It offends us, too, but our photographer's depiction of this anti-social behaviour says volumes about this man".

CONTEXT-EXCLUDED IMAGES

Michael Smith, photo director for the *Detroit Free Press,* was accused of glorifying a drug dealer by readers because of a photograph that was printed. Richard Carter, reputed to be one of Detroit's major cocaine dealers, was shot to death in a hospital bed.

He was buried in a $16,000 casket "customised to look like a Mercedes-Benz-complete with wheels, grill and headlights." George Waldman made a picture of Carter that showed his body lying in the open casket.

Although some readers objected to seeing a corpse, most complained that the picture glorified the drug dealer. Smith said that the picture "says a lot about the drug culture in Detroit in 1988." Reader representative, Joe Grimm admitted that the picture did no make it clear enough that the casket "symbolized unabashed arrogance and ignorance of drug dealers who have contributed greatly to Detroit's toll of young shooting victims".

The context of a picture, explained in a story or column, will diffuse much of the protest about a controversial picture. AIDS research and care are highly emotionally charged issues. When covering the AIDS story, photographers usually concentrate their efforts on those unfortunate individuals who are close to death.

Alon Reininger has traveled the world for many years to document the AIDS crisis. His portrait of Ken Meeks, who died shortly after the picture was taken, shows a man sitting in a wheelchair, lesions covering hi arms, and staring at the camera with a hauntingly vacant look.

During Nicholas Nixon's Museum of Modem Art show where he presented hi work, "People with AIDS," a protest group handed out fliers. The flier stated that photographers who portray the emancipated bodies of AIDS victims show "people to be pitied or feared, as people alone and lonely." The gallery exhibit "perpetuate general misconceptions about AIDS without addressing the realities of those of us living every day with the crisis."

According to the New York activist group, ACT UP, the reality of a life with AIDS is more optimistic, but less visually dramatic. Because of "experimental drug treatments, [and] better information about nutrition and holistic care," AIDS patients are living longer.

Editors should never publish shocking pictures for their shock value alone. No responsible editor would contemplate such an action. The days when a publisher can make a large amount of money with a sensational picture on the front page are long over. Publishers reveal that a newspaper's profits are made from selling advertising, not papers.

If anything, such a dependence would cause editors to be more conservative in their picture choices so as not to offend advertisers. Don Black and other photographers worry that editors are, in fact, too timid when it comes to pictures and stories that might shock or offend some readers. "Failing to run an important news picture for fear of reader response," Black says, "is indulging in a form of censorship". The public never learns the whole truth, however, when graphically visual images are devoid of a fuller context.

IMAGES OF CHILDREN IN DANGEROUS SITUATIONS

Occasionally, an editor will hear complaints from readers who object to the showing of children not playing safely. Human interest pictures of children jumping from a second floor window onto several stacked mattresses, playing with fire or guns, or floating on hand-made rafts on a river, might give editors problems.

The Florida Supreme Court recently ruled that a soft

drink company "is not liable for damages suffered by a teenager who broke his neck and was paralyzed when he copied a stunt he saw in a Mountain Dew television commercial".

The ruling could probably be applied to a parent's lawsuit if a child was injured copying an unsafe act printed in the newspaper. Responsible editors, however, will avoid such tragic confrontations.

EDITORS AND THEIR ETHICAL CONCERNS

Bill Phillips, director of photography and Bill Dunn, managing editor of *The Orlando Sentinel,* have come up with 16 areas of sensitivity "that should raise a flag on all desks-though not an automatic signal to kill."

The 16 subject categories that might give picture editors trouble include:

- Body shots,
- Gore, grief,
- The physically and mentally afflicted,
- Vulgar gestures,
- Cheesecake and beefcake,
- Otherwise sexually offensive pictures (includes see-through and sexy fashion photography),
- Racial or ethnic stereotypes (includes those that inflame),
- Pictures that embarrass or ridicule,
- Invasion of privacy,
- Trespass,
- Posing news pictures,
- Mechanically manipulated images,
- Kids doing dangerous things,
- Juveniles being arrested, and
- Dead animals.

Inevitably, there will be other, unique issues that will test the ethics of photographers and editors. With a solid and sure philosophical foundation, an understanding of the many conflicting opinions, and an emphasis on journalistic credibility, decisions can be defended with confidence.

ATTITUDES

Let's return to those years of yesterday when I made my first sales call and ask what I did wrong. The answer is easy – everything. But everything is not a helpful response, so we will put the responses into a context of a selling system to help you understand the elements of a successful sales call and a successful sales system.

To begin with, I did not plan my call properly did not have a framework, or a method for breaking down the sales call into component parts in order to analyse it. The AESKOPP system of selling provides such a framework. The AESKOPP system is a generalization, a simplification of some underlying, universal sales principles and provides a framework for coaching, planning, and evaluating sales thinking and action.

It posits that successful selling requires Attitude (A), Emotional Intelligence (E), Skills (S), Knowledge (K), Opportunities (O), Preparation (P), and Persistence (P): *A x E x S x K* x O *x* P x P = *Success* Notice that each element in the above formula is multiplied by the others. Just as in a mathematical formula, if any one of the elements is not present, then the result is zero success; any element multiplied by zero is zero.

Thus, all of the elements must be present for a successful result – getting customers and keeping them. Before making a sales presentation to a prospect or customer, salespeople should get into the habit of asking themselves the seven AESKOPP questions, and they should also evaluate their overall sales approach and performance by regularly asking themselves these questions. In addition, managers should continually ask these questions about their salespeople and their performance in order to coach them effectively.

THE SEVEN AESKOPP QUESTIONS

1. Do I have the right mental Attitude to solve problems and get results for my customers?
2. Do I have the Emotional Intelligence to understand people and build rapport with them?

3. Do I have the Skills necessary?
4. Do I have the Knowledge necessary?
5. Do I have the Opportunities?
6. Do I have sufficient Preparation?
7. Do I have the Persistence to never, never, never, never give up?

If the answer to all of the above questions is yes, you will make lots of sales. However, if you put a priority on closing a sale above all else, you put establishing and maintaining relationships, solving problems, and getting results in a subordinate position.

This means that sooner or later your customers will know you care more about yourself and your income than about their problems and their desired results.

THE AESKOPP SYSTEM

- Attitude: Attitude is having the desire and motivation to be a salesperson and having the proper mind set to do it. If you have the skills, the knowledge, and the opportunities to sell but have no desire to do so, you will not be successful.
- *Emotional Intelligence:* Emotional intelligence is the ability to understand yourself and others so you can develop empathy and rapport with people and manage relationships successfully.
- *Skills:* Skills are the ability, improved through practice, to use your knowledge of techniques, methods, and tools. For salespeople, it understands the techniques of prospecting, identifying problems, generating solutions, presenting, negotiating and closing, and servicing.
- *Knowledge:* Knowledge means knowing the product you are selling in depth – knowing more about it than your customers do so you can educate them. For salespeople, it means having information not only about their product, but also about research, about marketing and advertising, about customers' businesses, and about competitive media.

- *Opportunities:* Opportunities are the circumstances in which you can use your tools. Even if you have the tools and know how to use them, you cannot accomplish anything unless you have opportunities to put them to use. Salespeople may know how to solve problems and have a storehouse full of product, marketplace, and competitive knowledge, but if they do not make sales calls and find prospective customers, they will lack the opportunities to put their skills and knowledge to work.
- *Preparation:* Preparation is getting organized to solve customer problems. Even if you have the attitude, emotional intelligence, skills, knowledge, and opportunities to sell, you will not solve problems or make many sales if you forget your presentations and if you do not know anything about clients' businesses or personalities.
- *Persistence:* Persistence means never giving up. Salespeople need to continue working on prospects past any initial uninformed "no" they might encounter.

COMPETENCIES OF THE AESKOPP SYSTEM

Each of the seven elements of the AESKOPP system is made up of a group of core competencies – building blocks – that, linked together, lead to successful performance on that element. The core competencies are subject to change, depending on the media selling job involved. Some sales positions, such as in a large-circulation national magazine – *People,* for example – require a high level of knowledge, especially about national advertising, the product, and magazine research, plus very strong relationships with major advertising agencies and advertisers.

Other sales positions, such as in a local television station, might require an understanding of retail businesses – an automotive dealership, for example – and skills in negotiating with advertising agencies. Below is a list of core competencies for each of the elements the AESKOPP system.

- *Core Competencies Attitude:* Honest, positive/optimistic, committed, confident, courageous, competitive, coachable (open/non-defensive), self-motivated, assertive, flexible, cooperative, and nurturing.
- *Emotional intelligence:* Self-awareness, self-management, social awareness, and relationship management (internal and external).
- *Skills:* Communicating (internal and external), listening, understanding people, creating value, presenting (to individuals and groups), negotiating and closing, and servicing.
- *Knowledge:* Financial/economic/business/category, marketing/advertising, market, product, and competitive media.
- *Opportunity:* Prospecting/getting appointments, and identifying problems (discovery).
- *Preparation:* Strategic thinking, creativity/problem-solving, organization, planning, and time management. Persistence: Determined/never giving up, and follow-up. Each of the seven AESKOPP elements will be defined and explained much more thoroughly in subsequent chapters.

CORE COMPETENCIES

The next step in effectively using the AESKOPP system is to evaluate yourself based on your degree of expertise on each of the core competencies. I have assigned a percentage to each of the seven AESKOPP elements according to my perceived importance each contributes to a salesperson's ultimate success. These AESKOPP elements and their corresponding core competencies will change with the type of media selling job as will the percentages I have assigned, but the AESKOPP elements and core competencies are a good place to start in order to define and evaluate a media salesperson's job.

I recommend that salespeople and sales managers go over the list together and add or delete core competencies and put weights on each according to the needs of the medium they sell and the company they work for. Then, salespeople should study their modified and weighted list, evaluate themselves, and then develop a plan to improve those competencies in which they lack experience or have a deficit. Note the title "Salesperson Core Competencies."

The term salesperson is used because it is inclusive of a wide variety of titles salespeople in the media are assigned by their organizations: sales representative, account executive, account manager, sales consultant, radio marketing consultant, business development director, director of new business, and many more. The preferred title is Account Executive or Account Manager, which implies managing customers' accounts, schedules, and campaigns according to what is best for a customer.

Also, titles that include "consultant" should be avoided because customers need results more than advice. In this modern age of solutions selling, Results Generator might be a suitable title. But this euphemism is akin to calling a janitor a Maintenance Engineer, so Account Executive or Account Manager are more appropriate titles. However, in this book, to avoid confusion, salesperson will be used in order to encompass all titles.

Whoever tells the stories defines the culture. That isn't new. What is new is that we have delegated more and more of the storytelling function to mass media. Some of the media take the art to new heights. Too many, however, specialize in dishing out heaping servings of violence, mayhem and degradation.

In this presentation we will discuss the role of the media in creating and nourishing a "culture of disrespect" among young people. Combining the latest discoveries in brain science with cutting-edge research, we will discuss how media stories of disrespect, sex, and violence in television, video games and online affect our kids and what we can do to help our kids become MediaWise.

Advertisers spent $267 billion in 2005 to get their message out to the American public and the business sector, but a pressing question remains: given the dramatically changing media and cultural landscapes, what is the best way for firms to communicate messages to key audiences? This report examines consumers' attitudes towards television, Internet, radio, print, and public advertising.

Using exclusive consumer research, extensive analysis is devoted to how TiVo, DVRs, Internet video, and other technologies and trends have affected consumers' receptivity to commercials. This report also identifies which media channels are suffering as a consequence of these changes, and which media channels hold opportunities for advertisers seeking to reach various constituents.

Specific topics include:

- Groups most and least receptive to television commercials
- The emergence of new opportunities on the Internet
- Opportunities for reaching select groups via traditional media outlets

This report also features lengthy discussion on important trends in advertising in 2005 and 2006, along with related changes in the cultural fabric, such as the "iPod Effect" and the decline in leisure time.

This report analyses how demographic changes are reshaping the American population, the affluence of various sectors of the population, and snapshots of what the country's population will look like in 2012.

The media sector plays a crucial role in shaping public attitudes and perceptions around globalization, sustainable development and corporate citizenship. According to a comprehensive study released this year ("Good News & Bad: The Media, Corporate Responsibility and Sustainable Development"), media understanding – and, most importantly, sustained intelligent coverage – of these issues is a necessary precondition for real progress.

However, there exists a major disconnect: while these issues are arguably the most important of our time, many media watchers – and media representatives themselves – say that the press is generally abysmal at covering critical – but "slow burn" – issues, instead opting for sensational events and "headline-grabbing" news stories.

The big media story of the late 1990s was globalization – or, more accurately, anti-globalization. However, many observers believe that the anti-globalization movement is on its back foot as a result of September 11. Still, the issues remain real and urgent. They demand action, both in terms of coverage and corporate accountability mechanisms.

The media have a critical role to play in the transition towards the objectives of the sustainability movement, and in the fair and intelligent coverage of globalization issues so that citizens can make more informed decisions that influence policy making in positive ways.

For example, the media-sector study revealed that many media appear to be missing one of the biggest stories of our times, that of the progressive undermining of global ecosystems – with profound social and economic consequences. The assumption is that if the issues are real, we will have time to adapt.

But the sudden discovery of the ozone hole shows how even global problems can take us by surprise. There is a trend towards increased coverage of the corporate responsibility movement by media – some leading journalists are beginning to show interest in the "triple-bottom-line" agenda.

In general, European interest in CSR – both in the public mind and in the media – has been sustained at higher levels than in the U.S., Latin America and Asia. Among the issues that have driven the debate: child labour, climate change, and GM crops. One striking aspect of U.S. media coverage has been its "CSR blind spot".

Despite clear evidence that growing numbers of U.S. corporations are embracing CSR, U.S. media have largely ignored the trend – with the exception of widespread coverage of "corporate responsibility" in the wake of many high-profile business scandals. However, recently more U.S. media outlets have been showing interest in larger CSR and development issues, including Fortune, BusinessWeek and The New York Times.

Partly in the defence of media coverage, one of the findings of the sector study was that governments, companies, CSR groups and others interested in responsible globalization do a poor job communicating to media in an effort to raise awareness about pressing issues.

Many editors surveyed expressed a desire for more information. Interestingly, the NGO community is perceived as being much more effective in leveraging the media to communicate their messages. Another important finding was that, editorial coverage aside, media companies as businesses are among the least accountable institutions in the world.

While the sector is arguably poised to become the most powerful institution on earth, accountability mechanisms are generally weak. Few media companies, for example, produce CSR or sustainability reports. However, it is predicted that media will come under growing scrutiny as its influence grows.

And expect the spotlight to pick up other parts of the media ecosystem, too, including advertising agencies, PR firms and lobbyists. Finally, one must consider the impact of "new media". Technology – the Internet in particular – has given a powerful new platform to these agendas.

Niche electronic newsletters and websites convey a wealth of information that might otherwise fail to make it into the mainstream. And powerful search engines help people find them. Thus, new technology has changed the both how – and by whom – news is captured as well as how it is distributed. S hopping has indeed become the great American past time.

The number of consumers participating in this activity on an average day at a large mall overwhelms attendance at even the greatest spectator sports. America's continuing love affair with shopping is great news for retailers. However, "branding" their products and services on the minds of consumers is still a great challenge for them.

The competition for consumer attention and dollars is stronger than ever. Now retailers have to sell harder and smarter to increase brand awareness and market share. Much of this strategy relies on the best medium or combination of media to deliver advertising messages.

But the measure of a medium should include its ability to impact consumer buying decisions as well as reach wide and targeted audiences. An advertising medium needs to help consumers decide where and when to shop, and what to buy. It's important to know some of the drivers that impact shopping behaviour.

For example, almost four out of 10 consumers (38%) shop for the best price. So, it's important for a medium to enable shoppers to easily compare store prices. Almost half (49%) of shoppers go where good sales are. Thus, it's vital for a medium to proficiently bring sales information to the attention of consumers.

The following data shows that newspapers are clearly more favourable among consumers when it comes to various attitudes toward media advertising. This is where newspapers have an opportunity to shore up these strengths and maintain a competitive edge over other media.

In categories, such as service/utility, convenience, credibility and core values, newspapers are more challenged by other media. In these areas newspapers need to closely examine the attributes that are less favoured by consumers, to see where their product needs to be re-shaped to build consumer confidence.

The graphs in this report were created using data culled from NAA's 2000 "How America Shops & Spends" study and NAA's 2000 "Media Usage Study". They provide snapshots of consumer attitudes toward media's role in advertising, service/utility, convenience and credibility. There are also charts illustrating consumer attitudes toward different core values among media.

POWER OF THE PRESS

This year's campaigns are being more widely covered by the media than in any other election in U.S. history. Studies and reports continue to show that more people are tuning in and turning on their televisions, radios, and computers to receive, view, and respond to news about the race and the candidates. The cable news MSNBC reported that, in February, more than 8 million people tuned in to watch a debate between U.S. senators and Democrat presidential candidates Hillary Clinton and Barack Obama; the usual audience for the same time period is only one-tenth that number.

Foreign news agencies are also offering unprecedented, in-depth coverage of the elections to their own and U.S. expatriate markets. According to a recent national survey, current public interest in the campaigns is vastly outpacing comparable periods in previous presidential elections run-ups.

What is fueling this phenomenal interest is the subject to debate. Some experts chalk up the increased public interest in the election to media coverage that is more sensational and dramatic than in past campaign periods. Others contend that the news media's interest in the issues of race and gender because of the Clinton-Obama contest has generated greater levels of interest among a broader number of audiences.

According to historian and author Lee Edwards (a Hoover media fellow), the influence of mass media within any country—the United States included—cannot be discounted. In an article written for *Hoover Digest*, Edwards explains the mass media have become an "essential component of national power, as important to a nation's viability as natural resources, population, economic strength, military might, and political will."

Likewise, in an article published in the Hoover Institution's *Policy Review*, author and international affairs expert Robert D. Kaplan notes journalists and news show executives, because they control the "spin" and have ultimate authority over which stories are presented to the public, possess immense influence and power in today's society—more than the politicians they often cover.

TURN ON AND TUNE IN

In the United States and other industrialized nations, the pervasiveness of digital information has made media more accessible now than ever before. The National Telecommunications and Information Administration (the president's principal adviser on telecommunications and information policy) reports the number of people using broadband Internet connections grew 1,100 per cent between 2000 and 2006.

Broadcast news now cycles endlessly on a variety of 24-hour news channels; talk radio continues to be a rallying point for millions of Americans; and the Internet has spawned an entirely new culture of sites called "blogs" that allow anyone— from professors to athlete, scholars to politicians, stay-at-home moms to celebrities —to post information on myriad subjects.

Compared to only a few years ago, capturing and distributing audio and video files has become relatively simple and inexpensive. Video-hosting websites, such as YouTube, allow people to broadcast amateur videos to a worldwide audience. As a result, once-unknown individuals and groups have been able to reach vast audiences and rocket to fame (or infamy) virtually overnight.

Video clips of the Reverend Jeremiah Wright's fiery and controversial sermons have been extensively broadcast on YouTube, which led to Obama publicly addressing his relationship with the pastor. Activist organizations and individuals, taking advantage of the anonymity of the Internet, often use digital media to coordinate their efforts or broadcast their messages to supporters and the public at large.

Audio or video clips routinely appear on sympathizers' websites with messages from Osama bin Laden and like-minded extremists warning Westerners, non-Muslims, and noncompliant Muslims of impending doom. Print media are increasingly following the digital trend. Many of the world's largest and best-known newspapers and magazines have created online presences, and almost as many use bloggers to scour the net and report on news that the print venue does not allow.

Each year, the number of people who read their morning news from a monitor rather than the newspaper increases. A national report released in late 2007 showed that newspaper subscriptions fell 2.6 per cent during the previous six-month period. Data released by Nielsen/Net Ratings show that the number of visitors to online newspaper sites has increased from 41 million visitors in one month in 2004 to more than 63 million one month at the end of 2007.

PRESSING ISSUES

While print media becomes less utilized, alternate/new media outlets are gaining wider audiences. Coverage of the 2008 presidential primaries illustrates this shift; more people than ever are relying on nontraditional forms of media for news and information about the race and the candidates. A recent nationwide study found that 26 per cent of Americans receive information about the 2008 presidential campaign via the Internet on a regular basis, nearly twice that of the previous (2004) election.

Political candidates increasingly turn to alternative means to reach out to supporters and potential voters. All three top presidential hopefuls have created "MySpace" pages, where supporters can become virtual "friends" of the candidates, follow the campaign trail, download digital campaign images and slogans, and post and receive messages from the candidates and other friends.

These sites garner thousands of hits every day. Many of these new media outlets, especially blogs, openly espouse a particular political view, and attract readers who share similar views.

In contrast, traditional media outlets have generally touted their offerings—editorial content aside—as unbiased, balanced, and fair, a claim often challenged by politicians, pundits, and academics who question the objectivity of any given news source. Accusations of unfairness, interest pandering, preferential politics, and flat-out personal bias are plentiful.

Charges that mainstream media reflect a liberal or conservative slant are common among academics and politicians. Thomas Sowell, a Hoover senior fellow, agrees that many journalists are guilty of "filtering and spinning the news" according their own political agendas or that of the candidates they support. Such bias, according to Sowell, hurts the public that depends on "journalists to tell them the truth as they see it and to offer their honest opinion as to what it means."

Hoover senior fellow Morris Fiorina points out that bias in the media is to be expected because the experiences of journalists are limited to surroundings that are not representative of mainstream America. Thus, according to Fiorina, those providing the information cannot help but offer skewed observations.

CRITICAL MASS MEDIA

In today's media-saturated worlds, news outlets constantly vie for market attention. In an article written for the *Hoover Digest,* American legal history scholar and Hoover media fellow Morton Keller states "journalism is by nature contentious and opinionated. Gossip, sensationalism, and exposure are inescapable tools in the business of inducing readers to read (or viewers to view) media output."

Hoover research fellow and former journalist Robert Zelnick chalks up frivolity in today's news to an overriding shift in priorities. Zelnick believes many news outlets are forced to rely on "the shock value of things" to constantly feed the never-ending news cycle. To this end, news producers have a "tremendous need to break new information when there's no new information to break."

Zelnick argues that the news consumer is not a helpless bystander but rather is in control and, ultimately, responsible for media content. During a conversation with host Peter Robinson on *Uncommon Knowledge,* Zelnick remarked, "I think that the discipline that has to be exerted on the market has to be exerted by individuals who care about news. They have to seek out the better programming, they have to seek out the more erudite coverage, and that's the only type of noise that has any resonance in the rooms where decisions are made."

Chapter 9

Juggling Journalism and Humanism

A MURDER/SUICIDE INVOKES SIX PHILOSOPHIES

In the October 1989 issue of *FineLine,* editor Robin Hughes described a news picture that sparked controversy at the *Louisville Courier-Journal.* In "Anatomy of a Newspaper's Decision," Hughes reported editor and reader reactions to a staff photographer's photograph. The medium-distance picture shows an unidentified victim of a shooting spree by a disgruntled employee of a printing plant. The gunman killed 8 and wounded 12 with his AK-47 military assault rifle before he turned a pistol on himself. The picture by staff photographer Durell Hall Jr. shows a victim lying on his back with arms outstretched.

The image had been described by an editor as "a photo that had to be used" and by a reader as "obscene." The newspaper received more than 580 calls and letters, most opposed to the picture's use on the front page. The victim's family filed a suit "alleging that the newspaper intentionally and recklessly inflicted mental distress on the family and that publication of the photo was an invasion of their privacy."

Several weeks later the suit was dismissed. Although not invoked by name, editors and readers used all six of the major philosophies to support their positions. C. Thomas Hardin, photo and graphics editor, most likely used the Categorical Imperative philosophy to defend his printing of the image. When Hardin saw the picture, he knew that it was "a photo that had to be used. In 25 years, I don't remember a situation in our coverage area where an event was so tragic or public." Hardin continued, "Coupled with the national debate on automatic weapons, the use of the photo was validated." Hardin used the journalism principle of newsworthiness. A dramatic, local tragedy combined with a national concern for gun control, compels the editor to use the picture.

The Utilitarianism philosophy was probably voiced by the editor and two readers as a justification for printing the disturbing picture. Editor David Hawpe said that one of the reasons the picture was published was "the need to confront readers in our community with the full consequences of gun violence." Don Frazier, president of the Graphics Communications International Union, called the picture "obscene" and "was shocked to see it."

He later conceded that "maybe the picture did raise the consciousness of some about gun violence like [the editor] said he meant to do." A widow of one of the victims wrote, "I would want people to remember that my husband died violently- senselessly-and I don't want anyone to forget it." All three positions indicated that the public at large is served by the picture's powerful message.

Editors could have selected a less graphically violent picture for the front page, a largely Golden Mean position. Instead, the Categorical Imperative philosophy most often prevailed. "The photo did what I wanted it to do by showing the reality of what assault weapons are capable of," said Hawpe. "A less graphic photograph would not have been as effective."

Readers opposed to the picture were just as sure that their positions were correct. The Veil of Ignorance was probably invoked by a caller who asked, "How would you feel if it was your relative's body?" Most readers used the Golden Rule philosophy. One caller said, "Showing a body is in bad taste and insensitive to the victim's family and friends." Another man said, "I kept thinking what's this going to do to his family? Why did they have to show his face? They could at least put a shirt or a sheet over him."

Hawpe admitted that some callers "thought we ran the photo just to sell newspapers." Such a reaction comes from believing the publisher is guided only by Hedonistic concerns. The editors should have known that reader protests would be harsh. Six of the requirements for a reader firestorm had been met. The picture came from a staff photographer, was a local story, was printed on the front page, in the morning paper, and showed the victim's physically traumatized body.

Your own reaction to the photograph depends on your own ethical orientation. You might think that the picture is an example of hard-hitting journalism and tells the story well. On the other hand, you may feel that the photograph is much too gruesome to be published in a newspaper. Which reaction is correct?

YOUR ETHICAL PERSPECTIVE

A photojournalist who believes in the principles of telling the truth, objectivity, and newsworthiness will take pictures at the scene no matter how gruesome the subject matter may be. If a journalist relies on professional principles alone, however, there is a danger that a subject might be exploited.

A photojournalist who believes that victims of violence should be left to bear their grief privately without the prying eye of a camera's lens will not take pictures at a funeral or accident scene. If a journalist relies solely on humanistic concerns, however, readers will be denied information that is perhaps in their interest to know.

A photojournalist who believes that the sensitivity of readers should be a first consideration will not publish such pictures. Newspaper readers never complain about gruesome pictures that are not published. However, a journalist runs the risk of filling the publication with "happy talk" features.

An exploration of a photographer's ethical philosophy helps to decide the best course of action during a controversial assignment. Unfortunately, a survey of editors and reporters found that out of 153 respondents, only one referred to a "formal system of ethics outside the profession-Christianity" when responding to ethical situations.

STRESS RESULTS IN BURNOUT

A photographer who shoots too many stressful assignments that conflict with an ethical philosophy runs the risk of catching career burnout. About 14 photographers were included in a survey of Ohio journalists. More than 36% of the 252 journalists sampled "had suffered from burnout, either at present or in the past".

Many excellent and caring photographers have left the profession because of job-related stress. In a *News Photographer* article, Jerry Gay, a 1975 Pulitzer Prize award winner said that there is a need for balance in a photographer's life. A photographer concerned only for the next award-winning picture becomes, according to Gay, "insensitive to other people and their feelings, especially at home.

'They stop being people and start being as mechanical as their winder' ". Editors and photographers should work together to reduce one cause of stress-contests. The importance of photographic competitions for raises and promotions should be greatly reduced. A monthly clip contest in which first, second, and third places are chosen without points being awarded would relieve much of the stress associated with traditional contests.

Such a contest would award a photographer's effort and let others know what content is most respected by members of the profession. In other fields, job stress receives ample publicity with company-sponsored support programs. The NPPA and media organizations should recognize the problems that come from stress and offer support groups to all journalists.

If a particular assignment violates a photographer's ethical code, photographers should have the right to bow out gracefully. Some shooters are best at taking sports or feature assignments. Other photographers have worked for the coroner's office and enjoy driving around town listening to the squawk of a police and fire radio scanner.

A photographer should not have to cover an assignment that makes him or her uncomfortable. No reasonable editor will force a photographer to take a picture that is against a photographer's ethical philosophy. Such a statement should be a part of the NPPA Code of Ethics.

NEW TECHNOLOGICAL CONCERNS

When photographers and editors are asked to list their ethical concerns for the future, a dominant issue is the manipulation of subjects or images through computer, stage managing, or darkroom techniques. If a documentary photograph is altered through computer or more ordinary means, or if a subject is stage managed by the photographer, the publication has a responsibility to its readers to inform them of the manipulation.

Computer manipulation cannot be detected by an unsuspecting and trusting public. A photojournalist who believes in high ethical standards will not manipulate a subject even slightly. For once a minor manipulation occurs, ethical principles fall like a house of cards. Soon the photographer will justify writing words on feet, double printing, lying about a subject's location, and moving pyramids.

A STRENGTHENED ETHICS CODE

In the journalism profession, unlike the legal or medical professions, there is a problem of enforcement. Although a photographer is often criticized and sometimes fired for a blatantly unethical violation, he or she cannot be barred from the profession. The NPPA should have a committee for the ethics of photojournalism.

The committee would sponsor research, publications, lectures and workshops that would help spread positive ethical behaviour.

The committee could also investigate instances of questionable ethics with the power to censure offenders. An unethical photographer could be banned from entering the monthly clip contest for a determined number of months or even banned from the NPPA.

The public could then be informed that such behaviour is unacceptable and not representative of the membership as a whole. The "Code of Ethics" that all members of the NPPA must sign should include additional sentences:

- No photojournalist will intentionally add to a victim's grief for monetary or award-winning gains.
- No photojournalist will intentionally violate a subject's privacy for monetary or award-winning gains.
- No photojournalist will intentionally stage manage a subject or use traditional darkroom or computer technology to alter the meaning of an editorial picture. No editor will use traditional darkroom or computer technology to alter the meaning of an editorial picture.
- No editor will subject a photojournalist to the pressure of forced contest participation.
- No editor will demand that a photographer take a picture that is against that photojournalist's personal ethical code.

The new ethics code should be printed and sent to all members of the NPPA. The time has come for photojournalists to re-dedicate themselves to ethical behaviour by signing the new code. Despite the renewed interest in ethical issues, there is evidence that the profession has a way to go.

In a survey mailed to managing editors of newspapers across America, the respondents were asked to rank order the test elements given to prospective reporters. The top two test concerns were spelling and grammar.

Ethical considerations were at the bottom of the list. Only 15% of the editors reported that "their tests contained material of an ethical nature". Ethical issues need to be higher in the minds of those who hire journalists.

It is the duty of photographers with more experience to advocate ethical ideals to students and those new to the photojournalism profession. It is not enough to say that because ethical behaviour is an individual decision, photojournalism ethics cannot be taught. Ethical behaviour is taught by helping a photographer understand the underlying philosophies that shape a decision, by the ideals contained in a Code of Ethics, and through a discussion of specific situations.

The goal of a photojournalism ethics discussion is not to make right and wrong rules for every conceivable situation. Such a goal is not possible. Real situations are as complex as life itself and the responses are equally infinite. The goal is to help make sure that evaluations of photographers' actions are generally in agreement. When there is disagreement, the conflicting arguments should be based on sound ethical principles.

PHOTOJOURNALISM: A LESSON IN HUMANITY

A photojournalist is a mixture of a cool, detached professional and a sensitive, involved citizen. The taking of pictures is much more than F-stops and shutter speeds. The printing of pictures is much more than chemical temperatures and contrast grades. The publishing of pictures is much more than cropping and size decisions. A photojournalist must always be aware that the technical aspects of the photographic process are not the primary concerns.

A mother crying over the death of her daughter is not simply an image to be focused, a print to be made, and a picture to be published. The mother's grief is a lesson in humanity. If the photojournalist produces a picture without a thought for her tragedy, the lesson is lost. But if the photographer cares for her loss, is made more humane, and causes the readers to share in her grief, photojournalism has reached its highest potential.

Despite its frustrations and low moments, the lesson of humanity is why photojournalism is an extremely rewarding profession. For that reason, photojournalism is worthy of the best thought and actions possible by its participants.

NPPA CODE OF ETHICS

The National Press Photographers Association, a professional society dedicated to the advancement of photojournalism, acknowledges concern and respect for the public's natural-law right to freedom in searching for the truth and the right to be informed truthfully and completely about public events and the world in which we live.

We believe that no report can be complete if it is not possible to enhance and clarify the meaning of words. We believe that pictures, whether used to depict news events as they actually happen, illustrate news that has happened or to help explain anything of public interest, are an indispensable means of keeping people accurately informed; that they help all people, young and old, to better understand any subject in the public domain.

Believing the foregoing we recognize and acknowledge that photojournalists should at all times maintain the highest standards of ethical conduct in serving the public interest. To that end the National Press Photographers Association sets forth the following Code of Ethics which is subscribed to by all of its members:

- The practice of photojournalism, both as a science and art, is worthy of the very best thought and effort of those who enter into it as a profession.
- Photojournalism affords an opportunity to serve the public that is equaled by few other vocations and all members of the profession should strive by example and influence to maintain high standards of ethical conduct free of mercenary considerations of any kind.
- It is the individual responsibility of every photojournalist at all times to strive for pictures that report truthfully, honestly and objectively.
- Business promotion in its many forms is essential, but untrue statements of any nature are not worthy of a professional photojournalist and we severely condemn any such practice.
- It is our duty to encourage and assist all members of our profession, individually and collectively, so that the quality of photojournalism may constantly be raised to higher standards.
- It is the duty of every photojournalist to work to preserve all freedom-of-the-press rights recognized by law and to work to protect and expand freedom-

of-access to all sources of news and visual information.

- Our standards of business dealings, ambitions and relations shall have in them a note of sympathy for our common humanity and shall always require us to take into consideration our highest duties as members of society. In every situation in our business life, in every responsibility that comes before us, our chief thought shall be to fulfill that responsibility and discharge that duty so that when each of us is finished we shall have endeavored to lift the level of human ideals and achievement higher than we found it.
- No Code of Ethics can prejudge every situation, thus common sense and good judgment are required in applying ethical principles

Chapter 10

Research in Photojournalism

The research path in photojournalism ethics is neither straight nor narrow. It is strewn with pitfalls so large that sound methodology alone cannot be your guide. The purpose of this discourse is to help you avoid the primordial ooze that awaits unsuspecting researchers who venture out unprepared into the field of photojournalism ethics.

This is always a dilemma for ethicists and should be for researchers. Your moral judgment may be right for you or your newspaper, but it is wrong to deduce that your moral judgment, or that of your survey pool, is ever right for everyone. It is therefore particularly important to qualify your conclusions based on the demographics of your pool.

This is a particular problem in photojournalism research because often the situation in question will involve more than one person and therefore more than one perspective. The photographer may feel he or she acted in an ethical manner, yet the subject might feel that the photographer acted unethically. The real problem is that they may both be right. This can be a particular problem when you are doing research in areas of print journalism.

When you are judging a photograph or having others judge a photograph, are you judging the ethics of the photographer or the ethics of the picture editor? What policies guide the photographer and who decided to publish the picture in question? Has the photographer been told to photograph everything possible and leave the editing and ethics decisions to the editor? How should a photographer react to this directive? Was the photographer influenced by the actions of the competing newspaper's photographer who took a similar picture?

Can you, the researcher, make a sound decision about the photographer's behaviour when you were not at the scene and have not experienced the mood and external influences that may have guided the photographer to take or not take a certain picture? Does it matter when the picture was taken? Did the photographer make a decision to take the picture rather than to help the subject or did the photographer take the picture after the rescue squad had already arrived?

What about unpublished pictures? If an editor decides that a picture should not run, does that absolve the photographer of questionable ethical practices? Part of the researcher's role is to sort through this maze before bringing the issue forward for debate.

There are numerous examples in the literature of researchers who failed to present adequate information about an event to allow their survey participants to offer an educated opinion.

Are there degrees of ethical behaviour? Is it fair to ask your respondents to judge a particular set of circumstances as highly ethical versus ethical or as a numerical value on an ethical scale of 1-10? Is it even necessary to attempt to quantify your results or can the researcher draw adequate conclusions from answers to open-ended questions?

I don't believe something can be highly ethical or barely ethical and I have never seen an adequate set of definitions which differentiates between degrees of ethical behaviour. If you plan to use such a scale, be certain to include definitions of your categories. Some researchers examine actual events but generalize them within their study or survey.

The question will read "A photographer is photographing the victims of a car accident" or "A photographer crosses a police line." This assumes that all car accidents are the same or that all police departments treat photographers the same way. This type of generalized research can be valid, but the results should not be applied to any specific occurrence, even the one the original questions may have been derived from.

Perhaps we need to include a research docudrama disclaimer, "the study is based on actual events, but."

What influences have had a part in formulating the ethical standards of the participants you are studying and the members of your survey subject pool? If I was raised in the city and you were raised in a rural area; if I were raised as a Catholic and you were raised as a Baptist; if I grew up in Brazil and you grew up in Brooklyn; if I was a child of the 1960s and you were a child of the 1980s; if my father was a policeman and your father was a journalist; how might these external factors influence our ethical views?

Some or all of these, as well as other socioeconomic and demographic statistics, may skew our data. How do we know we have an unbiased pool if we do not even know what things influence our ethical decision-making processes? It may be important to modify how you measure for bias in a survey or interview pool. Do you need to know where your subjects fall on a societal scale of ethical/ unethical behaviour?

Do you need to pretest every subject and then factor their ethics rating against their responses? Although it is not possible to account for every possible cultural bias that your pool may contain, it is your responsibility, as a researcher, subject your study to the greatest possible rigor. The best we can hope for, in my opinion, is to identify issues that should be brought forth for debate and discussion.

Most photojournalists and picture editors receive their ethics training on deadline and may not have the time or historical perspective necessary to appropriately address the complexities of the situation. There is more to ethics than "use your best judgment" although many publications use this directive with their photographers.

The researcher's role is not to hand down judgments from his or her ivory tower, but to lend historical and philosophical perspectives to the arguments, gather data that supports or questions hypotheses, ask new questions about old beliefs, and interpret the results of research as it applies to the existing body of knowledge and the norms of the profession. The ethical behaviour of photographers and the use of their images has been a topic of debate for many years. In 1890, in *The American Annual of Photography and Photographic Almanac,* Henry Harrison Suplee wrote an article entitled "The Ethics of Hand Cameras" in which he advocated resistance to the nuisance of uninvited public snap-shooting and in 1899 in the *American Journal of Photography* there is an article entitled "The Casuistry of Photographic Ethics" that discusses how snap-shooters invaded the privacy of others in public places.

Much of the recent literature is case-study oriented and relies on expert opinion rather than quantifiable data. There have been attempts to research areas involving visual ethics that use traditional communication research methodologies. These studies form a foundation for additional research that will help decision makers formulate policy and judge individual images and events.

The following review provides an insight into the available source materials for practitioners and researchers. They are included for your consideration and to demonstrate potential areas of disagreement when researching this field. One of the best sources for juried research articles on visual ethics is the semiannual *Journal of Mass Media Ethics* that began publication in 1986.

Articles on visual ethics appear regularly and the fourth issue of the Journal, published in Spring/Summer 1987, was a special issue on photojournalism ethics. The author argues that the media has no right to bring moments of private grief to the public forum of the newspaper page or evening newscast. The article points a finger at organizations that award these pictures with the field's highest honours, including the Pulitzer Prize, and the failure of present media codes of ethics to adequately provide adequate guidelines for dealing with grief situations.

The author warns that "if the press does not clean up its act relative to the issue of privacy, the courts may decide to step in at some point in the not-too-distant future. While there is no precedent for the regulation of grief exploitation as an invasion of privacy, the vehicle for doing so already exists in common law privacy. A sub-section of privacy law prevents the publication of private matters, particularly when such publication violates ordinary decencies." I agree with many of the author's complaints and every editor, reporter, and photographer should read this chapter. I am still not convinced, however, that the answer lies in any one code of ethics or any one set of rules.

For example, the author believes that "the pain and tears of those who survived (the 1984 California McDonald's massacre) had no place in the national news" and that "while the massacre at Beirut was news of national and international significance as were those American soldiers whose lives were lost, the funeral services and the tears of family members were not." I would argue that the tears of the living are a more potent weapon against the wrongs of society than the blood of the dead. I would argue that the pictures from California might serve to convince my readers that the importing and manufacturing of semi-automatic weapons should be banned. I would argue that those servicemen belonged to all Americans and that my readers wanted to be at the funeral services and share in that grief, if only through a picture. I would argue that it is usually not the presence of the media at the event as much as it is the irresponsible behaviour of one or more members of the media at the event that causes the problem.

There are, no doubt, photojournalists who invade the privacy of their subject's grief, who make sensitive situations worse and who give the profession a black eye. But there are also many photojournalists who are sensitive, caring human beings, who struggle with the ethics of their profession and have shed many a sympathetic tear after a difficult assignment. Every grief situation is different. No one guideline will cover them all. We should continue to discuss these situations in our papers, and at our universities and seminars in order to establish precedents that will help guide us to be responsible journalists who are sensitive to our subjects and honest with our readers.

This chapter resulted from a participant-observation study at two anonymous major-market television stations for

21/2 months. The writer immersed himself in the day-to-day activities of local television news gathering and dissemination. He conducted in-depth, private, taped interviews with many photojournalists and journalists about their work, their attitudes, and their ethical beliefs.

The thrust of the study was to gain insight into the structure of ethical reasoning. This study provides an interesting look into the psyche of the television news photographer and explores some of the value judgments he or she faces while shooting on location. The researcher attempts to categorize certain patterns of ethical reasoning under such labels as veil of ignorance and utilitarianism and to isolate influences that cause certain behaviour patterns, including an interesting overview of the role of competition, peer pressure, and the role of producers.

This study is a good overview of the issues and provides future researchers with numerous paths to explore. The author concludes that the individuals he interacted with were generally acting in ways they felt were ethical. Researchers who wish to expand on this study should be wary of the participant-observation methodology. Even unethical subjects might tend to act ethically when working under the researcher's microscope.

This chapter is written in response to the study in the Steele chapter just discussed. It is a call for the inclusion of the photojournalist as an equal member of the production team so that his or her voice can be heard in the editorial decision-making processes. The premises of this response are that photojournalists are usually not as well educated through formal schooling as reporters and that managers often treat photographers as pieces of equipment and fail to include them in the ethical decision-making process.

Although these are presented under the subhead "A Few Generalities," it would have been helpful to footnote them to some quantitative data. The recommendations that the author provides to rectify this situation are excellent and should be considered by station managers, regardless of whether their staff demographics parallel the author's profile.

This chapter explores how new technology, particularly pixel manipulation and digital sound sampling, could open the field of journalism to a new genre of electronic ethics violations. The author explores the motivating factors of advocacy journalism, competition, career advancement, and ego gratification through four fictional case studies as driving forces toward the questionable use of these new technologies.

It is interesting that this chapter could now be re-written to replace each of the fictitious case studies with actual ones. This is true not only for the broadcast industry that the author explores but for the still photography industry as well. The once clear distinction between form and substance has indeed been blurred by technology as the author states. I would have preferred if the author had also included a discussion within the article on positive influences that might result from these technologies. It is also important to remember that these are not new ethical dilemmas, it is just becoming technically easier to trip into the existing ethical pitfalls. The article is a little hard to read because of the overabundance of quotes within the text, many of which could have been paraphrased or left for the "Notes" at the conclusion of the article.

This chapter presents the personal feelings, insights, and techniques of a newspaper staff photographer who covers spot news events as a regular part of his job. He discusses the credibility of the media, the perceived insensitivity of photojournalists at news scenes, the importance of news photographs as historical documents and teaching tools, and the societal good that has come the publication of many spot news pictures.

The value of this chapter is that it demonstrates how much thought photojournalists actually give to the ethics of spot news coverage. It belies the hard core, emotionless image of the news photographer and demonstrates that a camera is not always an impenetrable emotional shield. I would argue with the author when he states "I feel that we, the press and photojournalists, have done a very good job in educating the public about our job roles and our viewpoint." In most markets this is still not true. Many newspapers have not developed effective channels of communication for their readers and the educational role of the newspaper ombudsman is often not well defined.

The author attempts to design an early framework for the discussion of ethical problems brought about by the advent of digital retouching technology. Representatives from The Register (Santa Anna, CA), The Chicago Tribune, and USA Today, and three former presidents of the National Press Photographers Association, Gary Settle, C. Thomas Hardin, and Rich Clarkson were interviewed for this chapter.

The subjects agreed that any manipulation of news photographs would be unethical, but disagreed about using the technology on feature art and illustration. The chapter provides a glimpse of how the technology speeds up the production process and how newspapers are using it effectively without ethical violations.

The chapter is a good general discussion of the technology and successfully places a number of ethical questions before the reader. Unfortunately it fails to bring forth specific examples of questionable use of the technology for discussion by the panel of experts. The author briefly allows Rich Clarkson to defend the use of the technology to alter images in National Geographic but fails to solicit opinions from others about this controversial use of the technology.

The author also fails to adequately define the term feature photograph. In some cases it refers to photo illustrations and in others to the traditional definition of found moments. The text is hard to follow because of the constant intermixing of source people. It would have been better to let the reader learn the opinion of each expert rather than space short quotes throughout the chapter. I also question the author's conclusion that, "Now anyone in any department of a newspaper could decide on changes in photographic images by simply having access to the computer system." This statement is an oversimplification of the digital retouching process and not a very realistic scenario.

This interpretive essay explores the subtleties of

deception in photography and photojournalism. The author explores a variety of levels of viewer interpretation and photographic deception and concludes that any degree of direction on part of the photographer, when publishing within a context of expected truth, without a disclaimer, is a clear form of lying.

The essay compares numerous cinematic techniques to the working ethic of the photojournalist and argues that the symbolic implications of the photograph depend in part on what it is a photograph of-not simply on how it looks-and therefore depends on the literal accuracy of the print.

Although I do not totally agree with the author's strict literal interpretation of a photograph being dependent on its context or with his evaluation of the sophistication of the viewer, I do think this is an excellent article that should be required reading in this day of editorial illustrations and posed environmental portraiture. I admire the author's quest for reality, but question whether any picture can meet his standards. Can a two-dimensional picture ever accurately convey reality? Can a camera, even with a normal lens, ever accurately replicate the spatial relationship of object as perceived by the human brain? Can any one moment captured on film convey to a viewer how the subject actually felt? I agree that directing is different than recording but I question whether newspapers should contain cinema verite freeze frames.

This chapter explores the author's personal ethical guidelines for street photography, which he defines as, "photographs made of people on the street or in other public places without the consent of the subject." It discusses the Clarence Arrington photograph by Gianfranco Gorgoni for the New York Times and relates to a photo opportunity that the author prevented from occurring. The essay also explores, through example, the potential misuse and misrepresentation of stock photographs by publications seeking conceptual editorial illustrations.

The author's two examples effectively illustrate his point, but one involves a picture shot in a hospital, which is certainly not "street photography" and also not legal without permission and appropriate releases. The author concludes by stating, "The assumption that you waive your rights to control of your image and declare yourself to be free camera fodder by stepping out of your front door is an arrogance on the part of photographers; it has no legal basis.

The excesses committed in its name are legion, and extreme." This is a statement that invites further research in this important ethical area. The essay recalls the pain that this photograph has caused for the author and why she feels it misrepresents what actually happened. The author also includes comments from the victim's mother who disagrees with her opinion.

There is also discussion within the essay of other famous spot news photos that the author feels misrepresented actual events or that invaded the privacy of the moment and should not have been taken.

It is always important to consider the views of the reader, particularly those present at the scene of such events. It is also important to read the ethical views, as they relate to photojournalism, of a non-joumalist, nonacademic author, for it is all too easy to get lost in the cloak of professionalism.

Many photographs, however, are painful to look at, they are intended to be. I was very familiar with John Filo's photograph as a student at Ohio State University during the early 1970s. On May 4, many of my fellow journalism classmates and I would drive to Kent State to attend annual memorial services for the victims.

That photograph was a meaningful symbol to us. It did not matter that Mary Vecchio was not a student or that she did not know the victim. It only mattered that she was a human being watching another human being who was murdered for what he believed. I am certain that the pain of the author is real. But in this instance, I believe that the picture has served a greater good, and should have been published. The author also notes that the picture was used to advertise a television special on the shootings at Kent State and suggests that "exploitative photographs should never be used to advertise a product." This is an interesting question that deserves further discussion.

This chapter examines a variety of issues that relate to the shooting and publication of grief photographs. It explores the decision-making process in determining if a photo is fit to print, the problem of photographic cliches, the treatment of local versus national and international news events, the victims' right to grieve privately, the effect of privacy law on the publication of grief photos, and how such photos fare in photojournalist competitions. The author does not draw any specific conclusions on these issues other than that every day, photographs must be evaluated anew, with photographers and editors considering the important elements of taste, privacy, and news value. The author attempts to do too much in this overview.

The issues are introduced and sometimes referenced with an applicable quote, but never discussed in sufficient detail to make a contribution to the existing body of knowledge. Over 20 sources are referenced for this six-page study, which makes for a disjointed and difficult to read article. The author offers no interpretation of these numerous quotes and fails to state any hypothesis or conclusions.

This report shows a lot of work, especially from an undergraduate student, but she would have been more successful had she been advised to choose one area to explore within this broad topic.

As the introduction states, "this chapter focuses on the ethical and moral implications of findings from the authors' national survey of television news directors' policies, practices, and perceptions of good/bad news."

The four major research areas in this survey are:

1. Assessment of various mass media in terms of good news and bad news;
2. Assessment of participants' own local television station practices regarding selection of good news and bad news;
3. Whether established policies guide selection and presentation of good and bad news; and

4. Perceptions about balance, newsworthiness, and effects of good news and bad news on television and whether broadcast journalists have an ethical obligation in the daily mix of good and bad news.

The paper follows a traditional research format that includes an introduction, the methodology, findings, and an extensive discussion. As the authors note, the 31% return rate limits the generalizability of the results even though great care was taken to reduce bias within the sample.

The hypothesis of this study is that the ratio of bad news to good news on newscasts is greater than the actual societal ratio of such events and that this raises ethical and moral questions regarding the selection process. Unfortunately, the study revealed a large group of gatekeepers who do not consider these categories during the selection process and many who objected to the categorization of news along a good-bad scale.

The authors dismiss this view as reactive or defensive, but I think it deserves further study and discussion. I would have liked the authors to define the terms good and bad as they relate to news within this study.

Is it good news if interest rates fall or does it depend on whether you are a borrower or an investor. I think we could agree on some events that are universally good or bad, but that we would also find a large number of news events that are universally ambiguous.

The question this study begets, which I am not prepared to answer, is whether researchers should apply quantitative methodologies to qualitative ethical questions.

This study surveyed top-level management at 49 large-circulation consumer magazines in six areas of potential ethical conflict. The areas are:

- Freedom to choose editorial content without pressure from the advertising staff;
- Acceptability of set up photos or composite or fictional characters;
- Acceptability of gifts, tickets, and travel;
- Allowable outside activities for the editorial staff;

- Entering of nonjoumalistic contests; and
- Acceptable means for obtaining a story.

The author notes, based on the survey results, that editors differ greatly in their interpretation of what is ethical and that "arriving at any kind of a common code for magazines with different purposes may be difficult."

The participants in this survey were promised anonymity. We know that news magazines were not included in the sample, but otherwise, we do not know anything about content or demographics, other than a rough estimate of average circulation. Without this information it is hard to judge the relevance of the data unless we are willing to assume that a uniform code of ethics should apply to all large consumer magazines regardless of content, communication goals, and audience demographics.

The answer to one question, however, should cause some raised eyebrows among visual communicators. When asked; "Do you ever publish photographs that are set up without labeling them as photo illustrations?"; only 50% of the participants answered "No, we only use actual shots." It is hard to interpret what this really means because that was the only negative response among the multiple choice answers. There should have been an answer "no" for people who use illustrations and label them correctly.

In any case, 50% of the respondents use illustrations and do not label them as illustrations. Whether this is 100% of the publications that use illustrations as the survey reports or some smaller percentage, it is still a lot of people abusing the trust of their readers. The author conducted interviews with 11 photographers, editors, and educators and complied them to formulate a discussion of ethical issues photojournalists face with the emergence of electronic still cameras and digital imaging.

The discussion focuses around five question areas outlined by the author:

1. Will manipulation of images increase?
2. Will still photographers become disillusioned with their profession and with editors?

3. Will still photographers have less input into what type of image appears in the paper?
4. Will the public's trust in newspapers decrease as manipulation of photos increases?
5. What will be the legal status of images that exist only in computers?

The article includes an explanation of the technology and discussion based on controversial examples of its use as well as theoretical areas of potential ethical conflict.

This is an excellent discussion by people in the field, many of whom already has access to the equipment, and has had to make ethical decisions about the extent to which they would use it.

The author concludes his article with a series of disturbing questions: "If the leading experts cannot agree on what is or is not ethical, what constitutes acceptable manipulation or enhancement? How will they be able to set standards for the next generation when virtually all news gathering will be done electronically? The experts should draw the battle lines now, because the future is here . . ." I believe this is the wrong attitude for our profession to take. The battle lines were drawn long before digital imaging and long before electronic still cameras. They were drawn long before the 35mm camera ever became the tool of the photojournalist. Technology does not create new ethical issues.

The reader does not care if you spend 2 days or 2 minutes formulating a lie. It is still a lie and still a violation of their trust. The standards we have set and the issues that we argue will continue to evolve based on our actions and societal norms. There is no need to return to the mountain for a new set of commandments.

The Association for Education in Journalism and Mass Communication is an international association comprised of educators, universities, and affiliates. The organization's annual convention is an excellent forum for the discussion of issues in the field. During the past 20 years, many papers have dealt with the issue of visual ethics.

The following list includes those papers that were sponsored or cosponsored by the Visual Communication Division or the Radio-Television Journalism News Division. More information may be available from the authors or from the Association's national office at the University of South Carolina. Many sessions have been recorded and are available on cassette tape.

This study of the ethics of staged news photos was based on a survey of photojournalists, managing editors, television newsmen, and a sample of the upper strata of the public as measured by educational attainment. Participants were asked to rate the behaviour of the photographer in each of 10 examples (all versions of actual events) as either definitely unethical, doubtful, or no ethical violation.

The author found the four groups to be in "remarkable agreement" with the most pronounced agreement occurring at the extremes of the ethical-unethical continuum. Disagreement was greatest in those situations that involved hard news and that also were "somewhat complex."

If everyone who has done research on visual ethics since 1961 had taken the time to read the introduction of this chapter, we would have a stronger foundation of data to build upon. Therefore, I take the space to quote the first paragraph of the article.

The study of professional ethics in a systematic fashion poses a number of formidable problems. First, the notion of ethics itself is subjective and, in a marked degree, dependent upon notions of morals and of law. Second, the subject impinges heavily upon personal moral values and the translation of these values into professional conduct, where a number of additional, and sometimes competing, values are encountered.

Third, an ethic-defined as the rule governing application of personal and social morals to a professional act-has as its basis the moral values of society, which in turn, are constantly shifting. Thus, it can be said that, for the purposes of systematic study, the professional ethic is not independent of other variables, and must be treated as a manifestation of a rather complex set of values. Although the case situations in this study are, hopefully, no longer applicable, the methodology and philosophy of this research are as sound today as they were 30 years ago.

This comparative study of ethical values is based on results from a random sample survey of National Press Photographers Association members who work at publications and people listed in the Austin, TX telephone directory. Participants were asked to judge 19 hypothetical situations as either highly ethical, ethical, unethical, or highly unethical.

The study included questions of privacy, decency, faking, dispositions of negatives in court proceedings, legality versus ethics, acceptance of freebees, and the presence of photographers affecting news events.

In 17 of the 19 situations presented the difference between the photojournalists and the public exceeded the .05 significance level set for the study.

There are three things that bother me about this study. First, what is the difference between ethical and highly ethical or unethical and highly unethical? Second, some of the situations lack specific details that I think would effect the response of the participants.

For example, situation 15 states, "Photographer ruins one of two remaining frames of film in another photographer's camera." What was the reason for this bizarre occurrence and how did it occur? And situation 18 states, "Photographer decides not to photograph hobo killed by train, despite being sent out to do this task."

Did the photographer feel that the scene was too gruesome or that it wasn't newsworthy? His reason for this action would be important to know. Third, the author states in his interpretation of results that, "Many (photographers) shifted responsibility for their actions to the editor by saying they had a job to do, or it was the editor's decision. This is not valid reasoning."

At many papers this is very valid reasoning if the photographer desires to keep his or her job. It may not be ideal, but it is reality. Although 17 of the 19 cases showed a statistically significant difference among the two groups of respondents, it is important to realise that about half of these differences occurred on the same side of the axis and were merely a difference in the degree of ethical or unethical behaviour that the respondents perceived.

The author would have been well served by reviewing the Wilcox study prior to re-inventing the wheel. An important vehicle for educating students about visual ethics is the college textbook. The following list includes many of the textbooks used in visual communication survey courses and beginning photojournalism courses at accredited schools of journalism and technical schools around the country.

It includes visual and written examples and a discussion of the photographer's and editor's viewpoints. I do disagree with Hoy's definition of the "cornerstone of journalism ethics," within the text and question whether we, as educators, should teach ethics to students with the degree of certainty that the following selection implies.

The photojournalist's role on the scene is dictated by the cornerstone of photojournalistic ethics-to get the picture despite any obstacles. In general, it is not the photojournalist's job to decide whether to photograph or not. He or she is just too close to the drama and tragedy to know whether the photograph is in bad taste or is in reality an important news story that the public should know about.

Later the editor (or the publication's attomeys, if need be) can decide on whether the photo is invasion of privacy, libel, or even 'in good taste.' Yet, often the first thought of the beginning photojournalist-and rightfully so-is to sympathize with the subject and to decide not to photograph. But the responsibility is clear-if it is news, a photojournalist has the obligation to report it regardless of personal reaction.

Here the old adage 'shoot first and question afterwards' is a good policy. I am aware that this is the policy at many newspapers, but there has been sufficient argument over its merits to question whether it should be stated as an accepted policy throughout the field to photojournalism students.

There may, at some time, be an updated version of this book. Amphoto had planned publication in 1986 and again in 1987, but both were canceled. There is a 1983 printing, which is also listed as the fourth edition.

MacDougall's book was published by Journalistic Services, Inc. in 1971. It is a shockingly honest discussion of ethical considerations in news photography. This book is an excellent historical reference, based entirely on case studies. There is commentary from many of the journalists who took the pictures and were involved in the picture editing and publication decisions.

It is valuable to know from whence we came and it is all here-lynchings, disasters, Lindbergh, and wars. I recommend checking the library or used book stores if you are not familiar with this book.

Image Ethics, from Oxford University Press, 1988, provides a much more theoretical approach to the issue of ethics and also includes an excellent annotated bibliography. Most of this book deals with film, but the issues are easily paralleled in television and still photography. Most of the chapters confront the moral responsibility of preconceived visual representation, but public photography and documentary film-making are also discussed.

As you might expect from a compilation, this book wanders amidst the amorphous realm of moral convictions. Some of the chapters leave the reader feeling that artistic license supersedes moral responsibility, while others share with the reader the deepest sense of ethical consideration.

"The photojournalism ethics problem seems to be a lot deeper than we feared," said John Long, NPPA's chairman of the Ethics & Standards Committee, after the audience of photojournalists, editors, managers, and educators were asked for a show of hands to reflect how many of them believe that they currently work with, or have worked with, peers who routinely cross ethical boundaries. "The show of hands was a scary thing to see."

The ethics panel, part of the programme offered this week by NPPA at the Photojournalism Summit and Multimedia

Immersion programme, included Long and Dr. Julianne Newton, a visual journalism professor at the University of Oregon, and Kenny Irby, the visual journalism group leader and diversity programme director for The Poynter Centre for Media Studies in St. Petersburg, FL.

The panel was moderated by Jack Zibluk, NPPA's vice president and a professor of photojournalism at Arkansas State University. Long is recently retired from a three-decade career at the Hartford Courant and has been NPPA's voice on photojournalism ethics for decades.

"We need to examine the ethical issues involved in 'photo opportunities,' in picture editing and design, and in graphics," Newton said. "Images affect memory, and behaviour, and values. Images affect what you believe about yourself, about others, and about the world out there. Images are powerful, and visual ethics is about the appropriate use of powerful images."

For these and other reasons, Long responded, journalism is based on accuracy, including the accuracy of images. "If you can't use the picture as it is," Long said, "don't use it."Long, who has watched the ethical and unethical practices of photojournalists and editors over many years, believes that ethics has now become a huge and still-growing issue for the profession.

"Editorial control is being lost," Long said. "The problems we're having now are not just ethical violations by photojournalists. Now there are editors, designers, and others who are altering pictures. Photographers who alter photos get fired. But we're seeing editors and others who alter pictures, and there are no repercussions."

Long cited People magazine's recent decision to digitally alter a cover photograph from the Virginia Tech massacre to remove what they believed may have been the genitals of one of the shooting victims, when it fact the item was part of a tourniquet the student applied to stop the gunshot wound's bleeding. The decision to alter the image was made by People's top editors. "If they can't use the picture 'as is,' then don't use it. Use another picture," Long said.

Irby told the audience that there are two major concerns in the ethics decision making process. "Diversity, are we being accurate and inclusive about where we point cameras, and who we include and who we exclude; and journalistic integrity: are we as journalists keeping our own confidentiality?

"But the greatest challenge we're facing now is the arrogance of journalism," Irby said. "We're dealing with circumstances that require a new set of dynamic responses now that we're dealing with editors who are making these decisions to alter pictures." "Ego gets in the way of true ethics education," Newton added.

"The digital world has shown the public how easy it is for someone to manipulate what we show them. Studies have shown that college students today are less concerned about altering images because, to them, 'all images are subjective.' We need to find a way to enhance the intensity of how we educate the public [about ethics]. Professional journalists have the duty to put forth the best truth they can provide."

FAKING IMAGES IN PHOTOJOURNALISM

That the camera cannot lie is true only in the sense that the images it captures must have existed in one form or another at some particular time. But it is not always clear if those images have been manipulated in some way to alter or to stage an event which never happened.

We are familiar with historical photos that have been retouched to include or exclude political figures. We are less familiar with the potential of new technologies for falsifying images, particularly those that appear in newspapers and magazines. The following chapter introduces this topic and raises important ethical questions.

There were the huge printing shops with their sub-editors, their typography experts, and their elabouredately equipped studios for the faking of photographs. Photojournalism, photography that accompanies stories intended for newspaper and magazine readers, has a long and cherished tradition of truthfulness.

The faking of photographs, either through stage direction by the photographer or through darkroom manipulation, unfortunately, also has a long tradition. As a result, Pulitzer Prize-winning images, photographs that have moved people to action, and pictures that have been hailed as beautiful humanistic documents filled with hope and joy, have been questioned.

Consequently, their impact has been diminished by charges of photographic faking. Such accusations are usually easily proven unsubstantiated and are the exception rather than the rule for photojournalism images. However, computer technology puts photographic faking on a new level of concern as images can be digitized and manipulated without the slightest indication of such trickery.

Early photographic history is filled with artists turned photographers who set-up situations with models and backdrops and made elabouredate compositions from several negatives In 1857 Oscar Gustave Rejlander produced a picture with a documentary quality, "Street urchins tossing chestnuts." The photograph showed a child who looked up at a chestnut suspended in the air. Stopping a moving object in mid-air was a technical feat impossible with the slow film and lenses in use at that time. Rejlander produced the effect through the use of a fine thread. In that same year, he also made the controversial "The Two Ways of Life," an elabouredate story of a young man's decision to follow the good or evil way of life. Thirty separate negatives were combined to produce the single image.

Later, Rejlander denounced the process in a letter to H. P. Robinson, another early photographer known for his composite photographs. Rejlander wrote, "I am tired of photography-for-the-public, particularly composite photos, for there call be no gain and there is no honour only cavil and misrepresentation."

A curious and little mentioned photographic genre, spirit photography, had its beginning a decade later. Spirit photography, capturing on film a likeness of a deceased person, was proven through photographic experts as double exposure fakes. Nevertheless, many people, including Sir Arthur Conan Doyle, a strong advocate for the Spiritualism movement, believed in the truthfulness of the images. During World War I, many photographs were faked for propaganda purposes. For example, newspapers showed faked photographs of Kaiser Wilhelm cutting off the hands of babies.

April Fool photographic fakes were popular in newspapers during the first half of this century. Curtis MacDougall in his book, *Hoaxes*, details several instances where newspapers published such images as giant sea creatures, Viking ships, and a man flying by his own lung power. The Madison, Wisconsin *Capital-Times* went so far as to publish a photographic composite of the Capitol dome collapsing in 1933.

More serious fakes involved political campaigns. A 1928 campaign picture of Herbert Hoover and his running mate was faked because Hoover refused to pose with the vice-presidential candidate, Charles Curtis. *Life* magazine revealed a composite photograph of a Maryland Democrat running for office that looked like he was conferring with a Communist leaflet. He lost the election.

THREE FAMOUS PHOTOGRAPHS

Perhaps most troubling to the reputation of photojournalists and their photographs are reports that well-known and deeply moving photographs have been directed by the photographers.

Three famous photographs, Robert Capa's moment of death of a Republican soldier during the Spanish Civil War, Arthur Rothstein's skull on parched South Dakota land, and Joe Rosenthal's raising of the American flag over Iwo Jima, have all been reported to be photographic fakes. Based on misunderstanding or professional jealousy, these three historical images reproduced more times than probably any other photographs, have a cloud of uncertainty that surrounds each photographer's reputation.

Published in *Life* magazine in 1937, Robert Capa's photograph shows in one instant the suddenness and loneliness of an anonymous soldier's death. It has been suggested that the photograph was either a chance occurrence by the photographer shooting blindly, or it was staged for the benefit of the camera. Capa, whose motto was, "If your pictures aren't good you aren't close enough," would have been dismissed as a "one-shot wonder" had the "moment of death" photograph been the only image in this portfolio.

However, Capa produced extraordinary war-time documents throughout his career. He photographed in China, on the beaches of Normandy, in Israel, and finally in Vietnam, where he was killed by a land mine. Capa consistently produced images with strong emotional impact and high technical expertise. He was not a photographer who needed to fake a photograph in order to enhance his career.

Arthur Rothstein, a documentary photographer for the Farm Security Administration during the American Dust Bowl era, was accused of photographic faking because he moved a skull he found on parched South Dakota pasture land ten feet. The skull was labeled a prop by Republican politicians who used the Rothstein pictures to attack the credibility of the Democratic administration. The Democrats, it was argued, were using photographs to make environmental conditions look worse than they actually were in order to pass controversial legislation through Congress. Rothstein was accused of traveling around the country with his suitcase, his camera, and his skull. He denied the charge and regretted the controversy for the rest of his career.

Rothstein produced several memorable photographic documents including the classic Dust Bowl photograph of a father walking through a storm with his two young sons. He received more than 50 photography awards and has written several books on the subject of photojournalism and documentary photography. Given such a reputation, it is difficult to imagine him packing a skull with his clothes and cameras.

Associated Press photographer, Joe Rosenthal, made three photographs atop Suribachi, a Japanese observation post on the island of Iwo Jima during World War II. His first picture became the most reproduced photograph in history and won for him a Pulitzer Prize. His third photograph became the source of accusations that the first picture had been set-up. The first picture is the image most remembered. It shows six soldiers erecting a large, American flag on a long, diagonally slanted flagpole. Rosenthal's third shot shows 18 soldiers smiling and waving for the camera under that same flag.

The confusion over the authenticity of the famous photograph resulted from Rosenthal's casual response to a correspondent back at Guam. The reporter congratulated Rosenthal on the image and then asked if it was posed. Thinking that the writer meant the third picture, Rosenthal admitted that it had been set-up. Speaking of the famous picture, he rightly argues that "Had I posed the shot, I would, of course, have ruined it. I would . . . have made them turn their heads so that they could be identified for AP members throughout the country."

Writing of the Rosenthal image, picture editor, Harold Evans in his book *Pictures on a Page,* notes that "no genius could have posed the picture if he had spent a year in a studio with lights and a wind machine." Lucky for photojournalism, Rosenthal did not carry a wind machine to the top of Iwo Jima.

TECHNOLOGICAL THREAT TO INTEGRITY

There is currently a serious threat to the integrity of photojournalism images. Computer technology allows individuals to manipulate photographs to such an extent that alterations cannot be detected. As has been stated, such sleight-of-hand is not new. Those who believed in the Spiritualism movement believed in the photographs as well.

Those who were unsophisticated as to the double exposure and composite tricks that could be accomplished by a darkroom technician were fooled by the April Fool and political photographs. Those who are cynical and perhaps professionally envious believe that Capa convinced a buddy to act as if he were being killed by a bullet in the head, Rothstein carried a skull in his suitcase, and Rosenthal directed the flag-raising photograph. Computerized digital retouching involves more than suspicions about a photograph's authenticity. Companies such as Scitex, Hell Graphic Systems, and Crosfield have computers that can be used by newspaper, magazine, and book publishers to manipulate photographs that were originally intended to be classic, documentary accounts of real events.

The *A Day in the Life* books of America, Australia, and Canada have cover photographs that were manipulated by the computer. Likewise, the unsuccessful *Picture Week* magazine fused two different photographs in tabloid magazine style of Nancy Reagan and Raisa Gorbachev to portray a misleading attitude of friendliness.

National Geographic magazine, long known for its reputation of photojournalism excellence, used the Scitex computer digitizer on two recent occasions. On a cover story of Egypt, pyramids were squeezed together to fit the cover's vertical format. A picture story on Poland contained a cover photograph that combined an expression on a man's face in one frame with a complete view of his hat in another picture. Both cover images were altered without a hint of possible detection and without a note to readers that such manipulation was performed.

Throughout photography's history, an unsuspecting public has been fooled by manipulated images. What is of concern to modern media watchers is the justifications used to alter images through computer technology - not tile fact that such alterations can be published without detection. Rick Smolan, a producer of the *Day in the Life* books defends his use of the computer to alter the cover photographs.

"We are very proud of the fact that we were able to use this technology to make the covers more dramatic and more impressive," Smolan said. Likewise, Rich Clarkson, director of photography at *National Geographic* when the pyramid and Poland covers; were faked, said he had no ethical problem with combining two photographs into a single cover picture, although "some publications could start abusing."

Many journalists disagree with the practice. Jack Corn,

director of photography for the *Chicago Tribune* says that such manipulation is "ethically, morally and journalistically horrible." Robert Gilka, former director of photography at *National Geographic* magazine says simply that significantly manipulating images is "like limited nuclear warfare. There ain't none."

Photographs, particularly those used as accurate and trustworthy accounts of a significant event by respected publications, are our best hedge against the threat of devious editors and special interest groups who want to change truth and history. If the manipulation of photographs is accepted for any image, the public will naturally doubt all photographs and text within all publications.

Before computers were popular, the famous photojournalist, W. Eugene Smith said, "Let truth be the prejudice." Truth is the guiding principle - not layout efficiency, not magazine cover eye-catching ability, not political persuasion, but truth. When truth is the prejudice, photographs, and the stories behind them, can be easily defended and are a source for humanistic concern and inspirations.

Chapter 11

Photojournalism and the Internet

Ever since it became practical to print photographs on newsprint, photography has been an integral part of news media. Rhetoric can be slanted, quotations can be misrepresented, but (ostensibly) photographs were objective and reliable. At the same time, photojournalism (and photography as a whole) was solely the province of elite professionals, since most citizens did not have the equipment to take pictures—or, if they did, they had no means of disseminating them. Recent advances in technology, in particular the popularization of the World Wide Web, have challenged this authority from both sides.

Free and simple-to-maintain blog software has allowed anyone who cares to be heard by the world, amplify individuals' criticisms of foibles of the mainstream media. At the same time, citizen journalism of a variety of flavours has proliferated as ordinary people become accustomed to taking and uploading images of events that they witness. For the most part, mainstream media outlets seem to have adjusted to these trends, but what do they mean for the practice of photojournalism?

While photojournalism online may have some troubling consequences for ethics and privacy, overall it appears that the Internet's effect on photojournalism will improve the practice if not the profession. Photographic authority before the Internet because photographs are a mechanical reproduction, they have traditionally been accorded much more authority than other types of images such as drawings or paintings. According to an 1844 ad for the first book on photography, photographs "contain nothing but the genuine touches of Nature's pencil". A more modern proverb states that "the camera never lies."

Of course, this has never really been the case. Photographers choose when and where to take a picture; they decide how to crop it; they choose what lenses and lighting effects to use. Perhaps most importantly, they (or their editors) write the caption, fixing the meaning of a photograph that might otherwise be open to interpretation. Nevertheless, photographs were seen as more objective than purely human-mediated art, so they were favoured by news organizations. The increasing capability and use of photo manipulation software have decreased the authority of photojournalism in the public eye. The first publicly-acknowledged manipulation was the repositioning of one of the pyramids on the cover of National Geographic in 1982.

The editor defended the photo modification as a "retroactive repositioning of the photographer," but the act was nevertheless very controversial among the photojournalist community. Among the general public, Time's treatment of O.J. Simpson's mug shot in 1994 was one of the most well-known and contentious manipulations of a photograph. Time editors made the picture "darker and out of focus," bringing to mind "the stereotype of the darker, more sinister African-American as criminal".

Given the already racially-tinged nature of the case, for many onlookers this action confirmed that Simpson's arrest was the result of racism. As numerous incidents over time have show the difference cropping, manipulating, or otherwise enhancing photographs can make in how they are interpreted, the public no longer sees the authority of the photograph as inviolate.

THE WORLD WIDE WATCHDOG

The growth of the Internet has contributed to public skepticism about photojournalism. Numerous online communities, populated by thousands of professionals and amateurs, have sprung up around photoshopping, including

Fark.com, Worth1000, Something Awful, and many others. The contests that these communities sponsor, which reward realistic (and surrealistic) photo modifications, have increased public awareness of the power of Photoshop and the unreliability of images.

This skepticism has also found an outlet in the blogosphere, as Internet denizens critique inaccuracies in the mainstream media and out suspect photographs as fakes. One of the most infamous instances of this was the "Burning Building" photograph scandal during the 2006 Israeli-Lebanon conflict. Reuters circulated a photo of Beirut showing thick smoke billowing from "burning buildings destroyed during an overnight Israeli air raid," according to the caption. The problem? The smoke showed a pattern that clearly showed that it had been modified—sloppily—with Photoshop's "clone" tool.

Some bloggers also pointed out inconsistencies in the arrangement of the buildings on the ground with other Beirut photographs, suggesting that they also had been doctored. After this controversy billowed through the Internet, Reuters issued a "Picture Kill" and took the photograph down. However, the "Burning Building" photograph remained a hot topic as bloggers wondered why such an obviously doctored picture was able to get past the Reuters editors. Was it incompetence? Deadline pressure?

Or a sign of the purported left-wing, anti-Israel bias of the media? From an outsider's perspective, there was no way to tell—short of one's personal political ideology. Neither conclusion makes mainstream photojournalism look particularly appealing, however. The long-term effect of the presence of the Internet on the mainstream media's credibility is unclear. By giving a pulpit to anti-media commentators, it is quite likely to further increase the public's skepticism. It is all but certain that there will be future cases of photojournalists faking photos and other indiscretions, and each one takes the media's credibility down a notch.

However, one might hope that news outlets, aware that the blogosphere is watching, may tighten up their quality controls so that their photographic work becomes more accurate than before the Internet became popular. While reducing the number of actual photo doctoring incidents might not have much effect on audiences' perception of media bias, it would still be a positive result.

Grassroots photojournalism The Internet has also facilitated the distribution of ordinary citizens' photography, creating the possibility that their work may soon compete with traditional media outlets' photo essays. A myriad of Internet companies offer services allowing users to upload photographs and show them to the public.

One of the most popular photo hosting services, Flickr, has an online community-type feature called "pooling" which makes it easy for different users to group photos related to a particular interest or element. This has been used to bring together tens, even hundreds of different users' photos of events such as Hurricane Katrina's aftermath or the Day without an Immigrant protests.

This decentralized model allows amateurs to create an exhaustive record of an important event, accessible to anyone with an Internet connection, with little effort required from any one user. Not all amateur photojournalism is this decentralized, of course. The convergence of blogs and digital photography has allowed almost anyone to create and publish his or her own photo essays.

Most subjects are personal in nature, such as documentation of a birthday party or family vacation. (One might question calling these "photo essays," but that says more about the topicality restrictions of traditional journalism than about what a photo essay can or cannot be.) However, many photography enthusiasts choose to publish on broader topics with important social implications.

One example is Xeni Jardin's blog which documents culture and politics in Guatemala and the Himalayas. At the far end of the amateur photojournalist centralization scale are institutions such as Indymedia, which is a collabouredative, left-wing citizen journalism project contributed to by socially-minded individuals worldwide.

Founded to cover WTO protests, Indymedia relies on citizen journalists for its content. Anyone can upload photographs and other media to the Indymedia gallery, along with articles to accompany them, where they are visible to anyone; editors determine which photographs and articles appear on the Indymedia main page. Although decidedly non-mainstream and anti-corporate, Indymedia is respected by many on the left wing, especially for its international and protest movement coverage.

FROM THE MASSES TO THE MAINSTREAM

In many cases, the mainstream media has also encouraged its audience's participation in photojournalism. This phenomenon became apparent during the July 7 bombings in London when cameraphones "provided some of the most intense and immediate imagery from the scenes" (Dunleavy). Since professional photojournalists had little to no access to the blast sites afterward as security officials fenced them off, many news outlets relied instead on amateurs' images to illustrate news about the attacks.

Furthermore, since some of the victims also had cameraphones, they were able to document the moments after the bombing—images a professional photojournalist would never have been able to capture. Some of the bombing witnesses had embraced alternative copyright licensing schemes that gave them an additional advantage over professional photographers: "Stacey's picture was widely distributed, including onto the front pages of many newspapers, in part because he put it out under a Creative Commons license allowing anyone else the right to use it in any way provided they attribute the picture to its creator".

Typically, newspapers cannot use a photograph unless they get explicit permission from the copyright owner, which takes time and money. Because many Internet denizens have an interest in the free culture movement and use Creative Commons licensing, however, they can preemptively state specifically how they want their photographs used and thus quicken the dissemination of their work.

All of these factors led to enthusiastic collabouredation of mainstream news outlets and cameraphone-wielding citizens in the hours and days after the London bombings. Since the bombings, increasingly media outlets have explicitly called for viewers to send in photographs or other contributions to stories, especially for breaking news.

On the BBC's website, many news articles have a notice at the bottom: "Are you in the area? Have you seen anything? If you have any information you would like to share with the BBC you can do so using the form below..." Meanwhile, Yahoo has created "You Witness News" to handle user uploads related to sports and entertainment and Reuters is working on a "service devoted entirely to user-submitted photographs and video" which would pay users whose work was distributed to Reuters' clients. It is clear that the London bombings will not be the last major event to be covered via cameraphone.

The mass conversion of ordinary citizens into photojournalists, while potentially democratizing, could have some negative consequences. Amateur photographs pose the same credibility hazards as professional photojournalist work; news outlets will have to find ways to accurately determine whether or not a submitted image has been doctored. In addition, amateurs do not share professional.

While the BBC includes with its request for submissions an admonishment to readers not to "endanger yourself or others, take any unnecessary risks or infringe any laws," a citizen with a cameraphone is still prone to unthinkingly engage in ethically questionable practices as they document the scene around them.

This was seen in the citizen response to the July 7 bombings, when some passerby "vied to try and take pictures of the worst victims" with their cameraphones: Jardin compared [their] behaviour to the paparazzi that chased Princess Diana before her fatal car crash and noted that the ethical issues raised then are now applicable beyond just professional photographers.

"These are ethical issues that we once thought only

applied to a certain class of people who had adopted the role of news as a profession," Jardin said. "Now that more of us have the ability to capture and disseminate evidence or documentation of history as a matter of course those ethical issues become considerations for all of us." Unlike the professional paparazzi, there is no financial incentive for citizen journalists to produce gruesome or scandalous content.

Nevertheless, like rubberneckers on the highway, it is easy for people to let morbid curiosity get the better of them. Perhaps an unwritten "Golden Rule" regarding appropriate content will develop as more and more amateur ethical breaches become publicized. However, changing societal mores is a much slower process than editing a news organizations' ethics protocol.

The sheer ubiquity of potential photographers, while good for documenting news anywhere as it happens, also poses a general privacy threat. The same technology that allows people to identify criminals or document abuses of authority can be turned on ordinary citizens.

Kids snap cellphone pictures at parties and instantly put them on the Web; fans who nab photos of unsuspecting celebrities share them on celebrity-watch sites. The guy in the car next to you is leaning out of his window, taking a video that he later uploads to a video site where it could be seen by dozens or hundreds of people — maybe even millions.

(Kornblum) Amateur photographs of individuals in compromising situations, if released to the Internet and popularized, may do significant harm to their targets. An example is the case of a woman in South Korea now known as "Dog Poop Girl." Her dog defecated in a subway car and despite another passenger's offer of a tissue, she refused to clean it up. This would have been an unextraordinary if antisocial event except that one of the passengers took a picture of the girl on his cameraphone and uploaded it to the Internet.

The picture became a sensation in South Korea: "within days, her identity and her past were revealed. Requests for information about her parents and relatives started popping up and people started to recognize her by the dog and the bag she was carrying" (Krim). Eventually the woman was so stigmatized that she withdrew from university.

Perhaps most significantly, while most commentators on the incident thought that digging up "Dog Poop Girl's personal information was inappropriate, few criticized the act of taking and uploading the photograph itself. It seems that shaming people for bad behaviour is an acceptable use of the Internet—in this case it just went too far.

Incidents like these are likely to become more common. Half of the cell phones sold worldwide in 2006 were cameraphones, and analysts predict that cameraphones will make up 95% of the US cell phone market within four years (Corner). This trend could have a devastating effect on those who adhere to a traditional conception of privacy. Just the knowledge that cameras are everywhere...changes behaviour. "It forms an environment in which the assumption that there's a camera around is more and more part of your daily awareness.

This assumption you're being watched internalizes surveillance." The result: super-self-consciousness. (Kornblum) Yet it seems that there is a generation gap in how people have been responding to the increasing omnipresence of cameras. While older people are more likely to cover their faces or respond negatively when a camera is present, young people typically "wave, (flash) a peace sign, stick out their tongue or just yell 'Hey'" (Kornblum).

Many experts attribute young people's comfort with being photographed to their adolescent desire for attention and self-expression. However, since for people this age ubiquitous cameraphones and security cameras are the norm, it is unclear whether they will develop the same kind of privacy concerns as previous generations when they grow older. If not, the proliferation of amateur photographers will not have such a self-conscious, chilling effect; people will still do embarrassing things and just care less who is watching.

Generally speaking the public has the upper hand in getting pictures of news events, particularly ones that are fast-breaking or in restricted locations, because photojournalists simply can't be everywhere all the time. At the same time, the affordability of high quality digital cameras and web publishing has made it easier for aspiring photobloggers to produce artistic, narrative-style photo essays as well. So what is left for a professional photojournalist to do?

First, it should be noted that the emergence of the Internet and technological innovations has benefited professional photojournalists, too. Digital photography allows, for example, "a newspaper photographer to stay until the end of a baseball game since there is no need to develop film" and to take plenty of pictures without "the limitation of film roll length".

Whether through a satellite link, cell phone, or laptop, photojournalists can use the Internet to "send a high-quality image in minutes, even seconds after an event occurs" while on the go, making it easier to meet deadlines. Furthermore, the line between photoblogger and photojournalist is rather blurry. Many photojournalists, especially freelancers, have embraced the Internet as a place to promote themselves and post the photographs that didn't make it into newspapers. One example is Martin Fuchs' "Journal of a Photographer". He describes the site as "a resource for photographers," "[a] tutoria on my workflow," and "[his] personal endeavor...to write about [his] own experiences."

The site discusses the personal and business sides of working in photojournalism, with galleries of the photographer's work for self-promotion and sharing with the world. This seems to have worked; aside of any professional benefit to his online presence, soon after starting the site, he got an equipment sponsorship from Canon Europe.

He has subsequently received sponsorships from Lexar, ColourVision, and Digital Railroad. Clearly, the tools and users of the Internet are not strictly anti-photojournalist—they can be used to support traditional, professional photojournalism.

Second, it should be accepted that odds are, in the current social and economic environment most professional photojournalism is likely to go the way of the dodo. Newspapers and other news organizations are under a lot of budget pressure and already are cutting back staff. As they build ties with online communities and realise the wealth of photographic content available, staff photojournalists will probably be cut, too. Remember, there was once a fairly healthy community of portrait painters. When photography came along, a lot of them had to find other work; or at least their ranks were not refilled when they retired.

Professional portrait photographers, similarly, are less in demand today than a generation ago. But portraits have survived — and thrived. (Gillmor) What individual photojournalists will have to do, in order to compete with amateurs, is specialize and focus on quality. "Great feature photography is a special skill that amateurs won't match anytime soon"- -no matter how many megapixels your cameraphone has, it can't tell you how to frame a shot or tell a story (Gillmor).

As news organizations start paying citizen photographers for their photo submissions, the difference between a professional freelancer and an amateur photobug will all but disappear. If a skilled freelance photojournalist can effectively compete nowadays, one can expect that the cream of the photojournalism crop will be likely to remain so even as news outlets embrace the photography of the masses. On balance, the Internet and related technological innovations seem a positive development for photojournalism.

The problem of photoshopping will still exist, just as it does now, but between the possible technological solution sought by news agencies to detect image manipulation and the critical thinking offered by the blogosphere and other online communities, the deceptive power of such "faux-tographs" will hopefully be minimized. What photojournalism on the Internet means is a greater depth of material taken from many different points of view for easily-accessible events, and a few photographs of extraordinary circumstances when before there could be none.

It means changing public expectations of privacy—

though whether this is good or bad depends on one's age and perspective, the trend seems inevitable. And finally it means a democratization of news production and consumption. The click of anyone's cameraphone could be "the photograph heard around the world."

PHOTOJOURNALISM ON THE WEB

The Internet has made it possible to access images seen in newspapers, photojournalists' own Web sites, and compilations of photographs from history. The following is a selective list of Internet resources available to both practicing photojournalists and students of photojournalism.

STARTING POINTS

Atlanta Photojournalism Seminar: Photojournalism Resources

This nonprofit organization "promotes the highest standards of photojournalism through an annual educational conference and a photography contest judged by working photographers." The "Resources & Links" section is an annotated list of sites concerning photojournalism and photography.

PoynterOnline—Photojournalism Bibliography

As stated on the Web site, "The Poynter Institute is a school for journalists, future journalists, and teachers of journalism." This site allows you to do a subject search for photojournalism, where you will find links to current news items, seminars, and trends in the industry. Featured is a bibliography that includes online resources.

GENERAL

Americanphotojournalist

The site advertises itself as "for photojournalists, by photojournalists." The site, which is maintained by contributing members, began in 2002 and offers news, features, information, and portfolios from working photojournalists. The news section is an outstanding resource for current events in photojournalism.

Behind the Viewfinder: A Year in the Life of Photojournalism

This Web site documents one year in a photojournalist's life. Each photojournalist keeps a diary that illuminates us with the various duties, emotions, and stories that he or she encounters. We experience their pitfalls and triumphs, which allows us to look inside the world of a practicing photojournalist.

Editorial Photo

Known as EP, Editorial Photographer is a Web site for the practicing photographer, but is also valuable to the student.

EP has information not found at many other sites, such as copyright information, contract reviews, educational seminar information, and the EP Estimator—which is a pricing tool for editorial assignment. There are formal links to the events calendar, education, forum, business resources, assignment resources, and "Know Your Profession."

International Photojournalism Festival

This site presented by Visa PourL'Image celebrates and encourages press photography. The site archives past festivals, beginning with 1989, and includes galleries, interviews, and profiles.

NewsInPictures.com

This is a site that is dedicated to pictorial news stories. You can search under the following subject areas: news, sports, disasters, entertainment, history, science, and miscellaneous.

PDN Online (Photo District News)

This is an informative online resource for the working

professional photographer. PDN brings you the latest trends, news, portfolios, and event calendars.

Picture Editor

The site states, "PictureEditor.com was founded in 1998 to provide a place for documentary photographers to share their images and stories." This Web site has links to news, forums, articles, galleries, and resources. The site is for the practicing photographer and photo editor.

World Press Photo

The mission of the World Press Photo is "to promote a free and unrestricted exchange of information and to encourage high professional standards in photojournalism." This site is for both the student and the practicing professional and includes links to seminars, contests and awards, and galleries.

The link to "The Winners 2003" is set with the following subject headings: wpph of the year, children's award, spot news, general news, people in the news, portraits, sports, the arts, science and technology, nature and the environment, and daily life.

E-JOURNALS AND MAGAZINES

The Digital Journalist

This premier online photojournal is published monthly by photojournalist Dirck Halstead, who is the creator, editor, and publisher. The site features documentary work, editorials, columns, commentaries, product reviews, and illustrations of photographs in both still and video formats.

Eight: Photojournalism

This is the Web site to the magazine, which is in print format and published quarterly. It is based in the UK and has interesting photo stories concerning our world. The Web site itself gives subscription information, of course, but also contains a section for diaries, links, and reviews. The resources under the links category include agencies, photo festivals, publishers, photo collections, photographer sites, online journals, and organizations.

EPN World Reporter

"EPN World Reporter" is an online magazine for journalists, editors, and photographers. The journal covers news and events from around the world and is dedicated to the foreign correspondent. There are links to news, security, and an international job board. It actively encourages members to contribute opinions, advice, and news.

ETHICS

Ethics is an essential topic when it comes to photojournalism. Most newspapers have ethical guidelines printed on their Web sites. Below is a link to the monthly column that appears in the "News Photographer Journal," entitled "Ethics Matters written" by Deni Elliott, director of the Practical Ethics Centre at the University of Montana, and Paul Martin Lester, professor at Department of Communications California State University-Fullerton.

Ethics Matters

This column concerns itself with ethics and photojournalism, which is becoming a hot topic since many photographs are now being digitally enhanced. You can look, copy and distribute, for educational purposes, archival articles from this site.

AWARDS AND NOTABLE PHOTOGRAPHS

Alfred Eisenstaedt Awards for Magazine Photography

These awards are administered by Columbia University under a grant from LIFE. The awards are for excellence in magazine photography and are named in the memory of Alfred Eisenstaedt, who was a pioneer in photojournalism. The awards are given in 13 categories. Additional awards are also given for new talent and legend.

Capture the Moment: Pulitzer Prize Winning Photographs

Newseum, the interactive museum of news, hosts this exhibit. The exhibit brings together Pulitzer Prize-winning photographs from 1941 to the present day. There is a Shockwave version that includes narration by the actual photographers who have won the Pulitzer.

Pulitzer Prizes

Winning photographs can be searched by either category or year. Photographs are available for journalism winners from 1995 to 2002 only. Navigating the Web site can be difficult.

ASSOCIATIONS

American Society of Media Photographers (ASMP)

ASMP was founded in 1944 to promote the interests of photographers, which it continues to do today. The site gives you information under four specific categories: community, culture, commerce, and publications. There are links to business, legal, support, galleries, and industry. The site can be used by the casual viewer, but is more of a resource to anyone in photography from student to professional photographer.

National Press Photographers Association (NPPA)

NPPA, founded in 1946, sponsors this premier site for photojournalism. There is information and resources for NPPA members and the general public.

A login is required for access to member-only services, such as the Membership Directory and the Job Information Bank.

The Members Gallery is a directory providing links to the work of members, students, and other working photographers.

NPPA Listserv

This electronic list is dedicated to photojournalism.

VisCom Resources

The visual communications division of the Association for Education in Journalism and Mass Communication is devoted to study and discussion of all forms of visual communication. The division's members represent photography, graphic design, film, broadcast, and multimedia.

This site includes links to special collections such as September 11, 2001; photo competition sites; personal presentation sites; and large sites, such as Masters of Photography and American Photography: A Century of Images.

White House News Photographers Association

This site features a member's gallery, contest information, and links. The links section is an excellent compilation of photojournalism associations and informational Web sites.

HISTORICAL RESOURCES

American Memory

This site is part of the Library of Congress Web page. On the Collection Finder page click on "photos & prints." Each link retrieves a list of American Memory online collections. A significant collection is the Farm Security Administration-Office of War Information Collection.

International Centre of Photography

As defined by the Web site, "The collection spans the history of the photographic medium, from Daguerreotypes and real photo postcards to iris prints."

You can view current exhibitions such as "Bronzeville: Black Chicago in Pictures 1941–1943" and some of the recent exhibitions, as well.

Bibliography

Hornik Robert. Development Communication: Information, Agriculture and Nutrition in the Third World. White Plains, NY: Longman, 2001.

Kopper Gerd G. "Journalistenrolle und Journalistenausbildung in Japan." In Ausbildung für Kommunikationsberufe in Europa: Praktiken und Perspektiven, edited by Heinz-Dietrich Fischer and Otto B. Roegele. Düsseldorf: Droste Verlag, 2002.

McQuail Denis, and Karen Siune, eds. New Media Politics: Comparative Perspectives in Western Europe. Beverly Hills, CA: Sage, 2003.

Merrill John C. The Imperative of Freedom. New York: Hastings House, 2004.

New Trends in Journalism Education and Practice in Tanzania. Dar-es-Salaam: Ministry of Information, 2000.

Picard Robert G. The Press and the Decline of Democracy. Westport, CT: Greenwood Press, 2003.

Rugh William. The Arab Press. Syracuse, NY: Syracuse University Press, 2000.

Ruotólo A. Carlos. "Professional Orientation among Journalists in Three Latin American Countries." Gazette 40, no. 2 (2004): 131-142.

Sala-Balust Ramon. "Journalists' Training: A FIEJ Survey." FIEJ Bulletin 144 (September 2001): 9-12.

Tulloch John. "The United Kingdom." In Reports on Journalism Education in Europe, edited by Kaarle Nordenstreng. Tampere: University of Tampere Department of Journalism and Mass Communication, 2002.

Wicker Tom. 2003. On Press. New York: Berkley Publishing.

Index

E

F

G

H

I

J

K

L